Routledge Revivals

Shakespeare's Talking Animals

First published in 1973, this book is about Shakespeare, language and drama. The first part introduces some common ideas of anthropology and linguistics into an area where they serve as a base for the discussion of usually literary matters. It attempts to link language to our experience of speech — examining its range, texture, and social functions. In part two, the author argues that in Elizabethan culture there was a greater investment in the complexities and demands of speech due to the widespread illiteracy of the time. It examines eight of Shakespeare's plays, together with one of Ben Jonson's, in light of their concern with various aspects of the role of spoken language in society.

Shakespeare's Talking Animals
Language and Drama in Society

Terence Hawkes

First published in 1973
by Edward Arnold

This edition first published in 2017 by Routledge
2 Park Square, Milton Park, Abingdon, Oxon, OX14 4RN
and by Routledge
711 Third Avenue, New York, NY 10017

Routledge is an imprint of the Taylor & Francis Group, an informa business

© 1973 Terence Hawkes

All rights reserved. No part of this book may be reprinted or reproduced or utilised in any form or by any electronic, mechanical, or other means, now known or hereafter invented, including photocopying and recording, or in any information storage or retrieval system, without permission in writing from the publishers.

Publisher's Note
The publisher has gone to great lengths to ensure the quality of this reprint but points out that some imperfections in the original copies may be apparent.

Disclaimer
The publisher has made every effort to trace copyright holders and welcomes correspondence from those they have been unable to contact.

A Library of Congress record exists under LC control number: 74159556

ISBN 13: 978-1-138-23713-1 (hbk)
ISBN 13: 978-1-315-30059-7 (ebk)
ISBN 13: 978-1-138-23719-3 (pbk)

FOREWORD

The original dust-cover of Terence Hawkes' Shakespeare's Talking Animals encapsulates precisely the substance of this ground-breaking book: on the front, a still from the opening of the Olivier film of Henry V set in a mock-up of the Elizabethan public theatre, and on the back, a still from John Hopkins' celebrated television play, Talking to a Stranger. Drama, whose institutional home was once 'theatre', has now migrated to the modern technological media of film and television. Hawkes's strategy is to return to Shakespeare, and to the non-literate past from which the plays emerged, and to speculate upon a future in which the metaphor of the Globe might be realised in the global reach of new technological media.

  Shakespearean drama has become transformed into 'literature', a passage that occludes many of the distinct linguistic and thematic elements whose traces remain in the texts. Even more contentious, however, is the claim 'live' theatre is moribund and that its social role has been taken over by modern media. Shakespeare's Talking Animals appeared in 1973, in the aftermath of Richard Hoggart's The Uses of Literacy (1957), with its emphasis upon popular literacy, and before the seismic eruption of 'theory' into Literary Studies, in which Hawkes himself was centrally involved. His distinctive and abiding contribution is to recover the popular drama of a 'non-literate' culture, and to rescue Shakespeare from the clutches of an increasingly specialised vociferous literary criticism, while at the same time appropriating certain of its interpretative methodologies. Shakespeare's Talking Animals recovers an Aristotelian observation about what makes 'man' distinctively 'human', and uses it to explore the specific non-literate operations of 'language' within the 'popular' medium of Elizabethan theatre. Many of its arguments continue to remain both original and prescient, and they set a clear agenda for the upsurge of radical enquiry that accelerated in the 1980s. What was a novel thesis in 1973 has, in recent years, come to fruition in the recent practice of live streaming of theatre productions of Shakespeare to cinemas, and television, and the preservation of 'live' performances on DVD.

Hawkes' anthropological definition of 'culture' as a whole 'way of life' emphasises the distinction between the popular culture from which Shakespearean drama evolved, and the 'high' culture determined to transform these once popular, and necessarily ephemeral, 'oral' texts into a permanent Literature. What Shakespeare's Talking Animals amalgamates, uniquely, is the insights from historical linguistics, social anthropology, cultural history and criticism that extends imaginatively what might otherwise be little more than a bland literary ecumenicalism. What has now become a fashionable interdisciplinarity is offered here as a careful and persuasive integrated approach. While Renaissance commentators have always insisted on the period as a site of religious and philosophical crisis, and have sought to enlist the support of Shakespearean drama (tragedy in particular), the few earlier attempts to treat the plays as products of a 'popular' culture floundered on the rocks of a reductive formalism. In the fields of Classical Studies and Religious Historiography questions were beginning to be asked about the effects of the discovery of the technology of writing, an issue that has since exercised post-structuralist thinkers from Derrida onwards. The originality of Hawkes's thesis lay in his probing of the question of what life and 'drama' must have been like, and what its concerns were, in a largely 'non-literate' (as opposed to an 'illiterate') culture facing the onset of literacy, and to link the substance of a range of Shakespearean plays to a crisis that only more recently enquiries in to the History of the Book have begun (rather superficially) to investigate. His arguments also anticipated, and greatly assisted, the theoretical enquiries that were to sweep through Shakespeare Studies and beyond; indeed, his launching of the New Accents Series in 1977 with his own Structuralism and Semiotics (1977) emanated directly from the foundations that were laid substantially in Shakespeare's Talking Animals, and were to find their apotheosis in his championing of the project of Literary Presentism, and in books such as Meaning By Shakespeare (1992), and Shakespeare in the Present (2002) in his series Accents on Shakespeare.

This important book touches directly and indirectly, on the central arguments that have, since its first publication, raged throughout the Humanities, although it is Hawkes's supreme expository gift to have succeeded in communicating complex ideas while continuing to be readily accessible to all. Also, the book's careful methodology gives the lie direct to claims that a theoretically informed interdisciplinary practice pathologically eschews the close reading of texts. Indeed, at the same time that Hawkes deftly dismantles some of the deeply cherished prejudices of a literary and literate Establishment, he deploys his unique and pioneering combination of analytical skills to provide original, unique and memorable readings of particular plays.

Hawkes's own methodology, that he subsequently went on to refine, is one that has become the norm, and widely imitated in relation to the study of texts, and his particular emphasis on the various historical pressures that determine the operations of language in action, brings the specialised study of linguistics into a closer alignment with the wider concerns that have always been central to the Humanities. The result is a significant departure from the sentimental affection for particular institutions, or for their élitist investment in the value of 'high' culture. His distinctive approach to the seminal link between Language, Drama and Society, raises important questions about the distinction between 'populism' and the 'popular', something that has had a modernity thrust upon it by more recent political events in Britain, Europe and the USA.

Shakespeare's Talking Animals unashamedly, and unapologetically probes the question that doubters about the authorship of Shakespeare's plays have continued to challenge: how could a predominantly non-literate culture have produced work of such extraordinary quality? Hawkes's answer is that non-literate culture is much more sophisticated than those who espouse 'literacy' are prepared to allow, such that its complexity manifests itself, in political institutions, its habits of mind, its methods of recollection, and, of course, its art, especially its dramatic art.

Of course, the speed with which Information Technology has developed, and the political nuances that have made the concept of 'globalisation' a problematical category, have tended to weaken some of the idealism that fuelled part of Marshall McLuhan's enthusiasm for Television and the 'global village'. But Hawkes is too sophisticated to be caught on the wrong side of this debate. He recognises the shortcomings of 'mass' audiences, and he distinguishes clearly between populism, and the 'popular'. Much of what he says about Shakespeare is of direct relevance to the issues that we encounter in the present, and in Shakespeare's Talking Animals we have the first major foray into what he himself was later to inaugurate as Literary Presentism, a vibrant mode of historical criticism dedicated to enquiring about the ways in which the present imposes itself upon the past. It is fitting that in the year in which we commemorate Shakespeare's death, we should also commemorate one of the most distinctive and challenging voices whose widespread influence has done much to transform and to reshape the present and the future of Shakespeare Studies in particular and Literary Studies more generally.

John Drakakis
University of Stirling
March, 2016

Shakespeare's Talking Animals
Language and drama in society

Terence Hawkes

EDWARD ARNOLD

© Terence Hawkes 1973

First published 1973 by
Edward Arnold (Publishers) Ltd.,
25 Hill Street, London W1X 8LL

ISBN: 0 7131 5697 X

All Rights Reserved. No part of this publication may be reproduced, stored in a retrieval system, or transmitted in any form or by any means, electronic, mechanical, photocopying, recording or otherwise, without prior permission of Edward Arnold (Publishers) Ltd.

Printed in Great Britain by
Billing & Sons Limited, Guildford and London

Contents

	Acknowledgements	vii
	Introduction	1
	Part I: Language, Culture, Drama	
1	Language as Culture	9
2	Gesture as Language	15
3	Drama as Language	24
4	Drama as Culture	31
	Part II: Shakespeare	
5	Elizabethan Language, Culture, Drama	37
6	*Love's Labour's Lost*: rhyme against reason	53
7	*Richard II*: the word against the word	73
8	*Hamlet*: the play on words	105
9	*Othello*, *Macbeth*, and Jonson's *Epicoene*: the language of men	127
10	*King Lear* and *Antony and Cleopatra*: the language of love	166
11	*The Tempest*: speaking your language	194
	Part III: Conclusions; New Languages for Old	
12	Drama *versus* Theatre	215
	Index	243

Acknowledgements

It is a pleasure to record a general debt of gratitude to my colleagues at University College, Cardiff, who variously listened to, read, and commented on this material in its successive stages. Special mention should be made of G. Ingli James, Robin Moffet, and my sometime research student Malcolm Evans of the English Department who made particularly helpful observations. Needless to say, the many shortcomings which endure are my own responsibility. The typing skills of Mrs.I. Fawcett proved, as ever, exemplary.

An earlier version of Chapter 7 was originally published in *Language and Style*, parts of Chapter 10 first appeared in the *Review of English Studies*, and Chapter 12 incorporates material which began life as the basis of two B.B.C. talks, later published in *The Listener*. I am grateful for permission from these journals, where necessary, to reprint, refashion, or refurbish.

I am also grateful to the Cambridge University Press for permission to include at various points a modified version of some material taken from an essay, 'Shakespeare's Talking Animals', which I contributed to *Shakespeare Survey* 24; to Messrs. Routledge and Kegan Paul of London and the Humanities Press Inc. of New York, for permission to quote briefly from my book *Shakespeare and the Reason*; and to Messrs. Methuen & Co. (Associated Book Publishers) for permission to draw on a small amount of material which was presented in another connection in my book *Metaphor*.

Parts of this book have formed the basis of lectures delivered, in recent years, at various institutions in Britain and North America. As a result, I feel obliged to thank my hosts and audiences at the University of Waterloo, Ontario; the Shakespeare Institute of the University of Bridgeport, Connecticut; Rutgers University, New Jersey; the University of Stirling, Scotland; the International Shakespeare Conference and the Royal Shakespeare Theatre Summer School at Stratford-upon-Avon; and at the World Centre for Shakespeare Studies in London, for their benign tolerance of my inadequacy, as well as their condign commentaries on my argument. I have profited from both.

It is no less pleasing to acknowledge the profit I have gained from conversations over the years with scholars as munificent of their learning as of their hospitality: in particular, Maurice Charney, Bernard Beckerman, and Edmund L. Epstein. The beneficence, encouragement and friendship of Allan Lewis, John Drakakis, and Eluned Brown also demand special commemoration.

Finally, I must thank my own students at Cardiff, their amiable scepticism ever the best antidote for overweening confidence. They will discover that they are still owed a book worthy of them.

My greatest debt of gratitude remains, as always, to my wife: *sine qua non.*

University College   TERENCE HAWKES
Cardiff

Introduction

This is a book about Shakespeare, language, and drama.

I make none of the conventional apologies for writing about Shakespeare. His plays had a centrality in respect of Elizabethan culture that is palpable, and that culture has a very special relationship with our own. It experienced the beginning of a process whose end we now sense, and to study any aspect of it is to study ourselves.

Nor can I apologize for writing, however trivially, about language. If language is man's distinctive feature, as linguists tell us, it is far too important to be abandoned to them.

It follows that the case argued in Part I of this book is hardly for specialists, and certainly not novel. It tries to introduce some common ideas of anthropology and linguistics into an area where they may serve as a ground-base for the discussion of matters usually judged to be of a 'literary' nature. Their unfamiliarity to readers with a 'literary' background seems to justify the fairly full exposition awarded them, particularly as the argument aims to call aspects of that background into question.

In linking language concretely with our experience of speech in actual social situations, I am aware that I risk the enfiladed scorn both of linguists and of literary critics. Unrepentant, I affirm my belief that language consists ultimately of what happens when people talk to each other.

I also believe that what happens when people talk to each other constitutes the raw material of drama. Plays, after all, are made out of speech. Also drama, by definition, is a communal art by whose means a community 'talks' to itself. A good play 'utters' (or 'outers') the inward and formative presuppositions of its audience, confronts it with, and so potentially resolves, its own essential and defining tensions. This radical 'interlocutory' mode constitutes the foundation of the play's inherent involvement with language, with utterance, with the sound of the voice and the movement of the body.

It seems clear that a general awareness of such matters has implications for the study of drama, just as the study of drama in such a context has implications in turn for the analysis of the society that generates it. The four chapters of Part I set out to initiate that awareness by attempting to give some idea, however inadequate, of the range, texture, and social function of drama's raw material, and of the relationship it characteristically inculcates between plays and the way of life from which they originate and towards which they reflexively incline.

In an oral society, where utterance constitutes the basis of social life, the relationship between the society's language and its drama must obviously be raised to an even higher power. Part II of this book argues that, in the case of the culture which produced our greatest drama, we are confronted by a far more extensive investment in the complexities and demands of oral communication than custom admits. Shakespeare wrote, that is, for an audience most of whom could not have communicated effectively by means other than those of face-to-face oral encounter. As a result, his plays embody a discernible notion of language and its function in the community which illuminates both themselves and the way of life of their audience.

Of course, such an argument makes much of Elizabethan illiteracy. In fact, it deliberately risks over-emphasis in the matter in an effort to correct the covert presuppositions which, as an almost wholly literate society, we inherit and foster. I believe our own literacy blinds us to the nature of what must have been a central feature of Elizabethan life, and in that belief have devoted a number of pages at the beginning of Part II to an attempted description of the history, nature and extent of literacy's anaesthetic grip on the modern sensibility. I think that is the right way to put it. In the matter of literacy we represent, after all, a minority. Most people in the world have never been, are not, and will never be able to read and write.

This is not to presume the question of Elizabethan literacy to be a simple or a settled matter. Historians know otherwise and the pages of Chapter 5 respond, I hope, to the complexity they recognise, and which is recognised in their disagreements. It would be foolish to argue that the Elizabethans were completely non-literate. What makes for intricacy is the age's state of transition in the matter; the fact that literate and non-literate traditions coexisted and were intermingled particularly by a medieval and revived 'classical' tradition of education which stressed the importance of the spoken word far more than modern education does; and the fact that literacy *per se* did not then necessarily involve the massive commitment to printed material in English that we tend to presume it predicates. There is even a sense in which the issue has less to do with literacy than with the way in which the developing technology of the printing industry responded to it. Books, and not the ability to read them, seem to cause the impact to which *Love's Labour's Lost* offers a riposte.

As a result, a simple counting of literate heads tends to prove misleading. The question is not how many people *could* read and write, but the extent to which they *did* in a society in which books, candles, privacy and motivation were variously in short supply and in which, perhaps even as a result, the most vivid and rewarding form of popular entertainment was provided by the oral art of drama. We must allow, as the historians rarely do, that the plays themselves constitute a considerable body of evidence in the matter. Whatever the extent to which Elizabethan society was *actually* literate, their presence suggests that there was also a sense in which it never ceased to be *virtually* non-literate. It is the edging of virtual into actual truth that characteristically precipitates art.

The remaining six chapters of Part II make a close examination of eight of Shakespeare's plays (spanning the Comedies, Histories and Tragedies) together with one of Ben Jonson's, in the light of their concern with various aspects of the role of spoken language in society. As the implications of this concern unwind, a view of society and of drama in relation to it emerges which seems to lie, not only at their core, but at the core of the way of life from which the plays derive and towards which they are directed. They are seen to embody the notion that the essence of humanity lies in the efficacy of human communication: that man is the talking animal. In consequence, inhumanity often manifests itself most potently as the constriction or prohibition of talking and its concomitant activities. And as a result drama itself ultimately becomes a recurrent symbol of efficacious communication, as the plays indicate a firm faith both in the enabling capacity of man's 'talking' nature, and in themselves as the medium which best exemplifies it. Through art, pre-eminently the ephemeral art of 'playing', man talks to man, and so *is* man.

If this is so, it seems to follow that the study of the structures embodying drama in any society will afford a uniquely rewarding insight into that society. In any case, such can hardly be avoided, for to study a play is to study its audience. The difference between the nature of those structures in the Elizabethan period and in our own will in turn tell us a good deal about ourselves, and thus serve to reinforce both the necessity and the value of the special relationship between our society and Shakespeare's postulated above.

And so I make no apology for concluding this book in Part III with an attempt to say something however shallow about the general nature of the medium of television. It seems to me to have such obvious affinities with a popular tradition of drama and entertainment stemming directly from the Elizabethan theatre and its forebears that its persistent omission from the realm of scholarly discussion and analysis of that tradition by now almost occasions embarrassment. An understanding of the nature of the television medium undoubtedly both illuminates and is illumined by an understanding of the Elizabethan popular drama. More, it helps us to comprehend the complexities of the concept 'popular' which it has been our century's desperate lot shamefully to oversimplify.

That television connects vitally, formatively, and numerically with our own society in ways that the theatre can no longer hope to match is a situation that mockingly devalues the standard academic disdain which the medium encounters.

Recognition of that in no sense implies approval of the sort of television we have. But it is the first step towards improving it.

We force ourselves to carry so damagingly heavy a burden of history and of art that we may reasonably balk at the demands an entirely new medium makes on an over-crowded pantheon. This book ultimately suggests that, past-ridden as we are beyond any previous age, we might now allow some items which have served their excellent purpose to be surrendered to the ephemerality which their nature makes their right. We have Prospero's example. Meanwhile television, the new Ariel, remains. It is far too important to be abandoned to anybody.

Part I
Language, Culture, Drama

I
Language as Culture

When Ben Jonson nominated speech as

> ...the only benefit man hath to expresse his excellencie of mind above other creatures.
> (*Timber, or Discoveries*)

he was articulating an idea that has had modernity thrust upon it. In fact, the concept of man as the Talking Animal, with language his distinctive feature, marking him off from the other animals, is one of those currently fashionable notions redeemed, we might now profitably allow, by its antiquity. For the classification of man as *zoon logon echon* (a living creature possessing speech) enjoyed currency before Aristotle, and Cicero offers a formula as positive as Ben Jonson's when he claims that

> ...it is in this alone, or in this especially, that we are superior to the animals; that we can converse amongst ourselves, and express our thoughts in speech.
> (*De Oratore*, I. 8; 32)

Some three hundred years before that, the Athenian orator Isocrates had put the same point no less categorically:

> For in the other powers which we possess ... we are in no respect superior to other living creatures; nay, we are inferior to many in swiftness and in strength and in other resources; but, because there has been planted in us the

power to persuade each other and to make clear to each other whatever we desire, not only have we escaped the life of wild beasts, but we have come together and founded cities and made laws and invented arts; and, generally speaking, there is no institution devised by man which the power of speech has not helped us to establish.

(*Antidosis*, 253-7)

Such ideas obviously have particular force and relevance in societies where the act of talking, face to face, constitutes the fundamental mode of life and where speech seems not only to embody humanity, but to bring into being and reinforce all the communal social structures of 'civilization'. In such societies speech and man, language and culture, talking and 'way of life' must be very closely connected.

In fact, one might reasonably generalize on that basis. Most linguists would probably agree that man apprehends the world and is enabled to live in it by means of a complex network of communicative systems, in which language appears to predominate. His encounters with 'reality' take place in the context of the language of the community in which he lives. As Emile Durkheim has said,

> Language, and consequently the system of concepts which it translates, is the product of a collective elaboration. What it expresses is the manner in which society as a whole represents the facts of experience.[1]

In short, the structure of the 'real world' is largely predetermined by social forces. And the most powerful of these forces is language. In the words of Basil Bernstein,

> Language marks out what is relevant, affectively, cognitively and socially. . . . Speech is . . . the major means through which the social structure becomes part of individual experience.[2]

---

[1] *Cit.* Herbert Landar, *Language and Culture* (New York, 1966), p. 149.
[2] 'Aspects of Language and Learning in the Genesis of the Social Process' in Dell Hymes (ed.), *Language in Culture and Society* (New York, 1964) pp.

'Individual experience', it has been further suggested by Benjamin Lee Whorf, is itself embodied to a significant extent by the nature of the particular language spoken by the community, and in whose terms its individual members apprehend the world. Each language, Whorf argues, formulates experience in its own way, by means of its own structure, and is 'not merely a reproducing instrument for voicing ideas, but rather is itself the shaper of ideas, the programme and guide for the individual's mental activity, for his analysis of impressions, for his synthesis of his mental stock in trade'.[3] Thus the speaker of *Hopi* (an American Indian language) 'sees the world' through the lens of his own language, and that world differs significantly from the one seen by the native speaker of English.

Man, this seems to suggest, is very firmly a creature of his distinctive feature of talking. Culture, or way of life, and language, or way of speaking, appear to be coterminous. For man, language and reality interpenetrate, and seem all but inextricable.[4] The point is memorably made by Edward Sapir:

... Human beings do not live in the objective world alone, nor alone in the world of social activity as ordinarily understood, but are very much at the mercy of the particular language which has become the medium of expression for their society. It is quite an illusion to imagine that one adjusts to reality essentially without the use of language and that language is merely an incidental means of solving

---

251–61. Cf. Bernstein's 'Language and Social Class', *British Journal of Sociology*, Vol. II, 1960, pp. 271–6 on the relationship between language (especially vocabulary) and the social structure. In general, see J. R. Firth, *Papers in Linguistics 1934–51* (London, 1957), pp. 7–35.

[3] Benjamin Lee Whorf, *Language, Thought and Reality* (Cambridge, Mass., 1956) p. 212.

[4] For an expanded and provocative statement of this proposition (in which the phrase 'the talking animal' is coined) see George L. Trager's articles, 'Language' and 'Linguistics' in *The Encyclopedia Britannica*, 1956 edn., Vol. 13, p. 694; Vol. 14, p. 162.

I have argued the same case, drawing on much of the material deployed here, but rather more fully and in a different context, in *Metaphor* (London, 1972) pp. 78–83 *passim*.

specific problems of communication or reflection. The fact of the matter is that the 'real world' is to a large extent unconsciously built up on the language habits of the group. No two languages are ever sufficiently similar to be considered as representing the same social reality. . . . We see and hear and otherwise experience very largely as we do because the language habits of our community predispose certain choices of interpretation.[5]

This is not to say that no 'outside world' exists beyond our languages which we can call real: there are, after all, 'brute facts' that one bumps into. But we perceive these 'realities' through the spectacles of our languages, and there is no other way of perceiving them. Since there are no language-less people, each culture deals with the world, reaches it in fact, through its own linguistic structures, and it can hardly avoid imposing these on reality. And the 'brute facts' of life tend to appear in different guises and call forth different responses in different cultures. As Margaret Mead puts it[6] the notion we may embody in a simple statement such as 'Love will find a way' (one of our 'brute facts': either Love will or it will not) may simply not exist in some cultures, or may have an utterly different role (and so call forth appropriately different responses) in others. Hence in some languages it just would not be possible to make such a statement without 'labelling' it a bizarre and foreign notion. In effect, this is to say that English contains, as overt 'ways of putting' things, covert presuppositions about the nature of the 'reality' outside us which clash glaringly with the way in which other peoples perceive that reality. As Dorothy Lee found, an analysis of a language like *Wintu* throws the matter into relief:

> Recurring through all this is the attitude of humility and respect toward reality, toward nature and society. I cannot find an adequate English term to apply to a habit of thought

---

[5] Edward Sapir, 'The Status of Linguistics as a Science', in *Essays on Culture, Language and Personality*, ed. David G. Mandelbaum (Berkeley, Calif. 1964), pp. 68–9.
[6] *Male and Female* (Penguin edn., 1962), pp. 54 ff.

that is so alien to our culture. We are aggressive toward reality. We say, This is bread; we do not say, as the Wintu, *I call this bread* or *I feel* or *taste* or *see it to be bread*. The Wintu never says starkly *this is*; if he speaks of reality that is not within his own restricting experience, he does not affirm it, he only implies it. If he speaks of his experience he does not express it as categorically true.[7]

Whorf points out that English contains devices in its 'grammar' which impose a system of spatial and temporal relationships on objects and events (and these are part of 'brute fact' for us) that other languages, and other cultures, do not.[8] Our tense system for example imprints a dimension of past, present, and future on our experience which other languages (which do not by any means share a remotely similar system of tenses) take no account of. We speak of 'reaching' a 'point', 'coming to' a 'conclusion', 'higher' education, without recognizing the implicit linear notions of movement, along a graduated path or 'up' a scale and 'towards' a 'goal', presupposed by these and similar structures. And yet these presuppositions affect our lives as part of a 'reality' which seems to exist, concretely, 'brutally' and 'out there' beyond us. But it is not a question, ultimately, of there being different 'realities'. What is at issue is the existence of different perceptions of the *same* reality brought about by differences in language. Dorothy Lee puts it well:

> ... a member of a given society—who, of course, codifies experienced reality through the use of the specific language and other patterned behaviour characteristic of his culture—can actually grasp reality only as it is presented to him in this code. The assumption is not that reality itself is relative but that it is differently punctuated and categorized, by participants of different cultures, or that different aspects of it are noticed by, or presented to, them. If reality itself were

---

[7] 'Linguistic Reflection of Wintu Thought', *International Journal of American Linguistics*, Vol. 10, 1944.
[8] *Op. cit.*, pp. 134 ff.

not absolute, then true communication, of course, would be impossible.[9]

The metaphor of 'spectacles' applied to language thus seems to be a good one. Language, like spectacles, enables us to 'see', but it imposes on what we see certain of the properties of the lens. Yet without the lens we would see nothing: so we either see in the spectacles' terms or not at all. The language of the tribe, it seems, *is* the tribe.[10]

[9] 'Lineal and Nonlineal Codifications of Reality' in Edmund Carpenter and Marshall McLuhan, eds., *Explorations in Communication* (Boston, 1960), pp. 136–54.
[10] In Old English the word *geðiode* means both 'language' and 'tribe'.

2
Gesture as Language

Nevertheless, nobody just *talks*.

When we speak on the telephone, we engage in a communicative situation that ostensibly employs words alone as the sole and dominant factor. But even then we find ourselves using gestures, facial expressions, postures, as apparently vital and necessary adjuncts to our speech, impossible to abandon even in conditions of radical redundancy.

In short, patterned bodily movements, however slight, seem normally and invariably to accompany utterance. The comforting British conviction that only foreigners have recourse to gesture (or 'gesticulate' to use the term urged by prejudice) accordingly proves difficult to sustain. The Englishman's raised eyebrow and the Italian's vigorous hand and arm movements must rank (aesthetics apart) as degrees of the same inveterate activity—although those who consider it 'natural' to point with the index finger will always and inevitably regard as odd those who habitually point with another part of the body, such as the lower lip or the chin. Nobody *just* talks.

In fact, normal communication between human beings seems to draw upon a complex set or 'network' of inter-related non-verbal signalling 'systems', all of which we appear to learn, informally but decisively, along with the words of the language.[1] The particular form taken by the system of course

[1] See the extensive arguments of Kenneth L. Pike, *Language in Relation to a Unified Theory of the Structure of Human Behaviour* (Mouton; The Hague, 1967). Also Alfred G. Smith (ed.), *Communication and Culture* (New York, 1966) pp. 167–213, particularly the essay 'A Basis for Some Contributions of Linguistics to Psychiatry' by Robert E. Pittenger and Henry Lee Smith, and the essays collected in *Approaches to Semiotics* (eds.), Thomas A. Sebeok,

varies with the particular language in question, and the 'learning' consists in effect of the unconscious acquisition of patterns of physical behaviour congruent with membership of the language community. It involves, in short, unconsciously learning the 'rules' of the particular 'network' that enables one to be 'an Englishman' or 'an Italian' and so on. The commonly experienced distinction between knowing a language's words and grammar, and speaking these to a native speaker, has its gestural bearing, manifested in a feeling of imprecisely located 'awkwardness' which no amount of application seems readily to overcome. Even the native speaker of the language finds it difficult to teach what he is unaware of having learned himself.

If speech utilizes two major human instruments, the voice and the body in concert, then without too serious an involvement in matters that heavily engage both linguists and anthropologists, we ought to be able to attempt an amateur schematization expressive of the complexity of the relationship between them. The following rough categories suggest themselves by rule of thumb:

1 VOICE

a *Vocalization* (sounds made with the vocal apparatus, but which do not form 'words': voice 'quality': 'paralanguage').
b *Verbalization* (a 'system' of recognizable and isolatable 'words' with concomitant features of 'intonation', involving pitch, stress, and juncture).
c *Writing* (any quasi-phonetic scheme purporting to represent the 'sound' of words by systematic notation. This category would also include code systems representing the units of the phonetic writing system, or any 'imitation' of words by symbols systematically arranged).

2 BODY

a *Gesture* (including facial expression, posture, and all non-involuntary movement).

Alfred S. Hayes, and Mary Catherine Bateson (Mouton, The Hague, 1964). See also Roland Barthes, *Elements of Semiology*, trans. Annette Lavers and Colin Smith (London, 1967), pp. 23 ff.

b *Noises* (made with, 'on', and occasionally 'in' the body. E.g. clapping and rubbing the hands together, finger-snapping, back-slapping, coughing, inhalation and exhalation of air, as in sighing, whistling, etc.).
c *Spatial relationships* (with other bodies).
d *Temporal relationships.*

A few moments' observation in any situation where ordinary communication takes place should establish the existence of patterns of behaviour in something like these general categories, and their unconscious but fundamental function as part of the linguistic process.

For instance, a fairly large proportion of conversational exchange, however formal, characteristically involves vocal events and activities which may be grouped under 1a. The term 'paralanguage' (coined by G. L. Trager[2]) can perhaps helpfully be invoked here to refer to a wide range of phonetic phenomena normally and somewhat lamely termed 'tone of voice', whose rather complex conventions all normal native speakers of English (or any language) have mastered by an early age, and can manipulate and respond to with absolute and unconscious facility.

'Paralanguage' involves our ability to communicate complex information (perhaps about our emotional state, degrees of anger, affection, hatred, bewilderment) not by means of words themselves, but by the way in which we say them. A single word, whose literal meaning may have an indeterminate range—the word 'look' for instance—carries a considerable degree of 'paralinguistic' meaning over and above that given by its use in a particular situation through the 'tone of voice' in which it is uttered, and the way in which that interrelates with the social-cultural context of the utterance and all its attendant conventions. 'Look' said in a loud, argumentative tone of voice by a motorist to a policeman, communicates by means of paralanguage complexities of 'meaning' quite distinct from

[2] G. L. Trager, 'Paralanguage: a first approximation', *Studies in Linguistics*, Vol. 13, 1958, pp. 1–12. See also Trager's essay 'Paralanguage' in *Language in Culture and Society*, ed. Dell Hymes, *cit.*, pp. 274–9. Trager's term has a narrower meaning than is given here, and his analysis is of course much finer than I have attempted.

those expressed by the same word said in a soft 'wheedling' tone of voice by the same motorist to his wife. Even if the entire sentence were the same in each case, 'Look, I didn't realize it was a one-way street', it is the paralinguistic 'tone of voice', playing upon the social conventions of congruity relevant to the particular situation, that sophisticates the 'meaning' of the utterance, and makes it accusatory, or conciliatory, or whatever in its import.

In most interchanges between human beings, phonetic events of this kind constitute a good deal of what takes place on a level beyond the 'meaning' or accepted usage of the words actually exchanged. Moreover, even casual observation reveals that quite a large proportion of any conversation frequently consists not of 'words' at all, but of the sorts of vocal sounds which the limits of orthography force us to indicate as 'uh-huh', 'mmmm', 'ah!', 'ugh!', 'ha-ha', 'tsk-tsk-tsk' and so on. Sympathetic 'listening' employs them deftly.

Most cultures seem to make use of apparatus of this type as a kind of adjunct to the language. With it, we may perhaps group those patterns of vocal behaviour termed by the anthropologist Bronislaw Malinowski 'phatic communion'; that is, the use of words without regard for their conventional 'meaning'; 'a type of speech in which ties of union are created by a mere exchange of words.'[3] For example, in English, the words 'good morning' —typically used whether the morning may be expected to be 'good' or not—serve specifically to establish or reinforce undemanding 'ties of union' on one level. Their purpose, like most English pronouncements about the weather, is social rather than meteorological. The 'meaning' of the utterance, however complicated by its context, is conveyed paralinguistically and lies beyond the words themselves.

The activities classified under 1b and 1c, although both clearly connected with vocal communication, must be kept carefully separate. Words are one thing; writing, which 'imitates' words, is quite a different thing, and a confusion frequently occurs between the premises of each, whose signi-

---

[3] *Cit.* David Abercrombie, *Problems and Principles in Language Study* (London, 1963), pp. 3 ff. Abercrombie's discussion of the term is very illuminating.

ficance will be discussed later. For the moment it may be noticed that of all the above categories, only 1c, writing, can exist with any degree of significance by itself. When communication by means of any of the other categories is involved, more than one of them must be used: 1b (words) cannot, as we have seen, be separated from 2a (gesture). Indeed, whenever the voice comes into use, the body acts as context to and 'setting' for it. All events classifiable as 1a or 1b therefore imply a whole range of cognate and related events under the classification of 2.

Reference to the system of gesture has already been made, and it seems reasonable simply to say that a combination of vocal and gestural systems forms part of the equipment any encounter with a fellow human being will automatically call upon.[4] A sound such as 'mmm' accompanied, say, by nodding of the head and contraction of the brows clearly has potency as a communicative device, and Hamlet's advice to the Players to 'suit the action to the word, the word to the action' recognizes, in its warning not to exceed 'the modesty of nature' in this respect, the extent to which gesture invariably and 'naturally' modifies concomitant words, and *vice versa*. Horatio Hale supplies an example of such natural 'suiting' when he describes, in his *Manual of the Oregon Trade Language* (1890) the manner in which two Indians of the American North West, changing in the same conversation from their native language to the 'Chinook Jargon', a trade language used for business with strangers, felt impelled to change their gestures accordingly:

[4] The most extensive, precise, and valuable work on bodily communication or 'kinesics' has been done by Ray Birdwhistell. See his essays 'Kinesics and Communication' in *Explorations in Communication*, edd. Edmund Carpenter and Marshall McLuhan (Boston, 1960); 'Communication without words', *L'Aventure Humaine* (Paris, Societé d'Etudes Litteraires et Artistiques, 1965); 'Body Behaviour and Communication' and 'Communication as a Multichannel System', *International Encyclopedia of the Social Sciences* (New York, 1965). See also his earlier *Introduction to Kinesics* (Washington D.C., Foreign Service Institute, 1952). Birdwhistell's more recent work, together with earlier essays, is collected in his *Kinesics and Context* (London, 1971). The essay on 'Gesture' by David Abercrombie, *op. cit.*, pp. 70–83 gives a good introductory survey. For further implications see Jurgen Ruesch and Weldon Kees, *Nonverbal Communication* (University of California Press, 1956), Michael Argyle, *The Psychology of Interpersonal Behaviour* (Penguin Books, 1967), and Erving Goffman, *The Presentation of Self in Everyday Life* (1959; Penguin Books 1971) and *Interaction Ritual* (Penguin Books, 1972).

The countenances which had before been grave, stolid, and inexpressive, were instantly lighted up with animation; every feature was active; the head, the arms, and the whole body were in motion, and every look and gesture became instinct with meaning.[5]

With the 'noises' of 2b added (rubbing of the chin, coughing, clearing the throat, tapping of the knee, table, arm of the chair, blowing through the lips, snapping the fingers, etc.) new modes of communicable 'meaning' spring into focus. Most conversations seem to involve a certain amount of apparently gratuitous sound of this sort, and it characteristically escapes notice on one level. However, the congruence of such sounds with various affective or psychological states constitutes an area of knowledge, literally 'beyond' words, within which members of the culture will usually have learned unconsciously but adeptly to respond.[6] And since such events normally accompany words, only their absence or a perceived 'oddity' about them will make itself consciously felt, perhaps as a barely definable 'quality' the situation accordingly takes on. This would obviously prove the case if, for example, one or more of the participants, unaware of our culture's conventions in the matter, were to remain involved in a different 'set' or 'network' of his own. Normally, such eventualities enable us to distinguish 'foreigners' however perfect their command of the mere words of the language.[7] 'Membership' of a culture and native knowledge of its language clearly involves and necessitates the ability to recognize and 'decode' such communicative behaviour and to react appropriately to it.[8]

[5] *Cit.* Abercrombie, *op. cit.*, p. 74.
[6] See Peter F. Ostwald, *Soundmaking: the acoustic communication of emotion* (Springfield, Illinois, 1963).
[7] Cf. Ray Birdwhistell, 'The Kutenai Indian could tell the difference between a "Kutenai" cough and a "Shuswap" cough. It was a different type of cough and they coughed in a certain way. The Kutenai Indians coughed up their nose. This is part of being a decent Kutenai and not to have done so would mean being taken for a damned Shuswap!' (*Approaches to Semiotics, cit.*, p. 42).
[8] See the interesting essay by Roger W. Wescott, 'Introducing Coenetics', *The American Scholar*, Spring 1966, pp. 342–56, which suggests means whereby the totality of communicative behaviour may be analysed.

The events of 2c (spatial relationships) obviously form part of everyday experience. The distance maintained between human beings for the purpose of communication seems to be selected by the participants according to a reasonably precise 'scale', learned 'out of awareness'. As we would expect, its calibrations vary from culture to culture.

In fact they may range, self-evidently, from direct physical contact (hand on arm, arm round shoulder, hands held, mouth to ear, and so on) to a formally established and considerable remoteness (lecturer on a dais, preacher in a pulpit, etc.). Between these extremes there lie the various points of 'ordinary' polite conversation. In Britain and in the United States the degree of separation the participants 'choose' for the purpose (when standing, not sitting; that is, when the space involved can be controlled to a fine degree by each party) usually turns out to be roughly that of one arm's length. Spanish speakers, on the other hand, seem no less involuntarily to operate at approximately half this distance. Of course this brings the Spanish face uncomfortably close to the British and American one in conversation, so that the Briton and the American bears the reputation in Spain of being 'cold'—literally 'stand-offish'—since he 'backs away' from such an encounter.

In short, fairly precise conventions of 'spacing' apply, again 'beyond' words, as part of the total communicative process, to all social situations. One literally gets 'closer' to one's family than to one's employer in normal conversation. As Edward T. Hall puts it, space speaks.[9] Each of us has been 'trained' by our way of life to perceive its non-verbal messages, act on them, and transmit them ourselves in turn.

Finally, if space speaks, time talks. The category 2d (temporal relationships) refers to the kind of communication (again relative to the conventions of the culture) normally conducted through the medium of time. Our notion of what constitutes punctuality, the precise point at which one ceases to be 'early' or begins to be 'late', ultimately depends on our own culture's fundamentally arbitrary division of experience into units of time which, far from being 'natural', prove on examination to be highly conventional. That is, a 'coding' of time involves,

[9] Edward T. Hall, *The Silent Language* (New York, 1959), pp. 146 ff.

implicates and insulates us as thoroughly and as deeply as our native language.

And of course the code is cognate with and forms part of that language. In it, the 'time' words manifest a high degree of conventionalization by virtue of their obvious (to non-native speakers) subversion of the 'formal' measurement of time through a quite different but no less precise 'informal' measurement of their own. 'In a minute' does not mean 'after the elapse of 60 seconds' in English. In fact the phrases 'in a minute', 'half a minute!', and 'just a second!' all refer, bewilderingly, to approximately the same span of time: roughly between three and five minutes on the 'formal' scale. The 'meaning' of time, because of its wholly conventional nature, must be an elusive and protean entity in any language. Difficult to learn from the 'outside', its non-verbal role depends on the particular and relative classification of experience, 'formal' as well as 'informal', that it serves both to underpin, and to reveal.[10]

Human communication, then, comprehends much more complex and inter-involving activity than the interchange of words in grammatical patterns. However crude and imprecise the foregoing analysis and classification may be, it serves the purpose, as it were, of putting words in their place. Their use ranks as one of a number of interdependent communicative activities whose complex interaction makes up what we term 'language'. In our minds, for complex historical and social reasons, words may seem an exclusively dominant factor.[11] But this does not make language's non-verbal dimensions less than necessary to communication. Any event on the level of words will of itself call forth concomitant events of paralanguage, gesture, spatial and temporal relationships. In fact, if these and other events did *not* occur, then neither would meaningful communication, for meaning resides in the totality of their inter-relationships. As G. L. Trager puts it, 'language is always accompanied by other communication systems . . . all culture

---

[10] Cf. Hall, *op. cit.*, pp. 128–45.
[11] See Henry Lee Smith Jr., 'Language and the Total System of Communication' in Archibald A. Hill, ed., *Linguistics Today* (New York, 1969), pp. 89–102.

is an inter-acting set of communications and . . . communication as such results from and is a composite of all the specific communication systems as they occur in the total cultural complex.'[12]

We might now usefully begin to assess the implications of these matters for that art whose medium is language at large and whose concern pre-eminently is with the human situation. They reduce themselves ultimately to a consideration of the complexities inherent in this central principle: nobody *can* just talk and remain human.

[12] 'Paralanguage' *cit.*, p. 275.

3
Drama as Language

The apparent domination of words in human communications, together with the illusion that language consists solely of their systematic interchange in grammatical patterns, has none the less a powerful anaesthetic effect. As a result, we tend to disregard a good deal of communicative behaviour and in consequence risk the imposition of wholly arbitrary standards on what remains.

For, despite the fact that 'language', as we have seen, might be said to occupy an area no less than that of the full range of activities we term 'culture', and despite the fact that as a complex network of communicative acts it calls on the involvement of the whole man, voice and body, modern technological societies have seemed increasingly to promote a 'reduced' notion of language as simply the sequential occurrence of isolatable words, whose fundamental properties may adequately be reproduced by a system of writing.

But just as words hardly constitute the whole of language, so written words can scarcely be said to 'reproduce' it. Communication on the level of gestures, 'noises', paralanguage, etc., occurs spontaneously, instantaneously, and virtually subliminally in ordinary experience. To give an account of its details, word by written word, however deftly, imposes a single 'objectifying' dimension, a reductive linear sequence, and a flat depersonalized 'ordering' on events that operate in 'real life' in quite a different mode. It might even be argued that 'writing' fails to *record* language by paradoxically calling a different 'language' into being: one whose masking relationship to 'reality' can often prove misleading in a highly literate society which awards considerable esteem to the art of literature.

Of course, it would be short-sighted and foolish to dismiss the skills of writing and reading, and the art made of these, as of small value or significance to our own society. A compensatory insistence on the primacy of speech can result, as Margaret Mead has said, in 'the tendency to treat writing as if it were merely a system of phonetic transcription devised by linguists with no more separate and distinct evocative and communicative power than the linguistic text of a dictated cooking recipe is likely to have.'[1]

Nevertheless, in a society which prizes literacy, the opposite and equally mistaken assumption, that the language's 'secondary' written form must be primary, can and often does tacitly prevail. The notion of a *separate* 'literary' and ultimately 'correct' version of the language, reserved for and fostered by 'educated' speakers can attract unreasoning support.

Of course a 'literary' dimension of the language may exist, but it can have no status as a separate *linguistic* entity, for both the 'literary language' and indeed literature itself are the creatures of literacy; generated by the activities of reading and writing, not by language. As Harry Levin has remarked, 'The term "literature", pre-supposing the use of letters, assumes that verbal works of imagination are transmitted by means of writing and reading'.[2] And he points out that this fundamental misconception derives from the inevitable but misleading presuppositions of 'a culture based upon the printed book' such as our own.

In fact, the model of the printed book has proved deeply formative, even warping, in our culture, begetting in turn a discernible critical bias of the last century which characteristically treated all the manifestations of art in language as quasi-books, dealing in plots and 'characters' in the manner of the

---

[1] 'Vicissitudes of the Study of the Total Communication Process', in *Approaches to Semiotics, cit.*, p. 278. The essay repays study since it contains an appraisal of the value of the traditional Western belief in the idea of 'teaching language as a tool of civilised thought', particularly in its written form, as against the modern concern with 'multi-sensory face-to-face behaviour of interacting human beings'.

[2] Harry Levin, preface to Albert B. Lord, *The Singer of Tales* (Harvard, 1960), p. xiii.

B

novel. A. C. Bradley's famous lectures on Shakespeare (and their fame resides in their 'character'-analysis) were delivered, not insignificantly, at approximately the time of Henry James's later novels (with their intricacies of 'character'-construction).[3] The psychological interests of a society dedicated to literacy inform both, and the central modern objection to Bradley's criticism remains that it turns Shakespeare's plays into inferior novels; mere portrait galleries of various 'characters'.

In short, the simple assumptions either that the written text can communicate as 'language' does, or that any work of art which makes use of words can be treated as a written text, are both, as Harry Levin argues, misconceptions of a culture in which the printed book plays a dominant role. The situation of drama in such a culture is often paradoxical.

Quite clearly, drama is not literature. Edward Gordon Craig found that the point needed to be forcibly made:

> ... the Art of the Theatre is neither acting nor the play, it is not scene nor dance, but it consists of all the elements of which these things are composed: action, which is the very spirit of acting; words, which are the body of the play; line and colour which are the very heart of the scene; rhythm, which is the very essence of dance. ... A drama is not to be read, but to be seen upon the stage ... the word written to be spoken and the word written to be read are two entirely different things.[4]

Similarly, Arthur Miller has felt obliged to stress that

> A drama ought not to be looked at first and foremost from literary perspectives merely because it uses words, verbal rhythm, and poetic image. These can be its most memorable parts, it is true, but they are not its inevitable accompaniments.[5]

---

[3] A point made by John Holloway in his article 'Criticism; the Twentieth Century' in *The Reader's Encyclopedia of Shakespeare*, eds. O. J. Campbell and E. G. Quinn (New York, 1966), p. 158.

[4] *On the Art of the Theatre* (paperback edition, 1962) pp. 138, 140, 181. The whole book repays study, of course, for in it the implications of a non-literary theatre are fully drawn out.

[5] *Collected Plays* (London, 1958), p. 4.

Drama, in short, is made out of language. Acting is a stylization of linguistic 'interacting'. It depends, as communication outside the theatre does, on a good deal more than words set in the 'grammatical' patterns appropriate to writing and the literary notion of a 'text'.

In fact, of all the forms of art in which societies engage, drama remains the only one which wholly derives from and fully exploits the 'central fact' of man's 'talking' nature. In general terms, drama celebrates, manifests, and is 'about' the complex reality of man as the 'talking animal'. In particular, it draws upon the full range of verbal and non-verbal activities involved in 'talking'. If language is man's distinctive feature, drama is his distinctive art.

This represents a context in which the views of the French playwright Antonin Artaud might profitably be considered, as they raise issues that now centrally concern the argument. Always aware of the inability of formal 'literary' language to capture the essence of his own complex response to life,[6] Artaud was intrigued by the communicative possibilities of 'subtextual' lighting, music, bodily gesture, vocal intonation, dress, and the manifold potentialities involved in *mise en scène*[7] evinced by the theatre of Charles Dullin. Hence his notion that a non-verbal 'concrete' language peculiar to the theatre exists; 'a kind of unique language half-way between gesture and thought' intended 'for the senses and independent of speech' in a manner exploited by Oriental drama. The theatre of the western world, on the other hand,

> ... recognizes as language, assigns the faculties and powers of language, permits to be called language (with that particular intellectual dignity generally ascribed to this word) only articulated language, grammatically articulated

---

[6] See his *Correspondence avec Jacques Rivière* in *Oeuvres Complètes*, vol. I (Paris, Gallimard 1956, pp. 41 ff.). Also the informative essay by L. R. Chambers, 'Antonin Artaud and the Contemporary French Theatre' in *Aspects of Drama and the Theatre* (Sydney, 1965), pp. 113 ff.

[7] As the translator of *Le Théâtre et son Double* points out, Artaud's use of this term implies all that we mean by 'direction', 'production' and 'staging'.

language . . . it is an established spiritual value that the language of words is *the* major language.[8]

However, Artaud's subsequent insistence on a rigid division of language's unified and patterned systems into discrete and independent entities, with speech as an activity *separable* from gesture, paralinguistic 'tone of voice', spatial relationships and the other constituents of human *mise en scène*, seems to oversimplify the complexity of normal communication in pursuit of an otherwise wholly laudable attack on the moribund—because irrevocably 'literary'—*théâtre digestif* of our century. Man is certainly not the literary animal that such theatre presupposes, and Artaud's attempt to establish the theatre as a non-literary medium with its own unique characteristics and properties deserves approbation.[9] But man is the *talking* animal, which means that language constitutes his essence. To seek, as Artaud put it, 'to break through language in order to touch life', makes little sense if it means anything other than the rejection of a formal and entirely notional 'literary' or 'written' language. For man, language *is* life. Artaud's assertion that 'Dialogue—a thing written and spoken—does not belong specifically to the stage, it belongs to books',[10] fails to distinguish between the activities of speech on the one hand and of writing on the other. If language in its largest sense (that is, in the sense of what happens when people talk to each other) is life, the theatre can only 'touch' it by means which must be linguistic, although they need not rely exclusively on words alone.[11]

[8] *The Theatre and its Double*, trans. Mary Caroline Richards (New York, 1958), p. 117.
[9] Although he was preceded in this, as in many of his arguments, by Edward Gordon Craig: e.g. '. . . going through the stage door of the theatre I saw the following words, "Sprechen Streng Verboten" which means "Speaking Strictly Forbidden". The first moment I thought I was in heaven. I thought "At last they have discovered the Art of the Theatre!" ' *Op. cit.*, p. 131. And cf. his concept of the actor as 'Uber-Marionette', pp. 81 ff.
[10] *Op. cit.*, p. 37.
[11] In fairness, Artaud does seem to make this point, albeit glancingly: '. . . the fixation of the theatre on one language—written words, music, lights, noises—betokens its imminent ruin, the choice of any one language betraying a taste for the special effects of that language.' *Ibid.*, p. 12.

The theatre images man the talking animal. If this is so, the 'language' of the theatre cannot be peculiar to itself (paradoxically, it is the written language of the novel—against which Artaud reacts—that remains *sui generis*). On the contrary, the theatre's 'language' must essentially derive from the language of real life. Artaud's followers, Ionesco, Beckett, Genet, Adamov, seem more recently to have recognized this principle and, with greater success in consequence, to have explored and exploited it, making the analysis of words a major purpose of their plays (in the course of which it is pointed out that, on their own, in formal 'literary' guise, words hardly communicate at all).[12] Indeed, much of their drama centres precisely on the inadequacy of *mere* words.

Artaud's complaint that the theatre 'lives under the exclusive dictatorship of speech' which automatically relegates the 'language of gesture and mime' to the 'minor part',[13] has been felt by his followers to diagnose exactly and significantly man's own central inadequacy and dilemma. The theatre in our century is dominated by words because man is. But rather than construct a new theatrical 'language' they have—to much greater effect—used the theatre's accurate 'reflection' of man to explore just this problem of the 'dictatorship of speech' and the unpleasant yet fundamental fact that, as T. S. Eliot's archetypal talking animal recognized, 'I gotta use words when I talk to you' (*Sweeney Agonistes*).

Artaud's idea of 'trying to restore to the language of speech its old magic, its essential spellbinding power', together with his related notion of a non-literary theatre vitally concerned with the central elements of human existence, and by its nature reflecting these and providing a catharsis for them, remain penetrative concepts. Since they derive to some extent from his interest in and admiration for the Elizabethan drama, they have the immensely fruitful effect of sending us back to that drama with new insights into its nature. Certainly, Artaud is to be contrasted in this with Edward Gordon Craig, who found Shakespeare's plays 'unactable' and 'a bore' when

---

[12] This point is well made by L. R. Chambers, *loc. cit.*, p. 125.
[13] *Op. cit.*, p. 40.

staged. Uncharacteristically in tune with his time, Craig felt that they were intended for reading.[14]

However, Sweeney's principle holds good for all drama, whether the mode of the play is 'realistic' or not, since the persistence with which audiences identify the dramatist's creations as 'real people' derives much of its force from their enactment of the basic 'talking' form of human behaviour. Even Shakespeare's most unlikely 'characters' take on the 'reality' of life through poetic drama (though the event has many degrees of sophistication) in so far as in their behaviour they exhibit the unmistakable signs of 'talking' humanity to which our natures instinctively respond.[15] And as Artaud implies, when communication of this sort forms the ground-base and permeates the fabric of an art to such an extent, it cannot effectively be distinguished from it. Whatever those plays may have as their ostensible subjects, they are all in one way *about* language. That is, their subject is humanity.

[14] *Op. cit.*, p. 285.
[15] Cf. John Russell Brown, *Shakespeare's Plays in Performance* (London, 1966), pp. 22 ff., on the relationship of 'naturalism' to 'formalism' in Elizabethan acting styles, where he argues convincingly that 'Elizabethan acting aimed at an illusion of life' in which the verse would ultimately be 'enfranchised as the natural idiom of human beings'. See also B. L. Joseph, *Elizabethan Acting* (Oxford, 1951), pp. 113–40 for a different view which does not alter the main point: namely that, whatever *conventions* are at work, the actors function as 'communicators', as 'talking animals', whether 'naturalistically' or 'formally'. The difference in this respect is one of degree, not kind.

4
Drama as Culture

There remains the audience. As Artaud and his followers recognized, events in the auditorium form as much a part of of the play as events on the stage. A play hardly exists, it might be argued, unless and until it can be realized in the 'completing' presence of an audience.

This essentially symbiotic relationship between play and audience might also, by the same token, appear as interlocutory in character, informed by the same complex interactive processes that typify the act of talking. The 'dialogue' which takes place both on the stage and between the stage and the auditorium effectively involves a use of language in which words, gestures, sounds, paralanguage, all operate systematically and formally much as they do in informal human relationships outside the theatre. In this way, and at a deep level, drama could be said to represent a formal 'enactment' of a culture's language. It displays that language in action. And its action consists, after all, of nothing else.

The interpenetration of language and culture, the coterminous relationship of 'way of speaking' to 'way of life' has been noticed. It follows that if a 'consanguineous' interconnection pertains between drama and language, then drama and 'way of life' must prove inextricably linked. A culture's drama mirrors that culture. It becomes its members' 'second' nature.

All human societies seem to engage in drama of one sort or another. Ceremonies, religious or otherwise, ritually depicting human behaviour, assigning 'roles' realistic or symbolic, and thereby externalizing and 'bringing to mind' fundamental social and moral principles, have this function in societies apparently barren of 'plays'.[1] Games, contests, sports of all kinds, serve the same dramatizing, self-enacting, self-defining purpose elsewhere.[2] Social life itself necessarily imposes roles, offers cues, prompts lines. There is no non-dramatic dimension we can enter. Drama creates and reinforces the world we inhabit. We see no pristine 'first' nature. All the world's a stage.

However, there may be complications. For instance, as has been pointed out, in our society the written word enjoys a kind of 'official' primacy which in turn awards to literature a 'formal' status. As a result, we tend to classify drama as 'literature'. Not only does this mean that we usually first encounter Shakespeare's plays, say, as something 'written' and to be read, it also has the effect of transferring literature's 'formal' status to the theatre itself. Amazingly, the theatre becomes an institution in which literature somehow takes place.

The result, in a society where art has in any case come to occupy an area quite distinct from that of 'life', is that drama finds itself relegated to the 'official' or 'formal' or 'literary' part of most people's experience, and going to the theatre seems to fall on the same debilitating side of that unprofitable dichotomy. It becomes a 'formal' and quasi-'official' event, involving 'special' arrangements about 'ordinary' matters such as clothes, food, travel. And accordingly it occupies only a peripheral position in respect of the totality of informal activities that make up our way of life, and constitute our culture. In such circumstances, Artaud's diagnosis seems pertinent;

> If the age turns away from the theatre, in which it is no

---

[1] E.g. see O. B. Hardison Jr.'s chapter 'The Mass as Sacred Drama' in his *Christian Rite and Christian Drama in the Middle Ages* (Baltimore, 1965), pp. 35-79.

[2] This seems precisely the basis for rejecting Artaud's grandiose claim that 'the essential theatre is like the plague' in that 'it is the revelation, the bringing forth, the exteriorization of a depth of latent cruelty by means of which all the perverse possibilities of the mind, whether of an individual or a people, are localized' (*op. cit.*, p. 30). This function is partly and traditionally fulfilled in Western culture by football matches, wrestling bouts, bullfighting, and other spectator sports. The 1972 Olympic Games certainly exhibited the dimension of which Artaud speaks. See Lawrence Kitchin's article, 'The Contenders', *The Listener*, 27 October 1966, pp. 606-9.

longer interested, it is because the theatre has ceased to represent it. It no longer hopes to be provided by the theatre with Myths on which it can sustain itself.[3]

It seems not unreasonable to suggest that our treatment of drama as literature and not as 'language' must in part bear responsibility for such a situation and, in these days of public subsidy, its attendant ironies. We seem to have generated and fostered an enormous and enfeebling paradox in our society, whereby drama, far from mirroring culture, finds itself embodying Culture. Far from enacting language, and the total way of life yielded by our talking and listening, it finds itself immured within that intimidating area inhabited by 'works of art', their very remoteness and stony permanence underwriting a fearful standing. Man has not changed. He remains *zoon logon echon*. But in place of a culture available to and reflective of all speakers of the language, we have erected a culture to which, in the words of Claude Lévi-Strauss, we now unthinkingly accord 'the status of a national park'. And by a supreme irony, it has come about that that park's most prestigious inhabitant is our greatest popular dramatist.

[3] *Op. cit.*, p. 49.

Part II
Shakespeare

# 5
Elizabethan Language, Culture, Drama

We might now profitably remind ourselves that in terms both of the English language and of English culture, the situation represented above did not always pertain, and that Shakespeare's plays originally grew and flourished in quite a different context. They were written for an audience that did not regard them primarily as 'literature', and whose standards of literacy were in any case hardly likely to have been those of a modern audience. Shakespeare wrote, in short, for an audience of 'talking animals'.

Of course, an opposite notion seems to have prevailed over the years, and in its success lies the source of the paradox described at the end of the previous chapter. It may even point to a debate that lies close to the heart of the plays themselves, and relates them centrally to certain developments in the ideological climate of their own time.

One of the best accounts of the issues in question is given by Walter J. Ong's study of Peter Ramus (1515–72) the famous French philosopher and logician.[1]

Ramus's work raised for Renaissance Europe the whole question of the relationship of logic (reasoning) to rhetoric (speaking). His famous and formative 'method' took the elaborate structure of traditional Aristotelian rhetoric, and rigorously imposed on it a division whose educational implications remain with us to this day.

Aristotelian rhetoric was conceived in terms of five parts: Invention, Disposition, Elocution, Memory, and Delivery.

[1] Walter J. Ong, *Ramus, Method, and the Decay of Dialogue* (Harvard, 1958). See especially pp. 107–12; 149–65; and 288–314.

Each part was thought to make an indispensable contribution to the construction of a good speech. Ramus simply split these into two groups, shifting Invention, Disposition and Memory under a new heading of Dialectic (i.e. logic), and leaving only Elocution and Delivery under Rhetoric. This effectively split logic from rhetoric, 'reasoning' from 'speech', strengthening the former, and fatally weakening the latter.

The division was fully embraced by Renaissance pedagogy, and quickly became a principle of unquestioned, even anonymous, orthodoxy. The dichotomy seemed ultimately self-evident: and with 'logic' separable from speech, Ramist 'logic' quickly became logic itself.

Thus, where Rhetoric had formerly embraced the totality of the verbal arts, that is, the requirements for logical thought *together* with those for beautifying ornament, Ramus's division, reducing Rhetoric to Elocution and Delivery, made of it a mere cosmetic repertoire of 'figures' or trimmings that could be added to discourse after the logical arguments had been established. Rhetoric after Ramus becomes, in the words of Perry Miller, the 'sugar on the pill of logic'; a sort of decorative linguistic *appliqué* work; a kind of fancy dress in which thoughts may from time to time be clothed.

Ramists and others, particularly Puritans, were well aware of the absurd degree of embellishment to which this reduced notion of Rhetoric's function could lead. In fact the Ramist method of formal 'explanation' of an argument laid great emphasis on qualities of 'clarity' and 'distinctness' of a sort that Rhetoric could only seem to disrupt. Ong points out that in consequence the written text gained favour over the spoken utterance; the visual abstraction of writing began to seem preferable to the oral reality of speech. And by comparison with the written word, the non-visual spoken word began to appear ephemeral and fugitive. As a result the new Renaissance technology of print became gradually invested with a sense of permanence denied to the living language; the maxim *verba volant, scripta manent*, seemed irrefutable. As Ong expresses it,

> . . . at the heart of the Ramist enterprise is the drive to tie down words themselves, rather than other representations,

in simple geometrical patterns. Words are believed to be recalcitrant insofar as they derive from a world of sound, voices, cries; the Ramist ambition is to neutralize this connection by processing what is of itself nonspatial in order to reduce it to space in the starkest way possible.

Ramus, Method, and the Decay of Dialogue (p. 89)

The central impulse of Ramus's Method was towards order. The word *methodus* which made its first appearance in the 1546 edition of his *Training in Dialectic* came to signify the orderly presentation of any subject by means of a quasi-scientific 'reduction' of it from 'general' principles to 'specials' by means of definition and dichotomy. Everything could be 'methodized' after this fashion, and the process had a close link with that whereby language could be 'reduced' to writing. By means of 'method' and the written vernacular Bible, related agents of cultural reform, Ramists and Protestants proposed to eliminate the error and imaginative excess of what they considered to have been a 'barbarous' era.

Both 'method' and writing are of course visual and spatial in mode. Alphabetic writing seems to offer a visual counterpart of the spoken word: it purports to give sound a portable, quasi-permanent form:

> [Writing's] essential service is to objectify speech, to provide language with a material correlative, a set of visible signs. In this material form speech can be transmitted over space and preserved over time; what people say and think can be rescued from the transitoriness of oral communication.[2]

'Method', as Ramus conceived it, was also embodied in a visually perceived 'space'. Logical argument, by means of 'dialectical disposition', was seen to move through various box-like 'common places' to yield, eventually, a diagrammatic 'order'.[3] The whole theory of 'common places' as propounded by Agricola, and later by Ramus, represents, says Ong, not a 'settled philosophical outlook', but an 'inexorable disposition to repre-

---

[2] Jack Goody (ed.), *Literacy in Traditional Societies* (Cambridge, 1968), p. 1.
[3] See Ong, *op. cit.*, plates I and XIII.

sent thought and communication in terms of spatial models and thus to reduce mental activity to local motion'.[4] Writing, from this point of view, is language 'methodized'.

The gain, for language, purported to be a 'clarity' which, then as now, was held to be the first and principle advantage of writing. The *mode* of such clarity was, it follows, visual rather than oral. 'Method' naturally enough allies itself with the mechanization of writing in the form of the development of the printing trade during the Renaissance, as a central symptom of and a formative response to an essentially Protestant impulse to present 'knowledge' in a visual, quasi-permanent form: to 'package' it in physically and mentally 'portable' units, i.e. books, and to withdraw it from the apparently transitory world of sound.

Accordingly, as Ong argues, where communication in the pre-Ramist world was

> richly sonorous rather than merely 'clear' for it was the echo of a cognitive world experienced as if filled with sound and voices and speaking persons. . . .
>
> (p. 212)

the Ramist 'pedagogical juggernaut' eliminated sound and voice from man's understanding of the intellectual world, and created a situation in which 'Speech is no longer a medium in which the human mind and sensibility lives. It is resented . . .' (p. 291). As a result,

> By its very structure, Ramist rhetoric asserts to all who are able to sense its implications that there is no way to discovery or to understanding through voice, and ultimately seems to deny that the processes of person-to-person communication play any necessary role in intellectual life.
>
> (p. 288)

It is this situation which the modern world has inherited, in the form of a rarely questioned and educationally reinforced dichotomy between speech and writing which invests the

[4] Ong, *op. cit.*, p. 119.

latter with an authority in matters of 'correctness', 'grammar' and ultimately 'logic', that it systematically denies to the former.[5] It is the same dichotomy which persuades us to think of Shakespeare's plays as items of 'literature', designed for reading.

Nevertheless, the very vigour of the polemics surrounding Ramism and its adherents is sufficient to suggest a counterbalancing force of considerable proportions. As post-Ramists ourselves, products of the success of the 'pedagogical juggernaut', we find it difficult to 'see' that force—although it is probably more properly thought of as the accumulated tradition of centuries—in proper perspective, or indeed at all. Yet it is valuable to remember that the way of life which generated our greatest drama must have involved an investment in oral communication of a far greater order than we are accustomed to acknowledge. Anaesthetized as we are by our own educational experiences we tend, in short, to underestimate the nature and extent of Elizabethan non-literacy.

Of course, Elizabethan society was certainly not wholly oral in character. But equally certainly it was not wholly literate in any sense that would be meaningful to us. English then, as M. C. Bradbrook puts it, was still 'a tongue rather than a written language', and the most recent estimates suggest that only between 30 per cent and 50 per cent of males in Shakespeare's London were minimally literate (this using the dubious standard of their ability to write their own names).[6] In any

---

[5] An exact mirror of this process of 'reduction' in the matter of language can be discerned in the changing Renaissance notion of the role and capacity of man's cognate faculty of reason. The 'old' view, well expressed by Aquinas, conceived of the mind as a unity whose faculties were interdependent, and moved in complementary directions to perform the single function which was *ratio*. The 'new' view, in the interests of 'clarity' and 'distinctness', divided *ratio* into two separate and ultimately mutually opposed faculties, with 'reason' reduced to the function of one of these, the *ratio inferior*. The *ratio superior*, formerly considered part of 'reason', became by the same process an essentially 'irrational' faculty—like the modern notion of 'intuition'. For a detailed account see my *Shakespeare and the Reason* (London, 1964), pp. 1–38. For an account of a similar—perhaps cognate—process in respect of the faculty of memory, see Frances A. Yates, *The Art of Memory* (London, 1966).

[6] M. C. Bradbrook, 'St. George for Spelling Reform!' *Shakespeare Quarterly*, Vol. XV, No. 3, 1964, pp. 129–41. See Lawrence Stone, 'The

case, as Ong argues, oral habits and traditions still played dominant roles in spheres that were only potentially those of writing, and the writing of the period exhibits a formidable and formative 'oral residue' that he characterizes as 'heavy in the extreme'.[7] So it is not surprising to find the notion of speech as man's distinctive and 'civilizing' characteristic common amongst those who wrote of language at the time. George Puttenham comments

> what else is language and utterance and discourse and persuasion and argument in man, then the vertues of a well constitute body and minde little less naturall then his very sensuall actions.[8]

and in *The Arte of Rhetorique* (1553) Thomas Wilson sees speech, the raw material of rhetoric's oral art, as the means by which God redeems men from mere bestiality

> . . . such force hath the tongue, and such is the power of Eloquence and reason, that most men are forced, euen to yeeld in that which most standeth against their will.

Speech, said Edward Reynolds, was ordained by God 'to maintaine mutuall Society amongst men incorporated into one Body', and it is 'the Ligament and Sinew, whereby the Body of Humane Conversation is compacted and knit into One'.[9]

We have earlier noted Ben Jonson's nomination of speech as 'the only benefit man hath to express his excellencie of mind above other creatures'. 'It is', he continues,

---

Educational Revolution in England 1560–1640', *Past and Present*, 28 (July 1964) pp. 41–80; and 'Literacy and Education in England 1640–1900', *Past and Present*, 42 (February 1969) pp. 69–139. Also, Carlo M. Cipolla, *Literacy and Development in the West* (Penguin Books, 1969) pp. 38–61.

[7] W. J. Ong, 'Oral Residue in Tudor Prose Style', *PMLA*, Vol. LXXX, No. 3, 1965, pp. 144–55.

[8] George Puttenham, *The Arte of English Poesie* (1589), Book III, Chapter XXV.

[9] *Cit.* Perry Miller, *The New England Mind* (New York, 1939), p. 306.

... the Instrument of Society. Therefore Mercury, who is the President of Language, is called *Deorum hominumque interpres* (the intermediary between Gods and men)[10]

And the characteristically oral sense of identity between culture and language, man and speech, discussed in Chapter 1, lies behind the notion that Puttenham expounds so neatly when he writes that

> ... man is but his minde, and as his minde is tempered and qualified, so are his speeches and language at large, and his inward conceits be the metall of his minde, and his manner of utterance the very warp and woofe of his conceits.[11]

It is the same sentiment that is embodied in the commonplace stoic notion that Jonson expresses so memorably;

> *Language* most shewes a man; speake that I may see thee.[12]

It is difficult for us, who habitually read and write, to share Puttenham's and Jonson's sense of speech's revealing inward qualities. And it is no less difficult for us fully to accept the implications of the fact that Shakespeare's plays were written for an audience most of whom would have shared it.

In fact, scholars who write from the standpoint of our own highly literate culture tend to minimize Elizabethan illiteracy with a fervour and an abandonment of judgement that in its own way exemplifies the modern notion of it as a stigma. Thus, J. W. Adamson cites Sir Thomas More's pessimistic assertion made in 1533 that the people's souls should 'the moste part perishe' if they depended on 'the havyng of the scripture in englyshe' unless provision be made

> that all the people shall be hable to reade it when they have it, of which people farre more than fowre partes of all the

[10] *Timber, or Discoveries.*
[11] *The Art of English Poesie*, Book III, Chapter V.
[12] *Op. cit.*

whole divided into tenne coulde never reade englishe yet, and many now too olde to begynne to goe to schole.[13]

Yet his comment that this puts 'the number of readers of English at something more than half the population' is made in a spirit somewhat the reverse of More's account.[14]

In fact it is doubtful if the illiterate Elizabethan felt in any way deprived, let alone ashamed. Non-literacy, a less 'loaded' and so more accurate word in this case, simply implies a different 'set' or arrangement of responses to one's environment, neither more nor less appropriate or acute than those at work in our own culture. And such responses need not be denied or explained away, for they are not inferior to our own, simply different from them. It need not be asserted that 'the rank and file were more literate in the sixteenth century than in the eighteenth'[15] as it were in their defence. It is a delusion of the literate that the non-literate are dispossessed. In fact the reverse might be true. William the Conqueror was illiterate.

The evidence, such as it is, tends in any case to invite misleading interpretations, and clearly the age was one of transition in the matter, with accurate assessments very difficult to make. Peter Laslett speaks of literacy as the attainment of only a few at this time, claiming that 'Ordinary Englishmen three hundred years ago lived in an oral culture, that is to say one where most transactions went on by word of mouth.'[16] With writing a restricted accomplishment, 'Society as a whole was forced to rely upon its oral memory for many important things . . .'[17] But the very dimensions in which we see such a situation are deceptive if we import into it the notion that absence of literacy 'forced' on the people a certain way of life. In the terms of the present argument, non-literacy and 'way of

---

[13] J. W. Adamson, 'The Extent of Literacy in England in the 15th and 16th Centuries', *The Library*, 4th series, Vol. X, 1930, pp. 163–93.

[14] It is also worth noting Lawrence Stone's later judgement that More's estimate 'may confidently be dismissed as alarmist nonsense', 'The Educational Revolution in England 1560—1640', *cit.*

[15] Alfred Harbage, *Shakespeare's Audience* (New York, 1941, 1961), p. 146.

[16] Peter Laslett, *The World We Have Lost* (London, 1965), p. 194.

[17] *The World We Have Lost*, p. 98. See also Frances A. Yates, *The Art of Memory, cit.*, pp. 124 ff.

life' are coterminous; the one is not a lack whose necessities impose on the other. Non-literacy is rather the fully sufficient mode of an ancient way of life for whose participants no alternative could have been conceivable.

G. R. Owst's *Literature and Pulpit in Medieval England* (Cambridge 1933) demonstrates, in support of this view, the strength and vitality of the medieval oral tradition, and its shaping effect on the way of life of that 'bookless adult society' which immediately preceded that of the Elizabethan period: its vivid and living legacy can be clearly detected in the 'popular' elements of Elizabethan and Jacobean drama.[18] L. C. Knights says of the strong moral sense these elements exhibit '... it was not something imposed from above; it sprang from the wisdom of the common people, and it was only indirectly that it found its way into writing.'[19] Gladys D. Willcock speaks of the 'not yet broken strength of the oral tradition' in Elizabethan English. 'The tyranny, the drugging influence, of print were still in process of development.'[20] 'This strength of English', writes F. R. Leavis, 'belongs to the very spirit of the language —the spirit that was formed when the English people who formed it was predominantly rural ... speech in the old order was a popularly cultivated art.' [21]

Indeed, much of the 'writing' of the Elizabethan and Jacobean period proves to be a pale shadow of notions previously expressed orally with more powerful and ruthless realism in medieval vernacular proverbs and sermons, to an extent which makes questionable some of the presuppositions of those commentators for whom the literate few tend to obscure the non-literate many. Thus, Louis B. Wright, arguing rightly that the habit of reading became widespread amongst the middle classes in the century that followed the accession of Elizabeth, sees in the process the growth of an enlightenment amongst erstwhile deprived sensibilities:

---

[18] See pp. 471 ff. and 590–3.
[19] *Drama and Society in the Age of Jonson* (Peregrine Books edn., 1962), p. 161.
[20] Gladys D. Willcock, 'Shakespeare and Elizabethan English', *Shakespeare Survey*, Vol. 7, 1954, pp. 12–24.
[21] F. R. Leavis, *For Continuity* (Minority Press, Cambridge 1933).

... the patrons of the booksellers were not isolated villagers and countrymen, who probably got along with as few books as their ancestors, but the citizens of London and the commercial towns that had business intercourse with the metropolis. While, for the most part, the country squire remained sodden, with no more intellectual interest than Justice Shallow, his town-bred contemporaries were waking up.[22]

This sort of prejudice, unjustly dismissive of an extensive oral culture, and compounded by a tendency to speak of the undeniably literate Elizabethan middle class as 'the mass of Elizabethans', or 'the average man'[23] proves misleading in its estimation of the degree of 'waking up' (from what?) that the 'huge outpouring of books' could be expected to stimulate; especially when it is admitted that the 'average literate citizen' read more widely than well in such apparent best-sellers as Joseph Swetnam's *The Arraignment of Lewd Idle, Froward, and Unconstant Women*, or *The History of Tom-Tipler, the Merry Tinker of Banbury*.[24]

Joan Simon's claim that the printed book of the time gave an 'access to knowledge' that would otherwise have been denied to the non-literate, needs to be considered in this light. A good deal depends of course on what is meant by 'knowledge', and the degree to which a book can be said to 'contain' it as a commodity to which literacy of itself gives access. Non-literacy has its 'knowledge' too, and access to that comes from an intense experience of the concrete pressures of life no less valid than those offered by the printed book.[25] To regard knowledge as a single abstract entity, one which exists 'in' a book and not elsewhere, risks a considerable degree of over-simplification which casts its shadow over such statements as this:

[22] *Middle-class Culture in Elizabethan England* (London, 1935, 1938), p. 81.
[23] *Ibid.*, p. 91 and *passim*.
[24] *Ibid.*, pp. 83 and 88 ff.
[25] As V. H. Galbraith puts it, of an earlier period: '... there were vast possibilities of education through the eyes and ears, which have slowly faded out of modern life. Even today, as the picture paper, the picture palace and broadcasting remind us, there are substitutes for literacy.' 'The Literacy of the Medieval English Kings' in *Proceedings of the British Adademy*, Vol. 21, 1935, p. 204. A quarter of a century later television would certainly have to be added to this list.

The stream of books in English, which had reached respectable proportions in Edward's reign, had by the close of the century become a flood, giving the ordinary citizen an established share in the spread of knowledge.[26]

So many questions are begged by terms like 'respectable proportions', 'ordinary citizen', and 'established share', that the immense question of the *kind* of 'knowledge' that was 'spread' is never really put. In Peter Laslett's terms, this perhaps represents 'what it means to observe only the literate activity of a society most of whose life was oral'.[27] The principle that the larger the number of books published, the larger the 'share' of 'ordinary people' in 'knowledge' can be best assessed by reference to our own time, and a book such as Richard Hoggart's *The Uses of Literacy*. Most ordinary people are now literate. We publish an immense amount of books. Yet which of us would claim that the 'ordinary citizen' in our day has *more* knowledge of life (what other kind of 'knowledge' is there?) than the average Elizabethan?

The genuine repository of knowledge in any culture remains the language; that result of an immense historical interaction between all the members of the culture, and the living embodiment of their way of life. We who have replaced much of our own oral spontaneity by writing and its 'rules', and stored vast areas of our knowledge in books, where concrete experience of it is limited to the few whom we select and train to assimilate it through such media, may well reflect on literacy's capacity to *restrict* knowledge, and genuine collaboration in a language and its way of life, rather than the reverse. The simple optimism of

[26] Joan Simon, *Education and Society in Tudor England* (Cambridge, 1966), p. 383.
[27] *Op. cit.*, p. 195. Against the notion of a 'stream of books in English' there should also be set the conclusion of Douglas Bush: 'During the period 1500–1630 the annual production of books of all kinds rose from about 45 to about 460, and in what may be loosely classified as "literature" there was a corresponding advance from a dozen to about 115. . . .' This is not a particularly large number for a population of approximately 5 million. The catalogue of the Bodleian Library, printed in 1605, reveals that of nearly 6,000 volumes in the library, only 36 were in English. (See Douglas Bush, *English Literature in the Earlier Seventeenth Century*, Oxford, 1945, pp. 26–32.)

such as Jonathan Miller, who finds it 'hard to overestimate the subtle reflexive effects of literacy upon the creative imagination, providing as it does a cumulative deposit of ideas, images and idioms upon whose rich and appreciating funds every artist enjoys an unlimited right of withdrawal'[28] needs to be tested against everyday experience. As any teacher knows, the ability to read and write does not guarantee a person who habitually and with facility uses these skills. And those who do use them do not all by any means do so in pursuit of an 'improving' knowledge. Mr. Miller's remarks are perhaps true of the privileged. His fiscal metaphor is revealing.

The culture of the Elizabethans may have contained a relatively large proportion of people able to sign their names and to read, laboriously, passages of print (trade guilds made literacy at this level a qualification for entry to apprenticeship). It had also begun to give signs of a burgeoning interest in reading and writing in English (as opposed to Latin) on a significant national scale (although Harbage's evidence that 'In a period of eight months during the single year 1585, the publishers disposed of ten thousand copies of their reading primer *The ABC and Little Catechism*'[29] perhaps indicates the extent of non-literacy—and of the stringency of the trade guild regulations—rather than the reverse). And certainly, as Wright demonstrates, there was a considerable increase of interest in books of all kinds amongst middle-class men and women.[30]

But the number of people whose lives were dominated by print to the extent that ours are; or whose values were formed by it, as ours tend to be; or whose education was literally geared to, and whose spoken language was dominated—and impoverished—by the written word; and whose world was materially modified by the medium of books, journals, newspapers, and the skills connected with these, as ours is, must have been very small indeed.

Conditions were in any case crucially unpropitious. As Harbage allows, not only books, but candles and leisure to read them by were all in relatively short supply, and in a culture

[28] Jonathan Miller, *McLuhan* (London, 1971), p. 113.
[29] *Op. cit.*, p. 147.
[30] *Op. cit.*, p. 43.

which experiences a relative abundance of these things, the effect of their absence will be correspondingly difficult, even impossible to imagine. As Peter Laslett says, 'What we have to recall, to reconstruct, to make a present reality to ourselves is a time when most men and women could only think, and talk, and sing and play, and make things, and till the soil.'[31] In fact it might be concluded that of the many who could read, few actually did so to any extent that would seem significant to us.

Shakespeare's plays must have been written for an audience of people who communicated primarily by talking and listening, whether they could read or not, and in situations of personal confrontation, whose fundamental and permanent 'mechanics' I have tried to outline in the first part of this book. They retained, as we have not, what Walter J. Ong calls an 'oral set of mind'; a response to the world very different from that which we would regard as normal.[32] They lived in a culture dominated by the human voice and ear, an oral-aural world in which, without benefit of the telephone, the telegraph, the radio, the gramophone, communication was a face-to-face affair conducted with a degree of intimacy now foreign to the modern mind. As Ong explains, the sixteenth and seventeenth century non-literate mind and personality reserved far less of itself as 'private' and 'individual' than its modern counterpart does: 'This mind does not feel the exterior objective world and the interior personal world as distinct from one another quite to the extent that we do.'[33]

In short, they must have experienced a form of what Lucien Lévy-Bruhl has termed 'participation mystique', a special kind of unifying relationship between the individual and the 'objective' world 'beyond' him unknown to modern 'civilized' communities.[34] For them, as M. C. Bradbrook points out, 'the educational system was also very largely an oral affair. The

[31] *Op. cit.*, p. 195.
[32] Walter J. Ong, 'Oral Residue in Tudor Prose Style', *cit.* See also his *Ramus, Method and the Decay of Dialogue, cit.*, pp. 288–92, and Marshall McLuhan, 'The Effect of the Printed Book on Language in the 16th Century', *Explorations in Communication, cit.*, pp. 125–35.
[33] *Ramus*, p. 279.
[34] See the discussion of Lévy-Bruhl in Whorf's essay 'A linguistic consideration of thinking in primitive communities', *Language, Thought and Reality, cit.*, pp. 65–86.

dispute, the lecture with commentary, the *viva voce* examination predominated: reading and writing occupied correspondingly less time'.[35] Ong confirms this, speaking of 'the orientation of all academic instruction toward oral performance',[36] and ironically, as Perry Miller's arguments make clear, an interest in classical literature amongst the educated in effect reinforced the inherited and non-literate interest in actual utterance amongst the uneducated. After all, the second book of Aristotle's *Rhetoric* 'authorised Renaissance writers to view the art as primarily concerned with the spoken word' and

> With the rediscovery of classical literature humanism had come to a discovery of the majesty, the beauty, and the power of the word, in and for itself . . . to a sheer joy in words and word patterns of which euphuism and the verbal excesses of Renaissance drama were among the more extravagant expressions.[37]

Moreover, it was a world much more ambiguous and apparently confusing than the one we experience. As McLuhan puts it, in oral interchange

> there are numerous simultaneous vistas of any topic whatever. The subject is looked at swiftly from many angles: classic notions and insights concerning that subject are, via memory, on the tip of every tongue in the intimate group.

whereas in a world dominated by the written word

> The reader's eye not only prefers one sound, one tone, in isolation; it prefers one meaning at a time. Simultaneities like puns and ambiguities—the life of spoken discourse—become, in writing, affronts to taste, floutings of efficiency.[38]

Finally, and as a result, words in that world had a degree of

[35] M. C. Bradbrook, *The Growth and Structure of Elizabethan Comedy* (London, 1955; Penguin, 1963), p. 35.
[36] *Art. cit.*
[37] Perry Miller, *The New England Mind, cit.*, pp. 305 and 307.
[38] *Art. cit.*, pp. 125 and 127.

efficacy in respect of 'real life' that we would find difficult to grasp. M. M. Mahood says, 'When Elizabethan rhetoricians spoke of the power and force of words their meaning may have been as much literal as metaphorical . . . so Hamlet's words could wring his mother's heart or cleave it in twain.'[39] But it is already clear that, given such circumstances, the Elizabethan world would have been literally a 'dramatic' one, with the 'language' of its everyday interaction extremely close in mode to the 'language' of its stage. And of course the vitality and bulk of the oral art produced on that stage itself constitutes a large (and neglected) body of sheer *evidence* as to the central role of the spoken word in that society.

The essays which follow are not concerned with the plays' own use of language in this context, and the characteristically oral qualities of their style: the rhapsodic, formulaic, incremental and serial structures that occasionally baffled the highly literate Dr. Johnson. But they are interested in the ideas *about* language and its social role which they must in consequence implicitly manifest, and which constitute a neglected part of their world view, perhaps because we are anaesthetized to them by our own literacy. And these involve, primarily, a deep and almost certainly defensive commitment to language in its oral dimension: to the ideal as well as the idea of man as the animal that talks.

In the Elizabethan theatre, a predominantly oral culture, in which 'literature' did not include the drama anyway,[40] enacted its own 'shape' through the medium of words, gestures, sights, sounds, spatial and temporal relationships, which constituted, then as now, the spoken language. Because the drama was a formalized presentation of the culture's own

---

[39] *Shakespeare's Wordplay* (London, 1957), p. 171., cf. Perry Miller *op. cit.*, pp. 305–6.

[40] See Alfred Harbage, *op. cit.*, p. 11. In a more recent work, *Conceptions of Shakespeare* (Harvard, 1966) Harbage argues that 'although Shakespeare was recognised as the best of English playwrights in his own age . . . his standing was that of the popular entertainer rather than the literary artist' (p. 5). Unlike Ben Jonson, Shakespeare certainly never sanctioned his plays' status as 'literature'. The same point is made by Glynne Wickham: 'The fact has to be faced that the society in which Shakespeare lived did not admit plays as literature'. *Early English Stages* (London, 1963), Vol. II, p. 122.

'language', it faithfully reflected the culture and was thus enabled to handle the immense political, moral and social themes (without splitting these apart) that no drama in English has successfully dealt with since. In Leavis's words, '... people talked, so making Shakespeare possible'.[41]

To enter that sort of theatre was thus to engage with life, not to escape it: it was a *theatrum mundi*, nature's mirror. In fact the centrality of drama to human experience, its identity as 'language' with human 'culture', has received no better expression than that given by the plays performed in it—their best epigraph the motto of the aptly named Globe itself: *Totus Mundus Agit Histrionem.*

[41] F. R. Leavis, *For Continuity*, cit. The essay in question, with its 'brief reflection on the conditions of Shakespeare's greatness' is most penetrative on the issue of Shakespeare's language. It first appeared as a review-article, 'Joyce and "the Revolution of the Word" ', in *Scrutiny*, Vol. 2, No. 2, 1933, pp. 193–201.

6

Love's Labour's Lost:
rhyme against reason

It has been pointed out that one of the persistent delusions of the literate is that the non-literate are dispossessed. We are the children of Ramus. In consequence, a considerable effort of detachment is required of us before we can understand that the prospect of literacy may appear somewhat alarming to an oral culture. On the positive side, writing offers the possibility of a new and effective medium of communication which, by providing a visible and lasting counterpart of speech, apparently enables it to transcend ephemerality and to conquer space and time. Writing seems to make speech permanent and portable.

But a fundamentally non-literate community might well take a more negative view, seeing in writing a potential subversion of its established way of life. Far from reproducing speech, writing could be said to 'reduce' it. The full resonance of oral utterance, imbued with the personality, gestures, tone of voice and physical presence of its speaker from whom it is never separated, vanishes in the abstracted impersonality and sheer silence of marks on paper. The solvent of written 'clarity' disperses the richness of oral 'ambiguity'.

When we turn to one of Shakespeare's earliest comedies, exactly these tensions seem to confront us. In fact *Love's Labour's Lost* could be said largely to re-state and then to explicate a much older case in this connection.

In the *Phaedrus*, Plato presents a famous argument against writing. Re-telling the myth of its invention, he recounts the words of the Egyptian King to Theuth, who has invented letters:

If men learn this, it will implant forgetfulness in their souls:

they will cease to exercise memory because they rely on that which is written, calling things to remembrance no longer from within themselves, but by means of external marks. What you have discovered is a recipe not for memory, but for reminder. And it is no true wisdom that you offer your disciples but only its semblance; for by telling them of many things without teaching them, you will make them seem to know much, while for the most part they know nothing; and as men filled, not with wisdom but with the conceit of wisdom, they will be a burden to their fellows.[1]

In essence, that seems to be a reasonable account of what happens in *Love's Labour's Lost*, for in this 'the most linguistically oriented of all Shakespeare's plays'[2] the resonant world of speech is comically opposed to the silent world of writing. At its simplest, the action concerns a group of men who opt out of active oral society in pursuit of immortality, and in the name of what turns out to be the 'conceit of wisdom'. It tells the story of their realization that true wisdom, true 'civilization', true immortality, resides only within the oral community and its social and sexual processes which they have rejected. As 'bookmen' (as the play calls them) the members of Navarre's 'silent court' realize they have betrayed their true nature of 'talking animals'.

On another closely related level, the play also concerns itself with the relationship between the faculty of reason and that of language (the Greek word *logos* is the same for both faculties). A narrow concept of logical, or 'dialectical' reason manifested in the form of the sterile 'reduced' language of books, is set against its oral, rhetorical opposite symbolized by the music of rhyme: that 'fertile' language in which love manifests itself in the play, and which lies beyond the grasp of the reason, appearing in consequence 'mad' or 'foolish' to it. In short, the opposition of the world of speech to the world of books overtly proposed in the play finds itself covertly reinforced by a more contemporary tension between the rival claims of rhetoric and

---

[1] *Phaedrus* 275, a2–b2., trans. R. Hackforth (Cambridge, 1952), p. 157.
[2] M. C. Bradbrook, 'St. George for Spelling Reform', *cit.*

dialectic, itself a version of the immemorial linguistic opposition of rhyme to reason.

In general terms, then, the play explores and expands far beyond its ordinary boundaries the traditional thesis, most recently stated by George Steiner, that '. . . a trained, persistent commitment to the life of the printed word . . . diminishes the immediacy, the hard edge of actual circumstance'.[3] In fact, the 'unnatural' nature of such a commitment is stressed from the first. The courtiers begin by 'warring' against their 'own affections/And the huge army of the world's desires' (I, i, 9–10), in the prosecution of permanency through the written word. A clear conviction that *scripta manent* informs their pursuit of fame 'register'd upon our brazen tombs' (I, i, 2). They confidently expect such 'registration' to defeat 'cormorant devouring time' and to make them 'heirs of all eternity' (I, i, 4–7). It will of itself make the 'little academe' the 'wonder of the world' (I, i, 12–13) and bring a redemptive 'grace' to the 'disgrace of death' (I, i, 3).

Berowne's objections to the 'strict observances', the 'barren' regimen which requires him 'not to see ladies' (I, i, 47–8) and to which, significantly, he has had literally to 'subscribe', are standard objections of the 'active' man to the 'contemplative' life, and as such have many analogues in Elizabethan writing. However, the dominant theme they exhibit in this play has language at its core, and Berowne's liking for the active tends to manifest itself as a commitment to, and a reputation for vivacious oral communication. He is remarkable, we are told, for his 'fair tongue' which is 'conceit's expositor' and

> Delivers in such apt and gracious words
> That aged ears play truant at his tales
> And younger hearings are quite ravished;
> So sweet and voluble is his discourse.
>
> (II, i, 73–6)

---

[3] George Steiner, *Language and Silence* (Pelican edn., 1969) p. 23. Cf. Ralph Berry's view that 'words compose the central symbol' of the play. Berry's point that the play 'is about words' misses the larger one that the various attitudes towards words expressed in the play follow a sustained pattern of attitudes towards language and its social function. Ralph Berry, 'The Words of Mercury', *Shakespeare Survey*, Vol. 22, 1969, pp. 69–77.

Naturally enough, such a man will find that

> ... all delights are vain, but that most vain
> Which, with pain purchas'd, doth inherit pain:
> As, painfully to pore upon a book
> To seek the light of truth;
>
> (I, i, 72-5)

Many of the play's comic characters seem to be conceived in a mode appropriate to oral improvisation in the tradition of the *Commedia dell' Arte*. The text cites Armado as 'Braggart', Holofernes as 'Pedant', Costard as 'Clown', and so on. It is perhaps also worth noting that the play deploys these 'stock' figures amidst a group of perhaps recognizable Elizabethan upper-class courtiers or intellectuals; Armado as Ralegh, Holofernes as Harriot, Moth as Nashe, etc., so that one has the distinct impression of drama blending with—and becoming indistinguishable from—real life; of the speech of the play on the stage as part of the oral reality of the speech of life off-stage. The so-called 'contemporary allusions' which reach beyond the play, serve this artistic function within it.

Moreover, these 'oral' characters seem to be conceived exactly for the purpose of commenting on linguistic matters. The characteristically oral sense that speech is the man prevails. Armado's 'high-born' and 'fire-new' words (I, i, 171, 177) parody those of his betters, and constitute the essence of a language which is obviously 'literary' in its origin and function, and comically divorced from the real world of oral interchange. We encounter it first in its most characteristic form, as language written down, in a letter:

> The time when? About the sixth hour; when beasts most graze, birds best peck, and men sit down to that nourishment which is called supper: so much for the time when. Now for the ground which? which, I mean, I walked upon: it is ycleped thy park. Then for the place where? . . .
>
> (I, i, 230 ff.)

This reduction of the dimensions of nature itself to the level of

LOVE'S LABOUR'S LOST: RHYME AGAINST REASON   57

a horn-book of dialectical 'method' is comic because so much of nature's reality eludes the linguistic structures. And of course human nature eludes them utterly. The 'unlettered' Costard hardly recognizes the version of himself thus presented:

> *King:* (reading the letter) . . . there did I see that low-spirited swain, that base minnow of thy mirth—
> *Costard:* Me?
> *King:* that unlettered small-knowing soul—
> *Costard:* Me?
> *King:* that shallow vassall—
> *Costard:* Still me?
> *King:* which, as I remember, hight Costard—
> *Costard:* O! Me.
>
> (I, i, 240–8)

And in the difference between the 'small-knowing' soul's linguistically plain involvement, as he puts it, 'with a wench' ((l. 252) and the presumably large-knowing, literate version of the same

> with a child of our grandmother Eve, a female; or, for thy more sweet understanding, a woman.
>
> (253–4)

lies the nub of the play. Armado's language is a language of the book. As such, it is unable to cope with ordinary life, even on the level of the necessary social and sexual relationship between men and women on which society depends. Holofernes's designation of the 'wench' Jaquenetta as 'a soul feminine' (IV, ii, 80) indicates the same disabling characteristic.

In essence, then, Armado embodies a language appallingly, and so comically, 'methodized'. If to speak is to be human, he hardly achieves that status. He does not speak, so much as utter writing. The 'vulgar' tongue is not for him in any respect, either of number,

> *Moth:* Then I am sure you know how much the gross sum of deuce-ace amounts to.

C

> *Armado:*   It doth amount to one more than two.
> *Moth:*   Which the base vulgar do call three.
> *Armado:*   True.
>
> (I, ii, 42–7)

or of time (e.g. his reference to 'the posteriors of this day, which the rude multitude call the afternoon' (V, i, 84)). He does not laugh, but announces 'the heaving of my lungs provokes me to ridiculous smiling' (III, i, 74). And he is ponderously unable to deal with the wit of low-life characters such as Moth (III, i). Appropriately, the 'external marks' of the written word engage a good deal of his interest, and 'letters' constitute in great measure his way of communicating, and so his way of life. He writes, characteristically, of his love to Jaquenetta;

> The magnanimous and most illustrate king Cophetua set eye upon the pernicious and indubitate beggar Zenelophon, and he it was that might rightly say, *veni, vidi, vici*; which to annothanize in the vulgar (O base and obscure vulgar!) *videlicet*, he came, saw, and overcame: he came, one; saw, two; overcame, three. Who came? the king: why did he come? to see. . . .
>
> (IV, i, 66 ff.)

Such 'language' copes with reality by painting it over, in a 'cosmetic' process which requires ordinary experience to fit preconceived 'logical' structures. By means of such a process, the complexities of love can be dialectically 'reduced' to primary colours, and can seem 'most immaculate white and red' (I, ii, 86). Moth's jocular piercing of this painted linguistic veil notably takes the form as he puts it of setting a 'dangerous rhyme' against this 'reason of white and red' (I, ii, 101). Language used to 'paint over' reality, to reduce its complexities to a sinister simplicity, becomes a major and a tragic theme in Shakespeare's later plays, as we shall see. Here, it is sufficient to remark the process in its light-hearted aspect, as the comic means by which Armado tries rationally to cope with normal but apparently 'irrational' human emotions. His response to the inward animal disturbances of love is hilariously that of the 'book-man':

LOVE'S LABOUR'S LOST: RHYME AGAINST REASON 59

I am sure I shall turn sonnet. Devise, wit; write, pen; for I am for whole volumes in folio.

(I, ii, 173 ff.)

For Holofernes, as for Nathaniel, it is clearly *writing* not speech which distinguishes man from the animals, and both concur in dismissing the wretched Dull as one unredeemed by literacy's Eucharist:

... he hath never fed of the dainties that are bred in a book. He hath not eat paper, as it were; he hath not drunk ink. His intellect is not replenished, he is only an animal...

(IV, ii, 23-5)

Holofernes's contribution to the debate about orthography consists, predictably, of the assertion that the rules of writing ought to dominate and determine speech. He speaks, as Dover Wilson puts it, 'dictionary wise'. He 'abhors', he tells us,

... such rackers of orthography, as to speak dout, fine, when he should say doubt; det, when he should pronounce debt, —d,e,b,t, not d,e,t;

(V, i, 20 ff.)[4]

Of course, such 'book-men' are really no wiser than Dull, and share his dullness. When Holofernes chaffs him

---

[4] There was no 'standard' pronunciation in Elizabethan speech. Even noblemen tended to maintain their regional accents. Holofernes is asserting the priority of the written form of the language in a community in which the different forms of regional speech all still had equal validity, and where the standardizing of orthography was itself a matter of considerable debate. See Gladys D. Willcock, 'Shakespeare and Elizabethan English' *cit.*, and M. C. Bradbrook, 'St. George for Spelling Reform' *cit.* Holofernes's position is meant to seem ridiculous because it is so extreme. Richard Mulcaster's *Elementarie* (1582) contains notable contributions to the debate about 'right writing', and is prepared to give 'custom's consent' a major role. Shakespeare's own view is much more likely to have resembled Mulcaster's, or that of Ben Jonson, who claims that

'*Custome* is the most certaine Mistresse of Language,
as the publicke stampe makes the current money'
(*Timber, or Discoveries*)

Via goodman Dull! thou hast spoken no word all this while.

Dull's reply 'Nor understand none neither, sir' (V, i, 143 ff.) speaks for us. Nevertheless, the ordinary man's awe and reverence for book-learning is both recognized and satirized in the 'rational hind' Costard. His response to Berowne's request that he deliver a letter to Rosaline is the cant phrase 'I will do it, sir, in print' (III, i, 168; i.e. most carefully). And his malapropisms indicate his anxiety to rise to the level of the literate.

At that level, such 'taste and feeling' as Holofernes may be said to possess manifests itself in his poem on the pricket. His determination to 'affect the letter' (alliterate) in it makes it an absurd piece of 'lettered' writing, far removed from any oral reality. It is a superb example of language defeated by the 'rules' of writing, of rhyme made sterile by reason:

> The preyful princess pierc'd and prick'd a pretty
>   pleasing pricket;
> Some say a sore; but not a sore, till now made sore
>   with shooting.
>   etc.
>   (IV, ii, 56 ff.)

Predictably, Holofernes's critical response to Berowne's beautiful poem to Rosaline is wholly stilted, restricted to observations concerning the breaking of the 'rules':

> You find not the apostrophus, and so miss the accent: let me supervise the canzonet . . .
>   (IV, ii, 118 ff.)

As he begins to 'overglance the superscript' (l. 130) the inability of such literary standards to comprehend genuine emotion, genuinely expressed, is once more reinforced. In fact the play leaves us in no doubt that Armado and Holofernes are buffoons because they are 'lettered', as Armado puts it (V, i, 45) beyond reasonable bounds. They are 'bookmen', not human beings:

Moth: They have been at a great feast of languages, and stol'n the scraps.
Costard: O, they have lived long on the alms-basket of words.
(V, i, 36–40)

Berowne's rejection of 'speeches penned', the 'taffeta phrases, silken terms precise' of 'orthography', and his resolve to embrace their oral opposite, 'russet yeas and honest kersey noes', constitutes an important statement of the play's main theme. Access to reality, he discovers, lies not in books, but in involvement with other people: not in the domain of the eye, reading and writing, but in that of the voice and the ear, talking and listening.

What he discards could, it has already been suggested, be termed the 'cosmetic' quality of the language of books, of the 'academe', and of the Court world which combines both. The Princess has earlier referred to the 'painted flourish' characteristic of the courtier Boyet's speech (II, i, 14), and the King becomes more and more uncomfortably aware of the cloying quality of that 'sweet tongue' (V, ii, 335) which he wishes blistered. Berowne too has become increasingly conscious of the deficiencies of his own kind of 'painted rhetoric' (IV, iii, 236), and its unfavourable standing compared to the 'heart's still rhetoric' (II, i, 229) of true love.

Accordingly, his love for Rosaline makes a neat paradox out of the notion of 'breaking through' cosmetic 'painting' to the reality of nature beneath:

> Her favour turns the fashion of the days,
> For native blood is counted painting now.
> (IV, iii, 259–60)

Cognately, in linguistic terms, love's piercing of 'painting' is embodied in and expressed by a language which rejects the sterility of 'painted rhetoric' in favour of rhetoric of a truer sort, tempering the 'bookman's' words with the rhyme of the lover's sonnet. As Berowne puts it 'By heaven I do love, and it hath taught me to rhyme' (IV, iii, 12). All the 'bookmen' finally reach this conclusion, realizing, with Berowne, that 'rhymes are guards on wanton Cupid's hose' (IV, iii, 58) so that their commitment to writing is resolved by

> . . . as much love in rhyme
> As would be cramm'd up in a sheet of paper,
> Writ o' both sides the leaf, margent and all.
> (V, ii, 6–8)

Such fruitful rhetorical plenitude in rhyme 'completes' and so reverses the sterility of dialectical reason and writing, just as 'native blood', perceived by the lover's eye, defeats 'painting'.

The fundamental irony the play explores is that those who confine themselves to books, and to book-language, end up by being paradoxically and wittily 'caught out' by ordinary human language in its widest sense. In this way, as Berowne predicts from the first,

> . . . study evermore is overshot:
> While it doth study to have what it would,
> It doth forget to do the thing it should;
> (I, i, 140–3)

In short, man's 'affects' (emotions) cannot be mastered by rational 'might' (l. 151).

Indeed, much of the comedy derives from the fact that the 'affects' turn out to constitute an overriding and compelling 'language' of their own which is fundamentally human, though shared with the non-rational animals. The *leitmotif* of hunting scenes in the play carries this message forcefully: we are all animals in part, and should 'listen' to that part of our language. Thus the King's park, the setting of the play, becomes a microcosm filled with beasts and humans, all of whom 'hunt' each other. And of course the rhetoric of the hunting scenes manifests an appropriate sexuality:

> *Princess:* Was that the king, that spurr'd his horse so hard
> Against the steep-up rising of the hill?
> . . . .
> Whoe'er a' was, a' show'd a mounting mind.
> (IV, i, 1–4)

Also it is notable that a passage such as IV, i, 95 ff., with its profusion of sexual puns on 'hit', 'horns', 'prick' and 'rub' between the Princess, the ladies, Boyet and the rest, constitutes a more genuine language of love (and a highly rhetorical one) than the sterile 'logical' absurdities of Armado's 'methodical' letter, quoted above, which precedes it. Here, as elsewhere in Shakespeare, fruitful linguistic intercourse prefigures and mirrors its sexual analogue.

It also leads, inevitably and naturally, to the comic 'reversal' at the play's core, in which women first usurp, and then metaphorically *become* the books which the 'book-men' admire. In the event, the *real* 'book-mates' turn out to be women. They constitute the only legitimate repositories of knowledge, the only generative source of valid learning, the only fertile stimulus of rhetoric. They constitute the means 'by whom we men are men' (IV, iii, 357) and in so doing, they constitute the ultimate basis of social reality.[5]

We are back, after all, to Berowne's reasons 'against reading';

> Light seeking light doth light of light beguile:
> So, ere you find where light in darkness lies,
> Your light grows dark by losing of your eyes.
> Study me how to please the eye indeed,
> By fixing it upon a fairer eye,
> Who dazzling so, that eye shall be his heed,
> And give him light that it was blinded by.
> Study is like the heaven's glorious sun,
> That will not be deep-searched with saucy looks;
> Small have continual plodders ever won,
> Save base authority from others' books.
> These earthly godfathers of heaven's lights,
> That give a name to every fixed star,
> Have no more profit of their shining nights
> Than those that walk and wot not what they are.
> Too much to know is to know nought but fame;
> And every godfather can give a name.
>
> (I, i, 77–93)

[5] Bobbyann Roesen notes that 'the voice of Reality speaks' through the Princess and her retinue from the beginning. *'Love's Labour's Lost'*, *Shakespeare Quarterly*, Vol. IV, 1953, 411–26.

Access to reality lies not through study, but through life itself, through language. Berowne's sonnet to Rosaline has this as its theme:

> Study his bias leaves and makes his book thine eyes,
> Where all those pleasures live that art would comprehend.
> If knowledge be the mark, to know thee shall suffice;
> Well learned is that tongue that well can thee commend;
> (IV, ii, 108–10)

Women, in other words, make up the curriculum of *life's* 'academe' and once in love, the book-men of Navarre's academy find the world of books hardly appropriate to the demands of their 'affects'. The favours they send to their mistresses have a grotesque 'bookish' flavour, and the ladies not unnaturally find the comparisons 'Beauteous a sink' and 'Fair as a text B in a copy-book' (V, ii, 42–3) hardly appropriate. They demand 'some plain man' who can 'speak our language' (V, ii, 176–7).

The man who most fits this requirement proves to be Berowne. His long speech in Act IV contains the central thesis of the play; women are in essence the proper object of man's study, for

> They are the ground, the books, the academes,
> From whence doth spring the true Promethean fire.
> (IV, iii, 299–301)

Man, the argument seems to run, is naturally a social being, one that characteristically thrives in and adapts to a changing environment. He should not attempt to impose an unchanging, rationally conceived 'shape' on the world around him, for this violates his and the world's essential condition. The use of language which 'paints over' reality in false colours has been diagnosed as one of the major means by which the 'academe' and the court in this play have attempted to impose a narrowly prescriptive 'rational' scheme of things on the vagaries of nature and human nature; the imposition of reason without rhyme, of dialectic without rhetoric. Berowne's rejection of that involves his acceptance, and embracing, of the nature of the world as it is, for that is to accept and embrace his own nature. Fundamentally, this means embracing other people not books;

> For where is any author in the world
> Teaches such beauty as a woman's eye?
> (IV, iii, 309–10)

Knowledge, this seems to say, lies in life itself, in our interaction with others in the community, that talking-listening involvement which, the play has already made clear, precedes and prefigures its necessary sexual counterpart. Like love, knowledge is no abstract entity that books can 'contain', or reading give access to. In Berowne's words

> Learning is but an adjunct to ourself,
> And where we are our learning likewise is.
> (IV, iii, 310–12)

Our way of life, that is to say, constitutes our knowledge. And in an oral society, as way of life and language are intimately related, so the language embodies, and indeed *is* knowledge for the community. Knowledge thus resides in communal life. There is no other source.

The play is concerned to make very precise points in this connection. Thus, the immediate and untempered lust which afflicts Navarre and his bookmen presents itself as a distorting force which pulls the five senses out of a proper balance. Boyet says of Navarre's response,

> Why, all his behaviours did make their retire
> To the court of his eye, peeping thorough desire:
> His heart, like an agate, with your print impress'd,
> Proud with his form, in his eye pride express'd:
> His tongue, all impatient to speak and not see,
> Did stumble with haste in his eyesight to be;
> All senses to that sense did make their repair,
> To feel only looking on fairest of fair:

> Methought all his senses were lock'd in his eye,
> As jewels in crystal for some prince to buy;
>
> (II, i, 234–43)

Lust, thus described, brings about an imbalance of the faculties in the same mode as that attributable to book-learning. Both overstress the visual sense at the expense of the others. Both embody, by this, a disordering process wholly subversive of an oral community.

On the other hand, love orders the sensorium, and so life, properly (is this love's 'labour'?). It is deeply rooted in social reality, institutionalized by marriage, and is the means whereby man most fully becomes himself; properly ordered in his faculties, and so properly communicative:

> ... love, first learned in a lady's eyes,
> Lives not alone immured in the brain
> But, with the motion of all elements,
> Courses as swift as thought in every power,
> And gives to every power a double power,
> Above their functions and their offices.
> It adds a precious seeing to the eye;
> A lover's eyes will gaze an eagle blind;
> A lover's ear will hear the lowest sound,
> When the suspicious head of theft is stopp'd:
> Love's feeling is more soft and sensible
> Than are the tender horns of cockled snails:
> Love's tongue proves dainty Bacchus gross in taste.
>
> (IV, iii, 324–36)

Love necessarily acts as an ordering, harmonizing agent in man and in a world in which 'society . . . is the happiness of life' (IV, ii, 160). In that context, love affords the means whereby man is 'completed' by woman just as, so the analogy goes, books are complemented by speech, dialectic by rhetoric, and the mere 'reason' of language written down is redeemed by the humanizing acoustic qualities in which rhyme consists and deals. As love reconciles man to woman, rhyme, which only exists in that it has a vocal, auditory bearing, adds a human, reconciling, oral–aural dimension to speeches which are merely 'penned'. This is the significance of the sonnets in which love is finally expressed in the play.

Ultimately, as Northrop Frye says, the play's central theme is one of fruitful reconciliation, the result of Shakespeare's 'impersonal concentration on the laws of comic form'.[6] Life itself triumphs over human aridity, as love triumphs over letters. And at the very end of the play the two 'opposites' of nature itself, Spring and Winter, are finally seen to 'complete' each other, as part of the same total process. The songs sung in their name draw, linguistically, on the essence of ordinary experience. They manifest the texture of ordinary life, of icicles, frozen milk, coughing, cooking, birth and marriage; and they advocate acceptance of this life, of things as they are. Earlier, we might recall that (after recommending 'rhyme' against reason (I, i, 99 ff.)) Berowne was accused of being 'like an envious sneaping frost/That bites the first-born infants of the spring'. He replies with words that totally accept and affirm this chastening but necessary conjunction of one season with another, as part of the irrevocable 'completing' process of nature:

> Well, say I am; why should proud summer boast
> Before the birds have any cause to sing?
> Why should I joy in any abortive birth?
> At Christmas I no more desire a rose
> Than wish a snow in May's new-fangled shows;
> But like of each thing that in season grows.
> (I, i, 102–7)

Analogously, as Northrop Frye point out, the same principle applies to human affairs in Shakespearean comedy, and the genre's general epigraph might well be Terence's 'nothing human is alien to me'. So, on the level of the human world of social organization, the ultimate realization borne in upon Navarre and his 'bookmates' is that speech reflects, indeed guarantees the organic reality of the whole community and its

[6] Northrop Frye, 'The Argument of Comedy', in D. A. Robertson (ed.), *English Institute Essays*, 1948 (New York, 1949).

way of life; that consideration of 'each thing that in season grows' makes of the language of the 'unlettered' a necessary ingredient without which the writing of the 'learned' remains unredeemably sterile; that rhetoric is not alien to dialectic but adds to it its own kind of 'rhyme' as an essential social complement of learning's 'reason'.

The play quite deliberately avoids the conventional happy ending in order to make this point. In Berowne's words

> Our wooing doth not end like an old play;
> Jack hath not Jill.
>
> (V, ii, 864–5)

In fact, the punishment imposed on him has an emphatic linguistic aspect. His early love, on his own admission 'formed by the eye and therefore like the eye' (V, ii, 752) has proved shallow and vain. Now he is required to take up the implications of his commitment to 'russet yeas and honest kersey noes', to engage rhetorically with the speech-community, not deny it, to recognize its 'theatrical' dimension, and to involve himself in it as a 'player' or an 'entertainer'. His business will be oral interchange. He must

> . . . this twelve month term from day to day
> Visit the speechless sick, and still converse
> With groaning wretches. . . .
>
> (V, ii, 840–2)

That is, as the ultimate reality, in the form of death, breaks in on the love-making, he must experience the full force of his own dictum that 'Honest plain words best pierce the ear of grief' (V, ii, 743), and will be required to bring communication of a very basic kind into situations which badly need it. The former '. . . merry madcap lord/Not a word with him but a jest' (II, i, 216–17) must become aware of the *reciprocal* 'dramatic' nature of speech. He must learn, as Rosaline rebukes him, that an audience's listening necessarily complements the actor's oral art, that

> A jest's prosperity lies in the ear
> Of him that hears it, never in the tongue
> Of him that makes it.
>
> (V, ii, 851–3)

In the *Phaedrus*, Plato also makes Socrates say

> ... anyone who leaves behind him a written manual, and likewise anyone who takes it over from him, on the supposition that such writing will provide something reliable and permanent, must be exceedingly simple-minded. ...[7]

At the end of the 1598 Quarto, the earliest surviving 'written manual' of *Love's Labour's Lost*, this phrase occurs;

> The words of Mercury are harsh after the songs of Apollo.

It is attributed to no particular character, and is set in a type larger than that used for the printing of the main body of the play. In the Folio text the line remains, but is assigned to the 'Braggart' (i.e. Armado) who adds 'You that way: we this way' as an exit-line for the characters assembled on the stage. The various editors of *Love's Labour's Lost* have responded in different ways to this choice of endings. Dover Wilson and Quiller-Couch in the New Cambridge edition, and Richard David in the New Arden edition are the exception amongst recent editors in preferring that of the First Quarto. Most others tend to assign the line to Armado, thus reducing its prominence, and the peculiar quality given it by the larger type. Possibly they share with E. K. Chambers the feeling that 'Mercury has nothing to do with what precedes'.[8]

Yet Mercury, it will be remembered, was associated by Ben Jonson with language, being styled its President. In his role as messenger of the Gods, Mercury (or Hermes) was also firmly associated with writing, often as its inventor, a connection he

---

[7] *Phaedrus* 275 c5–d2, edn. *cit.*, p. 158.
[8] E. K. Chambers, *William Shakespeare, a study of Facts and Problems* (Oxford 1930), Vol. I, p. 338. In connection with the point that follows, I am greatly indebted to the hitherto unpublished work of my research student, Malcolm Evans.

shared with his Egyptian and Scandinavian counterparts. As the various avatars of Mercury merge into a single figure in the Renaissance, this association becomes more and more firmly established, so that, for example, Nashe's *Summer's Last Will and Testament* (1592–3), in the process of a satirical account of the history of writing, can tell how Hermes/Mercury

> Weary with graving, in blind characters,
> And figures of familiar beasts and plants
> Invented letters to write lies withal. . . .
>
> (1262 ff.)

Apollo, of course, symbolized no less a number of disparate ideas during the same period, but in respect of the contrast with Mercury here postulated will obviously primarily be connected with language in its oral form, and its tonal aspects; a relationship appropriate to his role as god of music and harmony. Robert Stephanus's *Thesaurus Linguae Latinae* (1573) assigns to Apollo the specific role, amongst others, of protector of the vocal chords. In short, both Mercury and Apollo could be said to have a good deal to do with 'what precedes'.

The line 'The words of Mercury are harsh after the songs of Apollo' perhaps constitutes not so much a comment on the *subject* of *Love's Labour's Lost*, in which Mercury as Mercade the messenger brings his harsh words into the Apollonian atmosphere of the play, as a comment on the *form* of this play, and on the nature of the drama which it embodies. The 'words of Mercury' are surely *Love's Labour's Lost* seen in written form; in its printed Quarto version. It is itself part of the world of books which the play has urged us to reject. The 'songs of Apollo' are those oral words heard in the actual performance of the play, of which the book is a 'harsh' shadow. The book cannot 'contain' the play, as Dover Wilson discovered for himself when he was 'converted' by Tyrone Guthrie's production in 1936,[9] and the words are printed in a larger type, separate from the words of the play for this reason. They constitute a comment on the *book* the reader of *Love's Labour's Lost* holds in his hand. Momentarily he is like the 'bookmen' of the play,

[9] J. Dover Wilson, *Shakespeare's Happy Comedies* (London, 1962), pp. 64 ff.

engrossed in a 'reduced' world of writing, not in the 'real' world of oral interchange, of which the play in performance is a compelling version. The play's epigraph, which these words are, is perhaps intended to jolt him out of that state; to force him to raise his eyes from the 'speeches penned' and to encounter the world with voice and ear, to add the reconciling vocal, auditory dimension of rhyme to the silent world of reason, to temper dialectic with rhetoric in the oral spirit intended by Berowne. The words thus use the functions of Mercury to achieve the purpose of Apollo, uniting these opposites in characteristically Shakespearean fashion. It is perhaps this aspect of his work that Ben Jonson celebrates in the lines he wrote for the great 'book of the plays' the First Folio, which refer explicitly to 'What He Hath Left Us';

> He was not of an age but for all time!
> And all the muses still were in their prime
> When like Apollo he came forth to warm
> Our ears, or like a Mercury to charm!

Nor is *Love's Labour's Lost* the only item of evidence he hath left us: there are the plays at large, the condition in which they have come down to us, and the point of view this condition perhaps embodies. G. E. Bentley has pointed out in some detail that for complex reasons Shakespeare manifests very little interest in his plays as works to be themselves read.[10] He was certainly interested in readers for his poems, but of the thirty-seven or so plays ascribed to him, he could never have seen twenty in print. Moreover, none of the plays printed in his lifetime gives any impression of having been overseen by the author with any degree of care.

We may, as T. J. B. Spencer puts it '... consider it incredible that he should not have expected his plays to be read as well as performed'.[11] It is indeed incredible. Yet the very *degree* of our incredulity testifies perhaps to the effectiveness of the anaesthetic of literacy that has us 'bookmen' in its grip.

[10] G. E. Bentley, *Shakespeare and His Theatre* (Lincoln, Nebraska, 1964), pp. 1–26.
[11] T. J. B. Spencer, 'The Elizabethan Theatre-Poet' in David Galloway, ed., *The Elizabethan Theatre* (London, 1969), p. 6.

For to suggest an opposite view is to do nothing more startling than to characterize Shakespeare as an artist supremely committed to the oral art of drama. ' . . . he was naturally learned' Dryden said of him in his *Essay of Dramatick Poesie* (1668); 'he needed not the spectacles of books to read nature'. He is the Theatre-Poet, that is to say, not the Book-Poet, and the sense of that distinction and its related commitment in these plays is perhaps one of their most underestimated ingredients.[12]

Because to be a Theatre-Poet is, after all, to manifest a personal faith in language's oral dimension. It is to believe that true immortality perhaps ultimately resides more in the apparent ephemerality of speech, less in the apparent permanence of writing. As Heywood, Shakespeare's contemporary, put it in his *Apology for Actors* (1612), the drama's vested interest in speech as its raw material actually expands and improves the language:

> Our English tongue, which hath been the most harsh, uneven, and broken language of the world . . . is now, by this secondary means of playing, continually refined . . . so that in process from the most rude and unpolisht tongue it is grown to a most perfect and composed language.

In a sense, it is *that* truth which we manifest in our daily lives. What links us with Shakespeare is exactly this reciprocal process, the oral process of the language that, 400 years since he used it, is still second—even first—nature to most of us. And in the matter of his aptest memorial we risk an overemphasis on the advice given in the First Folio to 'the Great Variety of Readers', to 'reade him, therefore; and againe, and againe'. On the contrary, let it be proposed, by one Talking Animal to others; *si monumentum requiris, audite.*

[12] We have, of course, lost sight of the aristocratic view of the situation. J. W. Saunders has pointed out that, in Court circles, publication of one's work carried a certain social stigma. A Court poet went to great lengths to *avoid* appearing in print, and adopted many conventionally apologetic stances when his verses were printed. '. . . for the amateur poet of the Court an avoidance of print was *socially* desirable.' 'The Stigma of Print', *Essays in Criticism*, Vol. 1, No. 2, April 1951, pp. 139–64. The point would not be lost on the highly literate, aristocratic audience for whose private enjoyment this play was perhaps first conceived.

7
Richard II:
the word against the word

I

Drama, it has been established, is not literature. In particular, Shakespeare's 'writing'—by definition, dramatic—leans in principle away from the printed page and towards the *spoken* language. The words themselves, as *Love's Labour's Lost* reminds us, have ultimately less to do with the 'book' in which they occur, than with the qualities of the human voice engaged in speech. They realize themselves aurally, rather than visually.

If Shakespeare's audience was at the very least residually oral-aural in character, committed far more to talking than to writing, then its speech, like all speech the fruit of a gigantic collaborative enterprise over the centuries, could be said to have generated the language Shakespeare found and used in his plays.

Given this, it seems not unreasonable to suppose that the relationship between the audience and its language must also to some extent be what the plays are *about*. Their concern with issues central to an oral-aural society must beget, reflexively, a concern with the nature, condition and role of the spoken language itself in that society.

We know, in fact, that Shakespeare's plays sprang from and responded to a theatre whose relationship with its own culture was one of unequalled reciprocity in respect of the spoken vernacular language. G. R. Owst has demonstrated that much of the 'free vernacular colloquy' of the medieval Miracle and Morality plays derived from the fact that 'vernacular preachers were daily proving the efficacy of this kind of speech in sermons on a level with the thought and expression of popular audiences'.[1] And he argues convincingly that this marks the beginning of an interpenetrative relationship between the oral-aural modes of the pulpit on the one hand and of the stage on the other, which extends unbroken up to and beyond Elizabethan and Jacobean times, constituting 'the emergence of a native school of vernacular comedy and tragedy, parent of our modern drama'.[2]

Naturally, the plays themselves form a large part of the evidence on which such a judgment must be based. Viewed in this light, their linguistic vitality seems a commensurate reflection of the largely oral culture from which they derived, and towards which they were directed. In it, words would characteristically have been a virtually all-embracing feature of life, inhabiting an acoustic and involving, rather than a visual and distancing space for the majority. When that language, that way of life, and the drama which comes out of these are those of an island people, circumscribed, self-sufficient, and hardly susceptible to outside influence for reasons of state and of religion as well as those of geography, then the interaction between these elements must prove correspondingly more fundamental. Language, way of life, and drama, will be more closely knit, the influence of each on the other more radically formative.

That the way of life of Elizabethan Britain was insular and self-sustaining, like its little-known language of English, needs no demonstration. What is of interest is the extent to which these factors act significantly as determinants in the plays, making not merely their use of English, but their attitude towards the language, and the social and political implications of its role, a major feature of their relationship with the society from which their first audiences were drawn.

In general terms, Shakespeare's history plays seem to embody and reinforce what might be called a fundamentally oral outlook. And of course it differs markedly from our own. Frances Yates has recently brilliantly reminded us that the faculty of

[1] G. R. Owst, *Literature and Pulpit in Medieval England* (Cambridge, 1933), p. 478.
[2] *Ibid.*, p. 591.

memory plays a crucial role in an oral setting, acting as the repository of the cultural tradition, and proving highly developed in response to that important function.[3] But memory's opposite, forgetting, is also important in the same process. Memory, it could be argued, acts collectively as a selective filter, storing experience of continuing relevance to the society. Non-relevant experience is then systematically forgotten, in what has been termed a process of structural amnesia. As a result, the present permanently imposes its own shape on the past, so that in an oral society the world seems always to have been as it is now. Its 'past' looks exactly like its 'present'. Myth takes the place of 'history', and the overwhelming bias towards consistency between past and present makes such societies normally deeply conservative. Such changes as occur tend to be redressive and reconciling, reinforcing rather than innovatory, and at their most extreme take the form of rebellion rather than revolution.[4]

A context such as this seems to have generated the history plays' view of the world. In them, myth and 'history' merge, and the shape of the present determines that of the past. The upheavals chronicled have a redressive, reconciling, reinforcing mode, and take the form of rebellion rather than revolution. The king is rejected, but not kingship.

In fact, the essence of what has been misleadingly termed the Tudor 'revolution' had been the establishment of the king as the vital and unifying communicative link between man and deity and man and man. Through him, men could symbolically 'speak' to one another, to God, and in English. And just as the Christian God is always characterized as a *communicator*, one who talks directly and personally to man so, as God's vicegerent, the Christian king ought ideally to manifest the same 'civilizing' quality.

[3] Frances A. Yates, *The Art of Memory*, cit.
[4] I am here drawing heavily on the essay by Jack Goody and Ian Watt, 'The Consequences of Literacy' in Jack Goody (ed.), *Literacy in Traditional Societies*, cit., pp. 27-68.

II

Richard II, of course, notably does not. And as one which focuses on a crucial turning-point in British social and political history, the play which tells his story invites examination in these terms. What immediately becomes clear is that a central dramatic concern with opposition, embodied in its most extreme form as a civil strife, is quite literally made manifest through the language of the play. In fact the social activity of language itself, which obviously always depends on an intrinsic and definining notion of reciprocity, of talking on the one hand and of responsive listening on the other, seems to take on almost opposite qualities here. Instead of reciprocity, antagonism; instead of talking and listening, ranting and deafness; in place of the warmth of human colloquy, the play coldly sets, in its own terms, 'the word against the word'.

Such a conflict (a fundamental infraction, after all, of man's natural role as *talking* animal) appropriately symbolizes the dehumanizing effects of civil war, in which the natural structure of the family, including the larger political family of society, is riven by the unnatural pitting of brother against brother, father against son. In Shakespeare's view, such a situation clearly violates rudimentary moral, political, and social tenets. The destruction of reciprocal talking and listening reduces man to the level of the beasts.

From the first, the play depicts Richard as a king ruling over a society in which truly sympathetic communication between the people has deteriorated beyond repair. He brings conflicting Bolingbroke and Mowbray together with the notion that, in his kingly presence, the loss will in some way be restored. They will 'freely speak' (I, i, 17) whilst he will 'hear' them. Yet in spite of this confident assertion of his traditional social role, certain qualities of Richard's own speech ironically point in an opposite direction. For whilst Bolingbroke and Mowbray are said to have abandoned the very bases of reciprocal communication—despite attempts at reconciliation they remain 'In rage, deaf as the sea' (I, i, 19)—Richard's assessment of the situation and of his own part in it itself exhibits a stultifying quality of rigidity, and suggests certain prevalent habits of conceptualization which seem happiest at the farthest remove from the complexities of actuality.[5] Beginning with his formal pronouncement to Gaunt,

> Old John of Gaunt, time-honoured Lancaster,
> Hast thou according to thy oath and band
> Brought hither Henry Hereford, thy bold son,
> (I, i, 1–3)

and ending with his shifting of the quarrel to the simplified level of a confrontation between opponents at the lists, Richard's method of dealing with reality is to abstract it from its human context and to reduce it to some formula that can be dealt with at a safe distance. His design so controls the situation that the participants can hardly be expected to 'freely speak' as human beings; they are forced simply to act out the reduced roles he imposes on them. Richard's own involvement, with Mowbray, in the murder of Thomas of Woodstock (a factor known to the audience) supplies a reasonable motive for such an approach on the level of the plot, but a good deal of support for it comes nevertheless from his interpretation of his own role as king in the matter, and responsive human contact plays no large part in that. As Mowbray comments, doubtless bitterly in the circumstances, Richard's kingship encourages not freedom of expression, but the reverse:

> ... the fair reverence of your Highness curbs me
> From giving reins and spurs to my free speech.
> (I, i, 54–5)

In the sense that Mowbray has acted as Richard's tool, the quarrel between him and Bolingbroke functions as a precursor of the later clash between Bolingbroke and Richard, and it helps to characterize that more momentous conflict in that the 'bitter clamour of two eager tongues' (I, i, 49) aptly describes a major aspect of both. Indeed, absence of the warmth of

---

[5] For an account of the way in which this point and others can be affirmed and underscored spatially by the staging of the play, see John Russell Brown, *Shakespeare's Plays in Performance, cit.*, pp. 115–30.

human communication receives specific stress, and acquires symbolic force, in the fliting which ensues. Both Bolingbroke and Mowbray use language as a weapon; their words become increasingly pugnacious, accusatory, alarming, and essentially uncommunicative. Neither really *listens* to the other. Thus Bolingbroke constantly offers physical violence in support of what he has to say:

> . . . what I speak
> My body shall make good upon this earth!
> (I, i, 36–7)

> What my tongue speaks my right-drawn sword may prove.
> (I, i, 46)

and Mowbray in return hurls back words which are 'cold' as well as essentially abusive. Communicative interchange is replaced by its opposite which would thrust 'These terms of treason doubled down his throat' (I, i, 57). Indeed, the very act and organs of speech themselves undergo metaphorical distortion. The throat becomes a 'false passage' by whose means lies are 'swallowed down' (I, i, 133); the tongue 'wounds' like a weapon (I, i, 191), and animal snarling replaces discourse:

> I do defy him, and I spit at him,
> Call him a slanderous coward and a villain.
> (I, i, 60–1)

The formality of the occasion, inspired by Richard and signalled from time to time by the rhyme which creeps into the combatant's speech (e.g. I, i, 41–6, and I, i, 150–1), of course further militates against any humanity that might have prevailed, even on the level of this becoming a 'woman's war' of mere words (I, i, 49). It does not do so, partly because more serious issues underly it, and to a greater extent because Richard seems determined to settle the matter by inappropriate methods—that is, by removing from the situation as many human elements as possible. The reductive structure of the verse reinforces such an approach:

> This we prescribe, though no physician;
> Deep malice makes too deep incision;
> Forget, forgive, conclude, and be agreed;
> Our doctors say this is no month to bleed.
>
> (I, i, 154–7)

Little human contact can be expected from this, and of course none comes. The throwing down of gages 'interchangeably' (I, i, 146) replaces responsive interaction. Words from now on act merely as the sheaths of swords. Animal violence lies beneath them, and becomes the real test of their truth. Each contestant 'will in battle prove' his utterances and, as Bolingbroke says, 'make good against thee, arm to arm/What I have spoke' (I, i, 76–7). The 'chivalrous design of knightly trial' (I, i, 81) thus serves to embody and abstract the conflict in terms which, from Richard's point of view, satisfactorily simplify it:

> We were not born to sue, but to command;
> Which, since we cannot do to make you friends,
> Be ready, as your lives shall answer it,
> At Coventry upon Saint Lambert's day.
> There shall your swords and lances arbitrate
> The swelling difference of your settled hate.
> Since we cannot atone you, we shall see
> Justice design the victor's chivalry.
>
> (I, i, 196–203)

Such unwillingness really to become involved in the complexities of human communication, and such a pathetic abandonment of what Shakespeare would regard as his true role as king in favour of a simple assignment of justice to the strong (compare the opposite in the hero-King, Henry V, who talks with humanity to the common soldier), indicates the root of Richard's tragedy. Genuine human communication with his subjects—and so genuine human reality—eludes him and, while he is King, remains absent from his kingdom. Within it, his subjects' lives come to depend on physical strength, not human contact. However much the formality of the lists attempts to conceal this, the combatants there fight like animals. However much the formality of rhyme attempts to conceal it, they snarl and roar at each other like beasts. Indeed, such formalities, representing as they do a considerable degree of abstraction from ordinary human life, perhaps suggest a peculiarly human form of self-debasement, and so of bestiality. For when talking and listening break down, when communication fails, man becomes less than man. The King, as the play frequently suggests (e.g. I, iv, 45) functions as a farmer, his country as a farm, and the 'divine' institution of monarchy is tragically debased. He is

> A king of beasts indeed: if aught but beasts,
> I had been still a happy king of men.
>
> (V, i, 35–6)

Thus when the actual meeting of Bolingbroke and Mowbray takes place at the lists (I, iii), its larger significance as an instance of Richard's failure lies behind the confrontation of the antagonists, and the nature of that failure and its cause overshadows the ensuing action. In fact, the confrontation merely produces so much verbal noise (I, iii, 22 ff.), itself paralleled by the communication-defeating din of physical conflict that, as Richard himself notices, denies any chance of men's peaceful communion, with its

> ... boistrous untuned drums
> With harsh resounding trumpets' dreadful bray
> And grating shock of wrathful iron arms.
>
> (I, iii, 134–6)

Richard's throwing down of his warder—the ultimate in wordless formality—of course solves nothing, and only serves to make permanent the rift between Bolingbroke and Mowbray, as well as, in the light of the effect of Bolingbroke's banishment, sowing the seeds of the gigantic rift of civil war. A kingly act which, in underwriting division, physical violence, and dehumanizing strife, betrays the institution's unifying function, it momentarily symbolizes Richard's rule and its social effects.

Typically, Richard proceeds to 'reduce' the situation one

RICHARD II: THE WORD AGAINST THE WORD

degree further. Confronted by estrangement of a fundamental sort, he deals with it by means of additional and more literal estrangement. Unable to bring the contenders together, he formally separates them from each other, and from himself, and from his and their own country, by banishment.

The degree to which banishment, far from curing lack of communication, serves only to reinforce it, of course undergoes examination in political terms throughout the rest of the play, and indeed the cycle of plays which succeeds it. For the banishment of the disaffected Bolingbroke not only precipitates the Wars of the Roses, it also initiates a social, moral, and economic disorder without parallel in the Elizabethan mind.

Appropriately then, the banishment also becomes symbolically relevant to the nature of Richard's failure as a king, for it takes the particular manifestation of a prohibition against speech itself. The metaphors exhibit a recurrent concern with language and the human voice. Richard 'breathes' the 'hopeless word' of 'never to return' (I, iii, 152) which Mowbray punningly calls a 'heavy sentence', one 'all unlooked for from your Highness' mouth' (I, iii, 154–5), and the full linguistic implications of the sentence are vividly brought out in the complaint which follows:

> The language I have learnt these forty years,
> My native English, now I must forgo,
> And now my tongue's use is to me no more
> Than an unstringed viol or a harp,
> Or like a cunning instrument cased up,
> Or being open, put into his hands
> That knows no touch to tune the harmony.
> Within my mouth you have enjailed my tongue,
> Doubly portcullised with my teeth and lips,
> And dull unfeeling barren ignorance
> Is made my jailer to attend on me.
> I am too old to fawn upon a nurse,
> Too far in years to be a pupil now;
> What is thy sentence then but speechless death,
> Which robs my tongue from breathing native breath?
>
> (I, iii, 159–73)

There is, of course, a sense in which such enforced dumbness also ironically mirrors Richard's own condition.

With equal irony, the play depicts him as no less tragically unable to listen, and his metaphorical deafness receives frequent comment. Even when Gaunt lies on his deathbed, about to speak those 'inspired' dying prophecies that tradition insists should be attentively heard, York says of Richard that 'all in vain comes counsel to his ear' (II, i, 4). Gaunt protests, expressing the hope that 'my death's sad tale may yet undeaf his ear' (II, i, 16), but that hope is never realized. Richard's ears remain 'stopped with other flattering sounds' (II, i, 17), and despite protestations to the contrary (e.g. III, ii, 93), his final account of himself in prison admits exactly this charge:

> ... here have I the daintiness of ear
> To check time broke in a disordered string;
> But for the concord of my state and time,
> Had not an ear to hear my true time broke.
> (V, v, 45–8)

Indeed, before Flint castle, Bolingbroke's sending of his emissary,

> ... to the rude ribs of that ancient castle
> Through brazen trumpet send the breath of parley
> Into his ruined ears. ...
> (III, iii, 31–3)

implicitly suggests the extent to which the civil war has maimed oral-aural communication in the kingdom at large.

Gaunt's prophecies do indeed prove inspired, for they give us an accurate picture of Richard as he really is. In the absence of genuinely communicative humanity, brutality and bestiality prevail in him. Vanity, like an 'insatiate cormorant' preys on his personality (II, i, 38), and England, the 'royal throne of kings' becomes 'leased out. . . . Like to a tenement or pelting farm' (II, i, 59–60). He rules over a less-than-human people who cannot reach him, or each other through him. His proper role of 'gardener' has been replaced by that of landlord: he who should tend now exploits. As Gaunt dies, human communication in England seems to die with him, and

> . . . all is said;
> His tongue is now a stringless instrument;
> Words, life and all, old Lancaster hath spent.
> (II, i, 148–50)

III

Richard D. Altick has argued that Richard's 'fatal weakness' lies in his 'propensity for verbalizing'. He '. . . cannot bring himself to live in a world of hard actuality; the universe to him is real only as it is presented in packages of fine words'. Altick goes on to suggest that the play is 'preoccupied with the unsubstantiality of human language', and that its characters 'By making the physical act of speech, the sheer fact of language, so conspicuous . . . call attention to its illusory nature. . . . That words are mere conventional sounds molded by the tongue, and reality is something else again, is constantly on the minds of all the characters.'[6]

Clearly, Richard's use of language does indicate a specific sort of response to the harsh world in which he finds himself, but perhaps it has a more complex quality than Mr. Altick's view allows. To refer to Richard's 'complacent enjoyment of the sound of his own tongue' surely oversimplifies the issue, for he is no self-satisfied blowhard. Also, words may be mere conventional sounds, but they are not that easily separable from reality. The notion that language is one thing and reality 'something else again', certainly is a view held by the play's main characters. But the play itself seems to argue the reverse case: that language and reality are indivisible, coextensive, and that communication by means of talking and listening embodies man's nature and constitutes his genuine reality. Indeed *Richard II* could be said, ultimately, to document the sort of tragic situation which comes about when that fact ceases to be taken into account.

[6] Richard D. Altick, 'Symphonic Imagery in *Richard II*', *PMLA*, Vol. LXII (1947), pp. 339–65.

Thus, when Queen Isabel encounters the Duke of York bringing news of war and social upheaval, she timidly tries to deflect his report, urging '... for God's sake, speak comfortable words' (II, ii, 76). The sense, of course, is that of 'comforting' in the way that the Anglican communion service uses the word. The notion that certain words can alter reality, modify it to the design of the speaker, is a very old one, with its roots in pagan thought, and it depends, obviously, on the notion of a relationship between language and reality which allows the former to be capable of significantly affecting the latter. It is a notion which presupposes that language is one thing, reality 'something else again', that 'comfortable' words exist whose efficacy can change harsh fact into a more pleasing shape.[7]

In all its superstitious crudity, this may be said to contain the key to Richard's view of the world for, far from accepting the necessity of man's having to use language in order to communicate with man, and so create the only reality, that of the talking-listening community, Richard acts on the principle that language serves as a 'comfortable' moulding device by whose means he *alone* can create his own kingly version of existence which can be imposed on everyone. Life, he believes, will become what his 'language', as King, makes it. His downfall springs from his inability to recognize any *communal* reality beyond that painted by his own 'comfortable words'.

So, when Aumerle tries to draw his attention to Bolingbroke's imminent rebellion, Richard dismisses him as 'discomfortable cousin' (III, ii, 36). Later when Salisbury, bringing bad news, affirms that 'Discomfort guides my tongue' (III, ii, 65), Richard, urged by Aumerle to remember the 'comfort' that lies in his kingship—'Comfort, my liege, remember who you are' (III, ii, 82)—does so by asserting the power that 'comfortable' words, such as his own title, have for him:

> I had forgot myself: am I not king?
> Awake, thou coward majesty! Thou sleepest.

---

[7] M. M. Mahood, *Shakespeare's Wordplay* (London, 1957) gives a striking account of the medieval 'faith in verbal magic' and the resultant belief in the immense efficacy of language. As she demonstrates, *Richard II* 'is a play about the efficacy of a king's words' (p. 73).

Is not the king's name twenty thousand names?
Arm, arm, my name!
>   (III, ii, 83–6)

Bolingbroke perhaps most aptly recognizes the relationship between language and 'real life' entailed in this when he wryly comments on Richard's somewhat arbitrary reduction of his sentence of banishment from ten years to six:

> How long a time lies in one little word.
> Four lagging winters and four wanton springs
> End in a word—such is the breath of kings.
>   (I, iii, 212–14)

He sees that the 'breath of kings', Richard's 'language', has power, not over reality, but over that part of it which society, by its structure and its laws, cedes to him.[8] Richard can 'end in a word' four years of banishment in that sense, and indeed, he has power of life and death. But his words have no genuine power over the reality of time—a point made by Gaunt only a few lines later:

> *Richard:* Why! uncle, thou hast many years to live.
> *Gaunt:* But not a minute, king, that thou canst give;
> Shorten my days thou canst with sullen sorrow,
> And pluck nights from me, but not lend a morrow;
> Thou canst help time to furrow me with age,
> But stop no wrinkle in his pilgrimage:
> Thy word is current with him for my death,
> But dead, thy kingdom cannot buy my breath!
>   (I, iii, 224–31)

It might be said that Richard's very existence traditionally depends on language and reality being indivisible in him: that he only exists as king in so far as he communicates as one. This is also to say that the monarchy's existence depends on the king's tacit acceptance of social contexts and sanctions which determine the range of actions that can properly be termed

---
[8] Cf. Mahood, *op. cit.*, p. 77.

kingly. The king, in other words, must behave *like* a king or he will cease to be one.

In so far as man is essentially a social creature, personal identity always depends to a certain extent on social identity. It is a matter of reciprocal communication with other people. Richard's notion that he can mould reality (and so society) as *he* wishes, simply by the use of 'comfortable' words, ignores a reality larger than himself: that of a society which creates the communicative fabric, the 'culture' or way of life which, in turn, creates him. A king, after all, has no reality outside the society that accepts him as king. In violating the language from which that society derives its corporate identity, Richard at once and cognately overrides its coterminous laws and customs, the fundamental interactive mechanisms making up the way of life which constitutes its reality and his own. As a result he puts himself outside that society's boundary, and so loses his identity as king.

And, of course, he has no other. It has already been pointed out that an oral society characteristically imposes fully involving *roles* on its members, rather than separate individual 'personalities'. The sense of a 'private' and 'personal' life lying 'beyond' a role would be foreign to it. The distinction we take for granted between an exterior, objective, 'public' world, and an interior, personal 'private' world is a fairly modern one to which literacy makes its own significant contribution. In a largely non-literate society, the king could have no private or personal life beyond his kingship. And Richard was, in fact, the last king of the medieval order, ruling by hereditary right. He did not hold an office that could be arbitrarily taken up or relinquished like a modern 'job'. Nobody could be an ex-king in Elizabethan England.

Accordingly, York sees Richard's appropriation of Bolingbroke's social rights as a violation of something far more fundamental than civil law: it strikes at the very basis of social 'language' and so of Richard's identity:

> Take Hereford's rights away, and take from time
> His charters and his customary rights,
> Let not tomorrow then ensue today;

RICHARD II: THE WORD AGAINST THE WORD

> Be not thyself. For how art thou a king
> But by fair sequence and succession?
> (II, i, 195–9)

Richard's attempt to impose his own order of things on the communicative structure of 'fair sequence and succession' causes that structure to cast him out. When he ceases to communicate like a king, he ceases to exist; and as we learn later, when 'fair sequence and succession' has been replaced by its opposite, then 'The King is not himself' (II, i, 241).

The misuse of language thus constitutes a major element in the crimes for which Richard loses his crown. For instance, the play insists over and again that his presence actually inhibits oral-aural interaction. Thus, in II, i, only when Richard leaves the stage do the disaffected nobles feel free to speak, a point which is almost laboured:

> *Ross:* My heart is great but it must break with silence
> Ere't be disburdened with a liberal tongue.
> *Northumberland:* Nay, speak thy mind, and let him ne'er speak more
> That speaks thy words again to do thee harm.
> *Willoughby:* Tends that that thou wouldst speak to the Duke of Hereford?
> If it be so, out with it boldly, man;
> Quick is mine ear to hear of good towards him.
> (II, i, 228–34)

Northumberland is urged 'be confident to speak' (II, i, 274) amongst the conspirators, whose purpose seems to them to be the restoration of the reality of communication to society, and to the institution of kingship:

> Redeem from broking pawn the blemished crown,
> Wipe off the dust that hides our sceptre's gilt,
> And make high majesty look like itself.
> (II, i, 293–5)

Meanwhile, Richard's efforts to change reality by means of language extend to the physical environment, the very earth of Britain itself. He personifies it, 'Dear earth, I do salute thee with my hand' (III, ii, 6), urges it to help his cause, 'Feed not thy sovereign's foe, my gentle earth' (III, ii, 12), and this not merely with the degree of licence to be expected in a verse play, for his own nobles clearly think that something odd prevails in this attitude. Richard feels constrained to abjure them;

> Mock not my senseless conjuration, lords:
> This earth shall have a feeling, and these stones
> Prove armed soldiers. . . .
>
> (III, ii, 24–6)

Such verbal 'conjuration' suggests nevertheless a degree of fantasy almost certainly fatal for a man confronted by an adversary such as Bolingbroke, and indeed his advisers do try to bring him literally 'down to earth', to make him cope with reality. But Richard's tendency simply asserts itself against all advice. He continues to try to impose the 'realities' of language on those of harsh fact, to make metaphors 'real' in a concrete sense. Thus the metaphor of king as 'Sun' takes on, as he uses it of himself, a note of delusion; he tries literally to become 'the searching eye of heaven' (III, ii, 37) whose divine power needs only to be affirmed:

> So when this thief, this traitor, Bolingbroke,
> Who all this while hath revelled in the night
> Whilst we were wand'ring with the Antipodes,
> Shall see us rising in our throne, the east,
> His treasons will sit blushing in his face,
> Not able to endure the sight of day,
> But self-affrighted tremble at his sin.
>
> (III, ii, 47–53)

This is the 'breath of kings', the words which, Richard imagines, by saying a situation is so, *make* it so. By contrast,

> The breath of worldly men cannot depose
> The deputy elected by the Lord.
>
> (III, ii, 56–7)

But that can only be metaphorically true: the harsh reality lies in the fact that 'the breath of worldly men' can depose, and does.

If talking about victory fails to produce it, the same attitude to language must attempt to make defeat over into something more attractive:

> For God's sake let us sit upon the ground
> And tell sad stories of the death of Kings.
>
> (III, ii, 155–6)

But the 'sad stories', inevitably self-dramatizations, lead far away, in the opposite direction from reality. Even momentary revelations of his own essential humanity,

> I live with bread like you, feel want,
> Taste grief, need friends: subjected thus
> How can you say to me, I am a king?
>
> (III, ii, 175–7)

do not fully grasp the situation's reality, for they dramatize Richard's ordinariness without reference to the fact that he has an extraordinary and all-consuming social role, which makes it impossible for him to be 'like' any commoner. Even when the 'ague fit of fear' that has produced such thoughts is 'overblown' (III, ii, 190), he persists in equating himself with his 'name':

> ... O that I were as great
> As is my grief, or lesser than my name!
>
> (III, iii, 135–6)

And his own impending deposition takes the form of a linguistic loss in which he must ultimately 'lose/The name of King' (III, iii, 144–5), that most 'comfortable' of words.

The climax of the use of 'comfortable words' perhaps

follows in Richard's final, almost wholly deluded configuration of himself in a 'Sun' image. Deposed, having transferred his 'name' to Bolingbroke (III, iii, 172), he sees himself involved in a metaphorical 'setting' of his power and status, linguistically signalled by an involved pun: if Bolingbroke is now the 'Sun', Richard is merely his charioteer, Apollo's 'son':

> Down, down I come, like glist'ring Phaethon
> Wanting the manage of unruly jades.
> In the base court! Base court where kings grow base,
> To come at traitors' calls, and do them grace:
> In the base court, come down: down court, down king.
> (III, iii, 177–81)

An almost hysterical over-adornment characterizes the language in its attempt to transmute base experience into the gold of something more heroic. As Northumberland comments,

> . . . Sorrow and grief of heart
> Makes him speak fondly like a frantic man.
> (III, iii, 182–3)

What follows in the play constitutes a complete dissolution of language in Richard, to the extent that he becomes unable to confront reality at all. Language for him speedily takes the form of a screen behind which he hides, posturing as Christ (IV, i, 169 ff. and IV, i, 239–41), and thus desperately trying (and failing) to impose some mythic as well as linguistic order on the facts of his deposition.

His discovery that reality has eluded him, and will no longer shape itself to 'the breath of kings' leads at last to his recognition that the rights attaching to the crown have a considerable linguistic dimension which must be discarded with it:

> With mine own hands I give away my crown,
> With mine own tongue deny my sacred state,
> With mine own breath release all duteous oaths.
> (IV, i, 207–9)

His deprivation, he insists, has to do with language as much as politics. His 'name' has been usurped as well as his throne:

> ... I have no name, no title,
> No, not that name was given me at the font
> But 'tis usurped. Alack the heavy day!
> That I have worn so many winters out
> And know not now what name to call myself.
> (IV, i, 254–8)

Standing before 'the sun of Bolingbroke', 'bankrupt of his majesty', his 'word' no longer 'sterling' in England (IV, i, 260 ff.) he commands a mirror to be brought so that, as ever, he can look inward, not communicating directly with the world, with reality, but with himself alone, like a reader who studies alone, without communicating outside the realm of the printed page, abstracted from the warmth of oral-aural contact. And, indeed, a glance at his own face in the mirror reveals the absence of a real and communicable identity: 'How soon my sorrow hath destroyed my face' (IV, i, 290). But, as Bolingbroke comments, the situation has a grimmer aspect even than that. Richard has become so far removed from reality that his world even now is one of mere shadows, and

> The shadow of your sorrow hath destroyed
> The shadow of your face.
> (IV, i, 291–2)

The spectacle of Richard staring at his reflection in the mirror perfectly symbolizes his inability to communicate as a human being. When he talks it is to himself; when he listens it is to himself. Thus it seems appropriate that when he ultimately speaks of himself as an actor, he stands in fact for the ultimate perversion of that art: the actor who has no audience but himself.

This, after all, provides the basis for the full irony of his earlier account of the 'hollow crown' (III, ii, 160 ff.). Literally a 'Globe-like' theatre, the golden circle within whose walls Death allows

> ... a little scene,
> To monarchize, be feared, and kill with looks,
>
> (III, ii, 164–5)

contains no audience, and the kings are merely actors whose acting fails to communicate with anybody. We are not surprised, later, to hear Richard's ride through London described in theatrical terms:

> As in a theatre the eyes of men,
> After a well-graced actor leaves the stage,
> Are idly bent on him that enters next,
> Thinking his prattle to be tedious;
>
> (V, ii, 23–6)

The 'well-graced actor' is of course Bolingbroke. Richard, as ever uncommunicative, utters only tedious 'prattle'.

The final sight we have of Richard confirms and restates all these points. His failure is a failure of humanity, because it involves a failure of language. Alone, unable to communicate, unable to face reality still, and still attempting to force external circumstances into a shape which his words have predetermined, he utters the final exhalation of the 'breath of kings':

> I have been studying how I may compare
> This prison where I live unto the world:
> And for because the world is populous,
> And here is not a creature but myself,
> I cannot do it.
>
> (V, v, 1–5)

He finds it difficult to produce words as 'comfortable' as he feels the situation demands. Yet he forces the language to this task:

> ... Yet I'll hammer it out:
> My brain I'll prove the female to my soul,
> My soul the father, and these two beget
> A generation of still-breeding thoughts;
> And these same thoughts people this little world,
> In humours like the people of this world.
>
> (V, v, 5–10)

The metaphor finally, and ironically, betrays him, for he finds that, mirroring the events of his own kingdom, the thoughts cannot live happily as a community but fight amongst themselves in a civil war which usurps the principle of order lying at the very basis of human existence, in language itself:

> For no thought is contented. The better sort,
> As thoughts of things divine, are intermixed
> With scruples, and do set the word itself
> Against the word. . . .
>
> (V, v, 11–14)

IV

From the very first, a distinction clearly emerges between Richard and Bolingbroke in the matter of language. As Gaunt points out, Bolingbroke 'hoards' his words (I, iii, 252) where Richard, by implication, 'spends' them. Where Richard's 'breath of kings' acts as an instrument for changing reality, a means of colouring it, Bolingbroke's view of the world seems to rest on the notion of a static reality which remains stable, unchanging, whatever may be said about it.[9] The same debilitating gulf between language on the one hand and reality on the other that was noticed in Richard clearly also operates in his usurper.

To Bolingbroke language consists 'merely' of words, and so words have no special value for him. He does not scatter them with Richard's profusion, for he has not Richard's ends in view. When, in the deposition scene, Richard says 'And if my word be sterling yet in England/Let it command a mirror hither straight' (IV, i, 263–4), Bolingbroke's words prove to be the ones which genuinely command, nevertheless: 'Go some of you, and fetch a looking glass' (IV, i, 267). The contrast between these two ways of speaking, the one formal and, in the circumstances, slightly ornate, pretentious, and ultimately

---

[9] Mahood argues forcefully that Bolingbroke 'knows words have no inherent potency of meaning, but by strength of character and force of arms he is able to make them mean what he wants them to mean', *Shakespeare's Wordplay*, p. 74. See pp. 73–7.

ineffectual, the other direct, homely, and effective, is ironic and sharp.

An earlier illustration of the same principle occurs in the scene (I, iii) in which Gaunt attempts to persuade Bolingbroke that his fate, the sentence of banishment, can be made to seem other than it is by means of the language in which one clothes it. He urges 'Call it a travel that thou taks't for pleasure' (I, iii, 261). Bolingbroke replies that this would be to 'miscall it', and in response to Gaunt's further suggestion,

> Think not the King did banish thee,
> But thou the King. Woe doth the heavier sit
> Where it perceives it is but faintly borne.
> Go, say I sent thee forth to purchase honour
> And not the King exiled thee; or suppose
> Devouring pestilence hangs in our air,
> And thou art flying to a fresher clime.
> (I, iii, 278–84)

—one which perhaps embodies a truer notion of language's role in society as we shall see later, Bolingbroke typically rejects such counsel on the grounds that reality cannot be changed by language. As he says,

> O who can hold a fire in his hand
> By thinking on the frosty Caucasus?
> Or cloy the hungry edge of appetite
> By bare imagination of a feast?
> (I, iii, 293–6)

In so far as their attitudes to reality so fundamentally affect one another, Richard and Bolingbroke seem set on a 'collision course' very early in the play, and nothing can stop the outcome, civil war. The war could thus be said in one dimension to be about the nature of reality, and the relationship of men and men's language to it, with the play focusing attention on the function of the institution of kingship in the matter. Both Richard and Bolingbroke ultimately realize that the whole truth of the situation has eluded them. Richard finds actuality much firmer, harsher, and more unchangeable than his belief in non-material, transcendental, and perhaps ultimately unknowable reality would allow. However much 'the breath of kings' attempts to reorder the things of this world, however Richard 'words' life, his deposition remains undeniable.

On the other hand, Bolingbroke discovers that reality is not firm, tangible, solid, and unmoving: it shifts as one alters one's point of view and one's way of talking about it. The clash between Bolingbroke and Richard, therefore, is oversimplified if stated as a clash between an idealistic king and a worldly usurper. In fact, the clash occurs between two opposed views of language. And the centrality of that issue to Shakespeare's culture emerges more positively when it is realized what is at stake. As M. M. Mahood puts it, 'Verbal authority passed to the king at his coronation . . . the king's word was immediately effective and so were the words spoken by those to whom he deputed legal authority. . . . In Shakespeare's lifetime the old hierarchy of delegated verbal authority was breaking up, and many words which had once seemed to hold magical efficacy were losing their connotative power.'[10] In such an atmosphere, 'To doubt the real relationship between name and nominee, between a word and the thing it signified, was to shake the whole structure of Elizabethan thought and society.'[11] This, in essence, is exactly what Bolingbroke does. Moreover, it is possible to characterize the same issue partly in terms of the momentous Renaissance divorce of rhetoric from dialectic mentioned earlier, with its subsequent and far-reaching effects on man's sensibility. Walter J. Ong writes of the divisive results of Ramus's 'method' in respect of speech itself:

> Rhetorical speech is speech which attracts attention to itself as speech—the showy, the unusual. . . . Dialectical or logical speech is speech which attracts no attention to itself as speech, the normal, the plain, the undistinguished, the reporter of 'things'. . . . 'Things' are constituted not in opposition to the mind, but in opposition to the word.[12]

---

[10] *Shakespeare's Wordplay*, pp. 171–4.
[11] *Shakespeare's Wordplay*, p. 73.
[12] Walter J. Ong, *Ramus, Method, and the Decay of Dialogue*, cit., p. 129.

It would be foolish to label Richard's language precisely as rhetoric to Bolingbroke's dialectic, but the division between them has this aspect quite firmly attached to it, and the position taken up by each in the matter of language—and therefore of response to reality—acquires this dimension in such a context. Both positions are, of course, shown to be extreme ones, and therefore as wrong as each other, in typically Shakespearean fashion. Richard's is melodramatically pre-Ramist and reactionary, Bolingbroke's post-Ramist and modern: neither can simply claim to be the right one, and each is as culpable as the other of the archetypally evil act of division, of splitting apart what ought to be unified.[13] The results of such a process, linguistically, politically, and morally, without presupposition of any division between these areas, are embodied in the chaotic horror of civil war.

Something of the nature of Bolingbroke's 'reality' emanates subtly from the scene which describes his farewell. Aumerle's account to Richard of their goodbyes reveals on the one hand Richard's notion of reality as he would like it to be, and on the other the reality of Bolingbroke's responses as in fact they are. Richard's somewhat melodramatic enquiry after 'high Hereford' receives a rather dry response from Aumerle:

> I brought high Hereford, if you call him so,
> But to the next highway and there I left him.
>
> (I, iv, 3-4)

Bolingbroke's linguistic simplicity accords ill with Richard's notions of what would be fitting in such a situation:

> *Richard:* And say what store of parting tears were shed?
> *Aumerle:* Faith, none for me, except the north-east wind

---

[13] I find it difficult to accept Miss Mahood's conclusion, 'we feel Shakespeare's conviction that it is better to have had and lost a faith in words than never to have surrendered to their magic' (p. 177), because it seems, by making Richard a linguistic 'hero', to pull the play from its necessary balance in this matter. I would not agree that he ultimately admits 'the discovery that the word and its referent are two things' (p. 85). He seems, on the contrary, to retain a deluded faith in 'the breath of kings' to the end.

> Which then blew bitterly against our faces,
> Awaked the sleeping rheum, and so by chance
> Did grace our hollow parting with a tear.
>
> *Richard:* What said our cousin when you parted with him?
> *Aumerle:* 'Farewell'.
>
> (I, iv, 5-11)

Significantly, Aumerle adds his own comment that the word 'Farewell' was in no way able to affect the reality of the situation:

> Marry, would the word 'Farewell' have lengthened hours
> And added years to his short banishment
> He should have had a volume of Farewells;
> But since it would not, he had none of me.
>
> (I, iv, 16-19)

Bolingbroke's subsequent accession to the throne provides the play with its deepest irony on the level of language. It has earlier been noticeable that for all his original bluntness, for all his interest in the unchanging nature of reality, Bolingbroke nevertheless becomes extremely concerned about names and titles when deprived of these by Richard. When Berkeley comes bringing a message, Bolingbroke will not reply to it unless addressed in what he considers a fitting manner:

> *Berkeley:* My lord of Hereford, my message is to you.
> *Bolingbroke:* My lord, my answer is,—to Lancaster;
> And I am come to seek that name in England,
> And I must find that title in your tongue
> Before I make reply to aught you say.
>
> (II, iii, 69-73)

and, as he later declares to York,

> As I was banished, I was banished Hereford,
> But as I come, I come for Lancaster.
>
> (II, iii, 112-13)

Such interest in names seems almost worthy of his antagonist, and in fact Bolingbroke in his own way quickly begins to exhibit Richard's worst faults. This point neatly emerges in a scene which echoes the play's first. Where, earlier, we had encountered an uncommunicating Richard ruling over a society in which truly sympathetic communication had decayed and all but vanished, now we find that, under a new king, the situation has not improved: the first scene of Act IV directly balances the first scene of Act I. Where Richard proclaimed that men might 'freely speak' (I, i, 17) in front of him, Bolingbroke now urges Bagot to 'freely speak thy mind' (IV, i, 2). The clash of nobles which follows exactly parallels the earlier clash between Bolingbroke himself and Mowbray. Accusations are made, loyalties denied, ears are said to be 'treacherous' (IV, i, 54), gages are hurled down as the prelude to combat, and true communication ceases: lying and snarling seems to fill the air (IV, i, 64 ff.). Clearly this company of men who, as Fitzwater puts it, 'intend to thrive in this new world' (IV, i, 78) will not find it much changed from the old one. In this atmosphere, Carlisle's attempt to 'speak the truth' (IV, i, 116) in his denunciation of Bolingbroke's intention to ascend the throne 'in God's name' (IV, i, 113) leads to very rough justice indeed. At the end of his prophetic speech, he suffers summary arrest on a charge of capital treason (IV, i, 150 ff.). Bolingbroke's later bald interjections between Richard's ornate abdication speeches cannot thus pass, as they often do, as the blurtings of a plain, blunt man. In context they suffer from the same fault as the words of Richard: a debilitating gap yawns between them and the reality of kingship.

Words dominate Bolingbroke's 'new world' then, as much as they did Richard's old one. And it may be noticed that, where Richard's world ends in silence (parting from his Queen he urges that they 'dumbly part' (V, i, 95), and resolves 'the rest let sorrow say' (V, i, 102)), we hear, moments later, the clamour of words which greets Bolingbroke's accession. As York puts it,

> ... all tongues cried 'God save thee Bolingbroke!'
> You would have thought the very windows spake.
>
> (V, ii, 11–12)

Richard's deposition puts him in Bolingbroke's former position; Bolingbroke's accession makes him another Richard, and he assumes Richard's linguistic mantle with his crown. Almost literally, he becomes the 'Richard the second' of the title. Under him, the communicative units of society begin to break up. Families divide as the great gulf between York and Lancaster begins to yawn. Aumerle literally cannot communicate with his parents (V, ii), and Bolingbroke's own son, Hal, proves notably disaffected from his father (V, iii, 1 ff.). The atmosphere swirls with plot and counterplot, and the scene in which Aumerle begs for pardon from Bolingbroke, only to have his father urge the new King to deny it (V, iii), seems to symbolize the dissension's intensity. Much is made of locked doors which keep people from contact with each other, and a climax of alienation occurs when York impeaches his own son, callously suggesting that Bolingbroke speak the promised pardon only in French, '.... say Pardonne moy' (V, iii, 118)—that is, 'excuse me, I cannot pardon you'. The Duchess's comment on this aptly suggests the whole scene's atmosphere; it is a mother speaking to a father about their son:

> Dost thou teach pardon pardon to destroy?
> Ah, my sour husband, my hardhearted lord!
> That sets the word itself against the word.
> (V, iii, 119–21)

The mutual incomprehensibility, as of French word against English word described here, takes us back to Richard's England of dissent, quarrels, gaps in communication, that, as he himself put it, 'do set the word itself/Against the word' (V, v, 13–14).

V

The setting of word against word signals the setting of brother against brother in civil war. Bolingbroke's accession brings in its train a sequence of riot, burning, and violence (V, vi) which reaches a climax in the news of Richard's murder. Carefully placed references to Cain and Abel frame the play's action and add an archetypal dimension to the prevailing lack of communication. Bolingbroke in the first scene had accused Mowbray of the murder of Woodstock in these terms:

> Which blood, like sacrificing Abel's, cries
> Even from the tongueless caverns of the earth
> To me for justice and rough chastisement.
> (I, i, 104–6)

and his reaction to Richard's murder at the end of the play strikes the same note:

> With Cain go wander thorough shades of night
> And never show thy head by day nor light.
> (V, vi, 43–4)

Nevertheless, the point remains that, just as Richard's 'word' caused Woodstock's murder, so his own death has come about as a result of Bolingbroke's 'word' (significantly, perhaps, because his words have been misunderstood, have failed to communicate). In fact, the murderer Exton claims the prime authority of Bolingbroke's own voice:

> From your own mouth, my lord, did I this deed
> (V, vi, 37)

and however much Bolingbroke may deny the murder the approval of 'my good word' (V, vi, 42), there can be no doubt that its source indeed lies there. After all, Bolingbroke's attitude to reality, and so his language, has involved a total 'murdering' opposition to that of Richard throughout the play.

The irony of the situation finally inheres in the fact that for both Richard and Bolingbroke, the institution of kingship seems to contain a self-destructive principle which makes one monarch hardly distinguishable from his successor. To place an immortal mantle on the shoulders of a mortal man seems in itself to cause that gap between words and actuality which, in both old and new king, impairs the sanctity of the office. The gap between words and things in the outlook of both Richard and

Bolingbroke mirrors and perhaps mocks at the gap between the *name* of king, which suggests harmonious social ordering, and the *nature* of man which causes the discordancy of civil war.

Where, then, does true reality lie? How can word and object, king and man, name and nature be reconciled? The play seems to argue that such a division can only be overcome by a refusal to recognize the terms in which it is cast; and it locates this 'right' attitude primarily in the character of Gaunt.

In Gaunt's view of the world, words and actuality prove not only inseparable, but coextensive: they contain and condition each other. His language not only touches reality, it both shapes and is shaped by it. In fact, words and things, names and nature, literally unite in his person:

> O how that name befits my composition!
> Old Gaunt indeed, and gaunt in being old!
> Within me Grief hath kept a tedious fast;
> And who abstains from meat that is not gaunt?
> For sleeping England long time have I watched:
> Watching breeds leanness, leanness is all gaunt.
> (II, i, 73–8)

The language goes beyond mere punning to the truth[14] a point which notably escapes Richard, who regards this as merely 'playing' with names (II, i, 84). But Richard, as Gaunt says,

> ... dost seek to kill my name in me,
> I mock my name, great King, to flatter thee.
> (II, i, 86–7)

and he continues, stating truth after truth about Richard and

---

[14] Cf. Mahood: Names 'seemed true to most people in the 16th century because they thought of them as at most the images of things and at least the shadows of things, and where there was a shadow there must be a body to cast it.... Name puns were serious for the Elizabethans on the same principle. The bearer of a name was everything the name implied' (p. 170). Cf. Harry Levin's arguments on the 'psychological onomatopoeia' of the names of Shakespeare's characters: 'Shakespeare's Nomenclature', *Essays on Shakespeare*, Gerald W. Chapman (ed.) (Princeton, 1965), pp. 59–90.

England, reaching to the heart of reality, by means of a probing of the resources of the language itself:

> *Richard:* Should dying men flatter with those that live?
> *Gaunt:* No, no, men living flatter those that die.
> *Richard:* Thou, now a-dying, sayest thou flatterest me.
> *Gaunt:* O, no, thou diest though I the sicker be.
> *Richard:* I am in health, I breathe, and see thee ill.
> *Gaunt:* Now he that made me knows I see thee ill;
> Ill in myself to see, and in thee seeing ill.
> Thy deathbed is no lesser than thy land
> Wherein thou liest in reputation sick.
>
> (II, i, 88–96)

This quality of Gaunt's language of course makes his long speech on England central to the play's linguistic as well as political themes. He speaks it as 'a prophet new inspired' (II, i, 31), and, significantly, its central concern is the relation of England to her kings, of the self-sufficient, circumscribed, tightly-knit island culture to its own little-known native language, of 'way of life' to 'way of speaking', of nature to name. Thus the main line of the argument claims that, under Richard, the 'royal throne of kings', the 'sceptred isle', the 'other Eden, demi-paradise', the England of numinous ineffable qualities, this 'fortress . . . Against infection' has been 'leased out. . . . Like to a tenement or pelting farm' (II, i, 60). The immeasurable, the non-negotiable, the cherished, has been assessed like a piece of mere earth; measured, weighed, rented. The communicative role of kingship, involving a liberating, life-giving interaction between crown and people, has suffered fatal violation.

Quite rightly, Gaunt expects words of this sort to become Richard's 'tormentors' (II, i, 136), and they linger in the mind throughout the rest of the play as standards against which the later speeches of both kings will be measured. Like the words of the Gardeners, they draw on and generate traditional and central metaphors about England, and make these part of the only reality; that which language and experience, names and nature, create by their fruitful interaction.

Appropriately, then, Gaunt's final metaphor seems to flow directly and poignantly from the heart of an oral community, to express a fearful sense of its own changed nature. Instead of a place of warm human colloquy, a resonant world of 'language', the 'little world' of Britain has become under Richard a stale, blotted, and badly bound book, a silent and cold world of written words. Once 'bound in with the triumphant sea', she

> ... is now bound in with shame,
> With inky blots, and rotten parchment bonds.
> (II, i, 61 ff.)

Significantly, Richard himself later employs a similar metaphor. When 'comfortable words' prove finally unable to stave off reality, he commands a new linguistic strategy, in a different mode:

> .... of comfort no man speak.
> Let's talk of graves, of worms and epitaphs,
> Make dust our paper, and with rainy eyes
> Write sorrow on the bosom of the earth.
> (III, ii, 144–7)

If the earth of Britain can shrink to the level of a page in a book, the metaphor can without strain be extended to the country's king who, confronting his own visage in a mirror, finds in the reflection

> ... the very book indeed
> Where all my sins are writ, and that's myself.
> (IV, i, 273–4)

Such 'writing' measures the extent to which, under that king, the vivid island language has indeed been grossly reduced.

As a result of considerations such as these, *Richard II* ceases to be a play concerned merely with politics in the modern restricted sense of the word, and exhibits a more complex interest in the fundamentals of human relationships: in particular in the role of that social institution which once seemed most positively to embody them. For above all others, the institution of kingship had, ideally for the Elizabethans, a communicative function. As was suggested at the beginning of this chapter, the purpose of what has been called unitary monarchy was to act as a focal, and so unifying medium through which men could symbolically 'speak' to one another, and also to God. The Tudor 'revolution' had established the king as the vital communicative link between man and deity and man and man. The intensely personal cast of the relationship between God and man in the Christian tradition stressed, then as now, the importance of language, of talking and listening, of the Word. The Christian God always speaks directly and personally to man. God calls to Abraham, 'Abraham!' and Abraham answers, 'Here I am' (*Genesis* 22:1).[15] And as God's vicegerent on Earth, Richard's shortcomings in this connection seem to supply Shakespeare in the second tetralogy with a crucial and illuminating purchase on the past. Part of that illumination derives from the fact that Richard's successor fares no better in this respect. It is Bolingbroke's son Hal, who, as Prince and 'the mirror of all Christian Kings' demonstrates a saving capacity for simple straightforward unifying oral communication with all speakers of the language from high to low, be they knave or knight, English, Welsh, Irish or Scot. His breezy inabilities outside his native tongue (exhibited in the courting of the French princess) serve decisively to emphasize his capabilities within it.

Meanwhile if, as this play seems to suggest, speech at all levels of society has a paramount status in human life as the essential element on which the entire moral, political and social fabric rests, then the setting of 'word' against 'word' must finally result in the dissolution of communal existence, and the consequent debilitation and ultimate destruction of the human nature dependant upon it. When the perpetrators of that process are themselves kings, the spectacle becomes a fit one for tragedy.[16]

[15] See Walter J. Ong, *The Presence of the Word* (London, 1967), pp. 12 ff. and 73.
[16] The body of this chapter first appeared in *Language and Style* Vol. 2, 1969. Since then, James L. Calderwood has argued a similar case in the different context of his interesting *Shakespearean Metadrama* (Minneapolis, 1971) pp. 149–86, and it is gratifying to note that his analysis of *Richard II* concurs in general so positively with my own.

8

Hamlet:
the play on words

I

The nomination of man as the talking, and also by definition the listening, animal locates his 'reality' in this mode of interaction. Talking and listening must rank as the *sine qua non* of manhood and womanhood, and of the societies in which men and women invariably live. The only man is oral-aural man.

In the course of their exhaustive probing after the nature of human reality, Shakespeare's tragic plays seem to take as their starting-point the notion that man is fundamentally a communicator; that talking and listening make man human. In them, the tragedy seems to involve a denial, by villainy or circumstance, of man's communicative functions; a prohibition of the essential 'talking and listening' aspects of his nature. Only when these are restored is society able to function again in harmony with, and as a collective expression of that nature.

To a considerable degree this may be said to be the subject of *Hamlet*. In a more complex sense than *Richard II*, it probes the idea of man as communicator. And so, as the question of the nature of reality lies very close to the heart of the play, a concern with the human process of communication involved in it becomes, appropriately, the means by which that question is explored.

If language is man's distinctive feature, drama is his distinctive art. And when *Hamlet* seeks deliberately to rephrase the amorphous and unanswerable 'what is real?' more practically and dramatically as 'what is the nature of true humanity?' it does so by focusing attention on the play itself as the artistic analogue of the communicative process. Seen in this light, *Hamlet* is a play about words and plays.

If we contrast Hamlet and Claudius in the matter (and thus follow the alignment of 'mighty opposites' which the play's structure requires), a major dimension of the conflict between them can be said to inhere in the use of and attitudes towards language characteristic of each side. Fundamental antagonisms are thus fundamentally embodied, for that conflict sparks the play.

In the very first scene, for example, we notice a certain quality of the Court's language as Barnardo, its sentry, commanded to 'unfold' himself, responds with the Court's password: 'Long live the King!' (I, i, 3). Francisco's opening query 'Who's there?' has posed a disturbing question which demands revelation, requires 'unfolding'. The Court's 'official' answer to it, ironic in view of recent events at Elsinore and ominous in the light of those which the audience, knowing the play's provenance, foresees, represents (if briefly and in miniature) a use of language for concealment which appropriately hints at a way of life, a culture almost, in exactly that mode. The Ghost may 'unfold' its tale, the Players may 'tell all', Hamlet himself may 'unpack' his heart with words (II, ii, 597) but however much Claudius's little world 'officially' appears to speak—to be garrulous, circuitous, 'wordy' even—it nevertheless conspicuously avoids genuine communication, and so genuine humanity. Conversely, Hamlet's own enforced silence, receiving early and memorable comment, weighs heavily on a heart desperate for human contact: longing to speak, he is forced to hold his tongue.

The Court's password typically disguises a king's murder by formal and 'official' talk of long life. On the other hand, the Ghost's appearance shortly afterwards becomes the occasion for a good deal of emphasis on its initial silence, its refusal, at first, to speak. Charged 'By heaven' to do so, it 'will not answer' (I, i, 49 ff.), and ignores Horatio's pointed demands: 'Speak, speak. I charge thee, speak' (I, i, 51), and 'Speak to me. . . . Speak to me. . . . O Speak! . . . Stay and speak' (I, i, 128–39). Yet it seems a Ghost which most certainly 'would be spoke to' (I, i, 44)—indeed it was 'about to speak' when the cock crew. So though it remains 'dumb to us' because the time is unpropitious, we know that it will later 'speak to him', Hamlet, as father to son.

In the scene which immediately follows, the old king's silence is notably replaced by its opposite in his successor. If old King Hamlet seemed reluctant to speak, new King Claudius seems only too willing.

An alarming aspect of Claudius's first speech overshadows all others. What ever else may be said of his words, they quite deliberately avoid direct revelation of the truth. The facts of murder, usurpation, incest—all known to the audience—are glossed over in polished depersonalized cadences designed to conceal them:

> Though yet of Hamlet our dear brother's death
> The memory be green, and that it us befitted
> To bear our hearts in grief, and our whole kingdom
> To be contracted in one brow of woe,
> Yet so far hath discretion fought with nature,
> That we with wisest sorrow think on him. . . .
>
> (I, ii, 1 ff.)

This impenetrable surface carefully defeats communication much as the password did, by using words (and in performance, gestures) which own a 'formal' status in the language (as, 'Long live the King!' is a formalized way of 'unfolding' oneself) but which remain, at any level beyond the merely formal, uncommunicative *formulae* none the less. Literally 'passwords', these act as signals designed to stimulate a prepared response; mere verbal noise, mere gesticulation. In fact communication-defeating noise seems permanently to surround Claudius in his pleasures:

> . . . the great cannon to the clouds shall tell
> And the King's rouse the heaven shall bruit again,
> Respeaking earthly thunder. . . .
>
> (I, ii, 126-8)

The noise which precedes the final duel is naturally arranged by him,

> ... let the kettle to the trumpet speak
> The trumpet to the cannoneer without,
> The cannons to the heavens, the heaven to earth
>
> (V, ii, 276–8)

—and with a predictability which suggests a way of life as much as mere ceremonial, so that we are not surprised to find, in the middle of the play, that even with the desire for communication strongest in him, Claudius's words 'fly up' like so much noise in his prayers, whilst his quite separate 'thoughts remain below' (III, iii, 97).

The Court's antipathy towards humanizing speech receives repeated affirmation from the first. Laertes, whom Claudius has assured 'cannot speak of reason to the Dane/And lose your voice' (I, ii, 44–5), nevertheless hastens to counsel Ophelia not to put too much credence in Hamlet's voice, especially 'if he says he loves you' (I, iii, 24). Under Claudius, letters have become a major instrument of diplomacy at Elsinore, replacing direct speech and constituting the means by which Hamlet's murder is arranged. Polonius's excess of 'talk' paradoxically signals an almost total breakdown in genuine colloquy. Even advising his own son (in a scene which provides an ironic contrast to the degree of communion pertaining between Hamlet and his father) Polonius counsels the avoidance of straightforward talking and listening between man and man. Laertes is advised to 'Give thy thoughts no tongue' and to 'Give every man thine ear, but few thy voice'. The fact that clothes 'talk', that 'the apparel oft proclaims the man' provides in this atmosphere an opportunity for proclaiming, not the real 'man', but the false image that one would like others to see. The restrictions placed on Ophelia notably refer precisely to speech:

> I would not, in plain terms, from this time forth
> Have you so slander any moment leisure
> As to give words or talk with the Lord Hamlet.
>
> (I, iii, 132–4)

'Plain terms' of course hardly constitute Polonius's own *forte*, and events such as his efforts to report on Hamlet's state of mind, garrulous, circular, impotent as they are, serve to indicate his almost permanent state of potential isolation from his fellow humans, much as Hamlet's own parody in his 'mad' conversation with Polonius in Act II contains an apt summation of the consequences of it. Verbosely uncommunicative, Polonius smothers himself in the dehumanized noise of 'words, words, words' (II, ii, 194).[1]

Genuine human colloquy between Hamlet and Gertrude proves equally impossible in this atmosphere. Despite his resolve to pierce her deceit with language, to 'speak daggers' to her, their words never connect, and there is no penetrative interlocution, only the circling assertions and counter- assertions aptly suggested by the device of *stichomythia*:

> 'Hamlet, thou hast thy father much offended'
> 'Mother, you have my father much offended'
> 'Come, come, you answer with an idle tongue'
> 'Go, go, you question with a wicked tongue'.
> (III, iv, 10–13)

Her threat, to 'set those to you that can speak' (III, iv, 18) clearly remains irrelevant, since genuinely communicative speech no longer forms part of her experience. Hamlet's words to her may be frank, direct and to the point,

> *Gertrude:* As kill a king?
> *Hamlet:* Ay, lady, it was my word.
> (III, iv, 31–2)

—but Gertrude's apprehension of such words makes of them (as Hamlet's parody has suggested) a meaningless and noisy gabble. 'What have I done' she asks,

---

[1] Polonius's obsession with 'clarity', 'distinctness' and the necessity of 'definition' is of course the cause of his own inability to communicate. As Ong points out, the notion that 'the great vice of all discourse is ambiguity', and the corresponding urge to pursue 'clarity' at the expense of genuine communication 'seems close to the view of a madman'—but it is typical of the 'Ramist mentality' (*Ramus*, pp. 191–2).

> ... that thou dar'st wag thy tongue
> In noise so rude against me?
> (III, iv, 39–40)

Hamlet's analysis of what she has done notably pivots on the central assertion that her actions, like those of Richard II, have defiled and debased language's function as the foundation of the social structure. She has made

> ... marriage vows
> As false as dicer's oaths ...
> (III, iv, 45–6)

—and her deeds have turned speech into mere formless noise, subversive of all civil and spiritual order, which

> ... from the body of contraction plucks
> The very soul, and sweet religion makes
> A rhapsody of words!
> (III, iv, 47–9)

At the height of the scene in her bed-chamber, when the Ghost, her former husband, urges her son, 'Speak to her, Hamlet' (III, iv, 116), even the intimacy of family bonds cannot induce real communication in Gertrude. She apprehends 'nothing at all' though the Ghost's 'form and cause conjoined, preaching to stones,/Would make them capable' (III, iv, 127–8).

In the case of Ophelia, the Court's prohibitions reach a more tragic pitch. From the beginning she has been the Court's tool, under orders not to communicate with Hamlet. As a result of this denial of essential human contact, all her communicative faculties have been inhumanly maimed, their scope narrowed obsessively to one (dead) object:

> She speaks much of her father, says she hears
> There's tricks i' th' world. ...
> (IV, v, 4–5)

Although Gertrude predictably 'will not speak with her' (IV, v,

i) she does nevertheless manage to essay talking, but only in the crippled and elliptical way forced by Elsinore:

> . . . Her speech is nothing
> Yet the unshaped use of it doth move
> The hearers to collection; they yawn at it
> And botch the words up fit to their own thoughts.
> (IV, v, 7–10)

Moreover, in a world which destroys words, reducing them to a formless 'rhapsody' incapable of a truly human function, gestures suffer a similar fate. Ophelia pathetically has lame recourse to what remains of the communicative apparatus when words have gone, to 'winks and nods and gestures' (IV, v, 11). Inevitably, she only succeeds in indicating 'nothing sure, yet much unhappily' (IV, v, 13). In her sifting of the disjointed parts of a broken language, with word and gesture utterly out of sequence, in her final pathetic embracement of the shallowly figurative 'language of flowers' (IV, v, 179), Ophelia constitutes a major example of the degradation of talking and listening man which Elsinore brings about.

At her burial, the Grave-diggers indicate by the ludicrous 'absoluteness' of their speech how difficult genuine interlocution has become at Elsinore. They force Hamlet to speak 'by the card'—with cold, inhuman technicality—to solve their riddling equivocations. The old fashion of responsive conversation, the play now hints, has long been dead. The skull they dig up may have 'had a tongue in it and could sing once', but now it only recalls violence and thus (in an archetypal form as in *Richard II*) the essence of non-communication:

> . . . as if it were Cain's jawbone, that did
> the first murder!
> (V, i, 76)

The memory of Yorick's voice, body, gestures, and once-kissed lips serves only to make the gorge rise.

Yet a further stage of deterioration reveals itself when in

response to Laertes's overblown rhetoric, Hamlet mocks and outdoes it in ridiculous screaming in the grave:

> Woo't weep? Woo't fight? Woo't fast? Woo't tear thyself?
> Woo't drink up eisel? Eat a crocodile?
>   . . . let them throw
> Millions of acres on us, till our ground,
> Singeing his pate against the burning zone,
> Make Ossa like a wart! Nay, an thou'lt mouth,
> I'll rant as well as thou.
>
> (V, i, 277–86)

Such mouthing and ranting is the opposite of genuine reciprocity. But one further stage in the decline remains, which Hamlet also parodies: the total degradation of meaningful language represented in Osric, the 'chough', the chattering jackdaw.

As Horatio suggests (V, ii, 126 ff.) it would at this level almost be preferable if everyone spoke in 'another tongue', so meaningless a noise does Osric make of English. Like his newly acquired 'dirt', language has become a commodity in which he speculates for social profit. Like land, it can be bought and sold. His own 'golden words' as money, are soon 'spent' (V, ii, 131 ff.), and the metaphor of coinage, with its ramifications of inflation and debasement, aptly applies itself to the discourse of this ultimate refinement of the 'drossy age'. His gestures, appropriately, prove no less flamboyant and void of genuine responsiveness. Instead of being integrated with, and meaningfully attendant on his words, they take on a separate and meaningless existence of their own, as a kind of manic gesticulation which inevitably draws Hamlet's scorn.

Of course, the process of deterioration takes other forms and different modes to suit the exigencies of the story, but the paradigm remains. Elsinore extirpates communication, and thus banishes the essence of manhood. One of the major instances of this can be seen in the prevailing habit of spying.

Spying must be regarded as totally opposed to language in a fundamental sense, for it constitutes an attempt to deal in

HAMLET: THE PLAY ON WORDS   113

human affairs by a circumvention of responsive contact. Indeed, absence of communication itself creates the need for the spy, and in trying to overcome it, spying serves to emphasize and confirm that lack. As a glance in the direction of our own popular literature on the subject reveals, the activity is necessarily a brutalizing one.

Hence, when Polonius sets Reynaldo to spy on Laertes in Paris (II, i), his orders typically require the spy to avoid true communication, and to dissemble his real purpose by 'encompassment' and 'drift of question', even to 'put on . . . forgeries' to Laertes's character for the purpose. That a father is here shown spying on his son helps to indicate the level of inhumanity at which the most personal relationships at the Court now operate.

As the supreme communicative instrument, then, the *sine qua non* of humanity, language at Elsinore has been seen to deteriorate progressively in the play, bringing with it a breakdown in exactly those personal relationships which underpin society and make man human. From the early formal blandishments of Claudius, their polish concealing the truth of murder and usurpation, through the 'indirections' of Polonius, which circle the truth but never approach it, down to Ophelia's ravings, the obstructive technicalities of the Gravediggers, and the 'civilized' gibbering of Osric, mirroring the culture that has produced him, the process is an accelerating one of descent to a level of uncommunicative brutishness, where spying replaces talking and listening, and men become hunting and hunted animals. As Laertes discovers on his return to Elsinore, linguistic chaos is come again. It is as if

> . . . the world were now but to begin,
> Antiquity forgot, custom not known,
> The ratifiers and props of every word.
>   (IV, v, 103–5)

II

The degree to which Polonius's relationship with Laertes represents the inhuman opposite of genuine communication between father and son can best be measured if we compare with it the relationship the play explores between Hamlet and *his* father. Communication between them, Prince and King, exhibits a warmth of 'family' contact, paradoxically triumphing even over death in being imbued with the humanity which Court life so patently lacks. Between these two, speech is direct, spatial relationship close and intense, intermediaries scorned. The play's first scene has indicated that King Hamlet will speak only alone with his son. Notably, one of Hamlet's first responses on hearing of the Ghost was 'Did you not speak to it?' (I, ii, 213), and he himself quickly resolves to 'speak to it though Hell itself should gape/And bid me hold my peace' (I, ii, 245–6). In fact, speech between them becomes a means of getting at the truth, not of hiding it, and the atmosphere has the same quality as that pertaining between Horatio and those who have reported the Ghost's visitations, with 'each word made true and good' (I, ii, 210).

Hamlet's resolve to confront the Ghost then, face to face, and to engage it in intimate speech, effectively becomes a reaffirmation of the human realities of social order and family relationships which his 'uncle-father' and 'aunt-mother' (who claim him as their 'son') have by their actions so inhumanly subverted:

> . . . I will speak to thee. I'll call thee Hamlet,
> King, father, royal Dane. . . .
>
> (I, iv, 43–4)

The Ghost's command is thus wholly appropriate,

> . . . lend thy serious hearing
> To what I shall unfold. . . .
>
> (I, v, 5–6)

as is Hamlet's response, 'Speak. I am bound to hear' (I, v, 7). He is in turn urged to 'List, list, O, list!' with his 'ears of flesh and blood . . ./If thou didst ever thy dear father love. . . . Now, Hamlet, hear' (I, v, 22–3, 34). Unlike the 'unfolding' of the Court world, heralded by its password of 'Long live the King', the 'unfolding' of the dead King's tale takes place, therefore, with talking and listening on the closest personal level emphasized as its mode. Accordingly, it seems fitting to find Claudius's crime depicted metaphorically as damaging to these faculties. We have seen how his Court maims the faculty of speech: now the Ghost tells us in a deliberately reverberating metaphor that 'the whole ear of Denmark/Is . . . rankly abused.' (I, v, 36-8).

III

The murder of King Hamlet—by poison administered to the ear—seems to hint symbolically at the murder of the aural counterpart of talking. As Paul Tillich says, 'No human relation, especially no intimate one, is possible without mutual listening.'[2] The Court does not listen in this communicative way. It deals in words which (like its 'password' in the first scene) deflect true communication, and which aim, as Hamlet jokingly remarks to Horatio, to 'do my ear . . . violence' (I, ii, 171). In fact, the Court's activity in that sphere exactly fits its mode of spying: words are overheard rather than heard at Elsinore, and it is a place in which the immediacy of talking and listening is replaced by the cold second-hand quality of the spy's reportage. 'Cold', because it abandons the warmth of face-to-face reciprocation for a one-way process of observation; 'second-hand' because it depends on subsequent analysis rather than simultaneous immediate response. This reductive process shares cognate features with what Walter J. Ong terms the Ramist mistrust of 'dialogue' and the oral-aural world of 'sound' consequent upon the 'shift towards the visual throughout the whole cognitive field' initiated by Ramism.[3] Certainly the human voice, and its complement the human ear, are replaced at Elsinore by the intensely 'visual' activity of spying, with its reduction of human relationships to 'clear' and 'distinct' categories. Under Claudius, as with Ramus, the voice and the ear are extinguished in this new world, which becomes, in Ong's terms, 'by that very fact depersonalized'.[4]

[2] Paul Tillich, *Love, Power and Justice* (Oxford, 1954), p. 84.
[3] *Op. cit.*, p. 281.   [4] *Ibid.*, p. 213.

Accordingly, when the King's ear is poisoned, 'the whole ear of Denmark' is violated, and this symbolic act stimulates an appropriate degree of horror in the play, effectively signalled by the Ghost's detailed account of the poisoning, and its revolting and dehumanizing effect on his royal body, itself a symbol of the body politic:

> And in the porches of my ears did pour
> The leperous distillment, whose effect
> Holds such an enmity with blood of man
> That swift as quicksilver it courses through
> The natural gates and alleys of the body,
> And with a sudden vigour it doth posset
> And curd, like eager droppings into milk,
> The thin and wholesome blood. So did it mine,
> And a most instant tetter barked about
> Most lazarlike with vile and loathsome crust
> All my smooth body. . . .
>
> (I, v, 63–73)

By contrast, the way of life Hamlet opposes to Elsinore is one in which talking and listening, voice and ear, hold their rightful cherished place as civilizing instruments. In Hamlet's world, speech is listened to, as Horatio puts it, 'With an attent ear' (I, ii, 193), and the prince's highest praise is reserved for Horatio, the good listener, '. . . e'en as just a man/As e'er my conversation coped withal' (III, ii, 56–7).

Ears properly used in the play's terms, thus symbolize effective and humanizing communication, and Hamlet, who in his own person can 'say nothing', and tends merely to fall 'a-cursing like a very drab' (II, ii, 598) whenever he tries to cope linguistically with his situation, seems to link the activity of attentive and receptive listening to the play's great metaphor of the theatre. Most significantly from Shakespeare's point of view, perhaps, its central location lies in the idea of an audience's sympathetic aural response to the oral performances of professional actors in their plays.[5]

---

[5] Ong remarks on Ramus's 'marked hostility to drama', *Ramus*, p. 287, and Frances Yates notes that he 'abolished memory as a part of rhetoric'

Hamlet has earlier invited us to think of Claudius in connection with acting, and his 'performance' has received bitter comment. For Claudius emerges not as a genuine 'player' as most Elizabethans would have understood that role and its responsibilities; that is, one whose acting makes use of imitation to reach reality, who 'pretends' as a means to the end of truth and whose ultimate aim is communication in the oral-aural mode. On the contrary, the play depicts him from the first as a mere dissembler; one whose goal is obfuscation. Hence Hamlet's sharp references to the acted 'trappings' of pretended woe, to the 'dejected 'haviour of the visage', the 'fruitful river in the eye', the 'actions that a man might play' and the 'forc'd breath' of 'seeming' (I, ii, 76 ff.) which characterize our first view of Claudius at work. To Shakespeare, 'acting' of that kind must have represented a gross perversion of the nature and social function of the art, and ultimately, as we shall see, a larger debilitation of manhood itself. But if the object of the amateur 'actors' of *Hamlet*, like Claudius who 'plays' at being a king, and Polonius who 'enacted' Caesar, is to cloak their puny reality with grandiose outward 'shows' in order to deceive their audiences, the professionals who play in *The Mousetrap* conversely deal in the truth. Their function, that of 'the abstract and brief chronicles of the time', is to communicate reality to the audience by holding the mirror up to nature.

Anne Righter has pointed out the extent to which Elizabethans were aware of the power of the professional play to invade life beyond the stage, and literally to change men's lives.[6] At Elsinore it is significant that the most effective exposition of Claudius's guilt is given by the professional performance of a play. And a good deal of emphasis is placed on the oral faculties in the matter; on the notion that a professional actor's speech makes serious demands on his audience's ears. Hamlet's rueful acknowledgement of the professional player's ability to communicate immediately and powerfully by means of his

---

op. cit., p. 229. The connection between the theatre, acting, and memory (a good actor needs a good memory) as a group of symbols for efficacious oral-aural communication is fully probed in this play. See below, p. 125.

[6] Anne Righter, *Shakespeare and the Idea of the Play* (London 1962), pp. 82 ff.

art; to 'cleave the general ear with horrid speech' (II, ii, 573), to 'speak out', to

> Confound the ignorant, and amaze indeed
> The very faculties of eyes and ears.
> (II, ii, 575-6)

provides a most effective contrast to the kind of 'acting' Elsinore has experienced hitherto, and is as striking as the claims made for the play's own capabilities in forcing oral communication on the guilty, making them 'proclaim' their malefactions so that 'murder, though it have no tongue, will speak/With most miraculous organ' (II, ii, 605-6). Not surprisingly, the sum of Hamlet's advice to the Players is that they speak distinctly, suiting gesture and bodily movement to word as human beings should (he decries those actors that have neither 'th'accent of Christians, nor the gait of Christian, pagan, nor man' (III, ii, 32 ff.))—and that they pay due respect to man's talking-listening nature, so that they do not 'split the ears of the groundlings' (III, ii, 10).

On the other hand, the 'players' of the Court typically abuse the listening faculty. They set Rosencrantz and Guildenstern to spy on Hamlet. In despite of friendship, their relationship becomes less reciprocal than parasitic. To Hamlet, they become, as he puts it, 'at each ear a hearer' (II, ii, 390). Laertes finds that rumours of Claudius begin

> . . . to infect his ear
> With pestilent speeches . . .
> (IV, v, 90-1)

Polonius obtrudes himself 'in the ear' of Hamlet's conference with his mother (III, i, 187) and at that meeting Claudius himself becomes, in Hamlet's alarmingly appropriate pun (resonating self-evidently, far beyond its literal frame of reference),

> . . . like a mildewed ear
> Blasting his wholesome brother.
> (III, iv, 65-6)

Gertrude's infatuation with Claudius is represented throughout the play as involving a disruption of her communicative faculties: she has been playing with the 'devil' at 'hoodman blind', and the result is

> Eyes without feeling, feeling without sight
> Ears without hands or eyes, smelling sans all.
> (III, iv, 78–80)

—a total and dehumanizing disorder of the relationship between the senses on which communication depends. At the play's end, the English Ambassador remarks fittingly on Hamlet's death:

> The ears are senseless that should give us hearing
> (V, ii, 370)

IV

If Claudius's grief at the beginning of the play is inhumanly 'acted' then something of the quality of his language is given by the similarly derived notions of 'make-up' or 'cosmetics' as these are later perversely used by the 'actors' of Elsinore. For as part of its emphasis on the merely visual aspect of communication which its spying celebrates, the Court's language may be said to 'paint over' or 'cosmeticize' reality, and to substitute an illusion for it. Claudius's first speech, clear and confident as its 'acted' grief is, owes little to brute fact, much to a process of linguistic 'making-up' befitting an occasion as 'theatrical' as this accordingly becomes:

> Though yet of Hamlet our dear brother's death
> The memory be green, and that it us befitted
> To bear our hearts in grief, and our whole kingdom
> To be contracted in one brow of woe. . . .
> (I, ii, 1–4)

The image is of a deliberate 'donning' of grief, of an actor's face contorted, to order, in simulated sorrow as unreal as that sketched in the 'mechanical' ordering of gestures which follows:

> Have we, as 'twere with a defeated joy,
> With an auspicious and a dropping eye,
> With mirth in funeral, and with dirge in marriage,
> In equal scale weighing delight and dole. . . .
>
> (I, ii, 10–13)

Nothing escapes the process of painting-over, of re-ordering reality to fit a pre-ordained *kosmos*. The climax of the scene comes when the disaffected figure in black, whose 'nighted colour' signals its own comment on the gaudy scene, is embraced in the new order as a 'son' (I, ii, 64 and 117) and urged to reinforce that context; to 'think of us/As of a father' (I, ii, 108). Hamlet's brusque rejection of such offers—'I shall in all my best obey *you* madam'—is unerringly 'cosmeticized' to 'a loving and a fair reply' and 'gentle and unforced accord' (I, ii, 121 ff.). A good deal of aptness thus sharpens Hamlet's later derisive reference to Claudius as a 'payjock', a posturing figure of absurdly colourful plumage, rather than the simple 'ass' called for by the rhyme (III, ii, 290).

The process reaches its climax at the beginning of Act III, with Polonius and Claudius appropriately engaged in their self-appointed roles of 'lawful espials' on Hamlet. Polonius urges Ophelia to 'act a part' by certain gestures in front of the Prince:

> . . . Read on this book
> That show of such an exercise may colour
> Your loneliness. . . .
>
> (III, i, 44–6)

—and having urged her dissembling with an appropriate cosmetic image adds,

> . . . We are oft to blame in this,
> 'Tis too much proved, that with devotion's visage
> And pious action we do sugar o'er
> The devil himself.
>
> (ll. 46–9)

The metaphor, characteristically mixed, lies in general terms in the realm of cosmetics, of 'painting over' unpleasant physical realities. At this, Claudius is moved to utter an aside:

> O 'tis too true . . .
>
> The harlot's cheek, beautied with plast'ring art
> Is not more ugly to the thing that helps it
> Than is my deed to my most painted word.
> (III, i, 49–54)

This metaphor, now precisely 'cosmetic', accurately illuminates Elsinore's use of language. 'Painted words' describes perfectly the kind of speech and gesture in which the Court deals. And Hamlet himself neatly takes up the theme when, shortly afterwards, he is himself confronted by an Ophelia whom he knows to be the Court's tool, and who has accordingly rejected his 'words of so sweet breath composed'. His accusation is precise:

> I have heard of your paintings well enough. God hath given you one face, and you make yourselves another . . .

The cosmetic process extends to her use both of words and gestures;

> You jig and amble, and you lisp; you nickname God's creatures and make your wantonness your ignorance.
> (III, i, 144 ff.)

Osric's own 'painted words' and gestures set the seal, if one is needed, on this aspect of the Court's attitude to language. Hamlet's mockery of him mocks precisely that quality which, in accordance with the 'tune of the time', makes of language a means of disguising reality rather than revealing it. Claudius's resolve,to Laertes, to

> . . . put on those shall praise your excellence
> And set a double varnish on the fame
> The Frenchman gave you. . . .
> (IV, vii, 131–3)

both aptly introduces us to Osric's 'varnishing' function, and trenchantly comments on it.

V

It has been said that the false 'acting' of Claudius's Court removes its participants from the realm of that humanity whose basis lies in genuine communication. In as light extension of the metaphor, the play ultimately removes the status of manhood from them altogether.

Indeed, in so far as Osric is less than a man, the dehumanizing effects of the Court's world are finally and fittingly recorded in him, and emerge as the result of that accelerating decay of talking and of listening which has been chronicled. Ironically, those thus denied manhood consistently assert its opposite: the spurious 'manliness' of the truly inhuman. Claudius calls Hamlet's grief 'unmanly' (I, ii, 94) at the very point when he 'cosmeticizes' himself, an incestuous murderer, as Hamlet's father and Denmark's king. And when Laertes is at the point of revolt, Claudius enjoins him to a 'man-to-man' talk, urging him to 'Speak, man!' and 'now you speak/ Like...a true gentleman' (IV, v, 127, 148–9). A powerful irony pervades that scene, for the play's false king inevitably reminds us there, at his most false, of the play's 'true gentleman', king Hamlet, who was, taking him for all in all, really 'a man' (I, ii, 187) and we shall not look upon his like again in this play. Claudius may 'play' at the king's role, as has been said, but Hamlet expressly makes the point that 'he that plays the king' thus in the modern world is likely to be literally less than a man; in fact, a child. Just as the men actors have been replaced by boys (II, ii, 346 ff.) in the world outside the play, so at Elsinore legitimate manhood has been usurped and replaced by puny actors who deal in a painted 'manliness'. A general degradation is hinted at; 'it is not very strange', as Hamlet says, for

> ...my uncle is King of Denmark, and those that would make mouths at him while my father lived give twenty,

forty, fifty, a hundred ducats apiece for his picture in little.

(II, ii, 371 ff.)

Claudius's 'littleness', compared to King Hamlet, becomes of course a major theme in Hamlet's accusation of his mother. Even in miniature, the one's picture gives the world 'assurance of a man' (III, iv, 63) whilst the other, 'mildewed', is as a moor to a mountain. Claudius becomes, by these metaphors, a kind of child-actor playing a man, a comic figure, a 'Vice of Kings' (III, iv, 99). His 'acting' degrades the manhood of the whole Court just as, to Shakespeare, the acting of child-actors might have seemed to degrade the status of the theatre in society. Polonius, who childishly boasts of his own acting, becomes in Hamlet's words, 'That great baby' (II, ii, 391).

VI

In previous chapters I have attempted to outline the nature and function of the communicative faculties, and to suggest the degree of significance that must have attached itself to these in a largely pre-literate society, such as that from which *Hamlet* springs. Its communicative mode was still oral-aural, its world a multi-dimensional unity in which the spoken language had a 'resonance' operating on simultaneous 'levels of meaning', which our more 'visual' world, with its one-dimensional sequential ordering born of literacy and the separation of the faculties from a subtler interplay, finds it difficult to comprehend.[7]

Thus *Hamlet's* concern with the symbols of oral-aural communication has the status of a concern with the very fabric of life in its own time, and the play consequently exhibits a degree of interest in the matter much of which is likely to escape the notice of a literate modern audience (of whom the majority must first encounter the play misleadingly as a printed text—or even, such is our educational system, as a *test*

[7] Cf. Marshall McLuhan, *The Gutenberg Galaxy*, (London, 1962), pp. 72 ff.

of literate skills!). For the same reasons, the play is unlikely to treat such a subject *separately* from its concern with other matters of moral and political importance, and is accordingly more likely to make metaphorical use of it, as part of the then possible analogical inter-relating of various 'subjects' which, to the modern mind, constitute quite different issues. It thus becomes necessary to isolate the strain of 'talking and listening' unfairly and artificially in order to perceive it at all.

Nevertheless, even seen in these unfamiliar terms, *Hamlet's* ending follows the typical and confirming Shakespearean pattern in that, whilst showing the final degradation and decay of talking and listening it insists at the same time on the necessity of their preservation. Thus, whilst the duel, its antagonism parodying communication, reduces talking-listening man to the level of a fighting struggling beast, a good deal of emphasis is placed on the fact that Horatio (whom Hamlet addresses as 'a man' (V, ii, 343)) will absent himself from felicity in order to speak the truth; will 'unfold' and report 'aright' the true 'story' to the human beings who enter at the end. Talking and listening must go on, in order that the apparently inexplicable carnage which the eye coldly sees on the stage may be explained and redeemed by the warmth of the spoken word sympathetically heard. Horatio will 'speak to the yet unknowing world/ How these things came about' (V, ii, 380–1)—and his audience will 'hear' what he will 'truly deliver'. Fortinbras, the new representative of manhood who has been appropriately elected by Hamlet's 'dying voice' properly resolves to

> ... haste to hear it
> And call the noblest to the audience.
>
> (V, ii, 386–7)

The theatrical connotation of 'audience' suggests that the 'hearing' will be warm, responsive, alive, as that of the theatre ideally should be.

As for Hamlet, death brings him victory in the sense that both manhood and communicative speech are asserted by his funeral. He is borne, in true 'manliness', 'like a soldier' to the stage. There, though unable to talk or listen further,

> The soldier's music, and the rite of war
> Speak loudly for him.
>
> (V, ii, 400–401)

In a world of 'broken' words, he has fulfilled his earlier promise to 'take the Ghost's word' (III, ii, 292), and a genuine and truly communicative order prevails.

Perhaps because it is truly communicative, Shakespeare invests that order with a positive 'theatrical' colouring. For Hamlet, it seems, the essence of genuine humanity ultimately lies in the basic 'playing' situation itself, in the 'talking-listening', oral-aural interaction of the actors and audience across a stage: a process that, to an oral community, might not inappropriately seem the ultimate symbolic representation of itself. In the theatre, as outside it, people talk, others listen, as evidence of their humanity, and the player's oral art does indeed show 'the very age and body of the time his form and pressure'. Moreover, in a society whose investment in memory must, as has been said, be very great, the theatre will have the added role almost of a 'memory-bank'; a place where memory literally resides, is stored, and in performance is brilliantly displayed by the actors. Hamlet's promise to the Ghost to

> ... Remember thee!
> Aye, thou poor Ghost, whiles memory holds a seat
> In this distracted Globe.
>
> (I, v, 95–7)

has, not merely by means of the oral device of the pun, this enlarging aspect. And it hints at such a theatre's immense but informal educative function in an oral culture as an institution serving to *remind* its members of accepted common values, and to confront them with a dramatic affirmation and confirmation of these, almost as a unifying and preservative act of *anamnesis*, of 'bringing to mind'.[8]

Thus in the final analysis, *Hamlet* becomes charged with a

---

[8] For an account of a similar process in respect of poetry and drama in Hellenic culture, see E. A. Havelock, *Preface to Plato* (Oxford, 1963) pp. 41–3 and 48.

total responsibility for communication far in excess of that borne by any of its characters, and the Prince thereby gains his release. His dying words draw attention to the 'play' in which he finds himself, and which bears his name.[9] Accordingly, they are directed much more towards the audience in the theatre than towards the one which surrounds him on the stage, in making exactly this point:

> You that look pale and tremble at this chance,
> That are but mutes or audience to this act,
> Had I but time . . .
> . . . O, I could tell you;
> But let it be.[10]
>
> (V, ii, 335–9)

Where Hamlet leaves off, *Hamlet* takes over. The play's own talking-listening relationship with its audience unfolds a 'story' which in one sense must lie beyond the scope of the Prince's voice, and in another can only exist within it. Hamlet's own commitment to direct face-to-face oral communication has been aptly manifested in the play by his frequent resort to the device of the soliloquy, in which he addresses the audience directly. So the play, in becoming 'the thing' whereby consciences are caught, ends appropriately by pointing to itself and urging us to respond attentively and directly to it: to listen, and to remember, whilst it 'talks'.

Release from the tyranny of 'words, words, words' remains the reward of the dead Hamlet, for whom the rest is silence. *Hamlet* on the other hand, perhaps as the ultimate play on words, continues to try to speak.

[9] Cf. M. M. Mahood, *op. cit.*, pp. 127–8.
[10] 'Mutes' here is a technical term referring to non-speaking 'walk-on' parts in a play. E.g. in the Folio edition of *Hamlet*, the Poisoner in the Dumb Show enters 'with some two or three Mutes' (III, ii, 140). See Maurice Charney's account of the 'quantity of professional allusions to art, acting and the theatre' in this play, *Style in Hamlet* (Oxford, 1969) pp. 137–53.

9
Othello, Macbeth, and Jonson's Epicoene:
the language of men

I

What (a) peece of worke is a man, how noble in reason, how infinit in faculties, in forme and moouing, how expresse and admirable in action, how like an Angell in apprehension, how like a God. . . .
> (*Hamlet*, 2nd Quarto, II, ii, 307 ff.)

The idea of 'manliness' has been mentioned, and its close connection with language and way of life has been said to make it a factor in our understanding of *Hamlet* in its own time. The notion of what a 'man' is naturally occupies a position of importance in all cultures, especially once it is allowed that mere sexual status has little to do with it. To be male is to exhibit simple and (normally) universal biological characteristics. To be a 'man' on the other hand, and to adopt and fulfil an appropriate social, moral and political role as a result is quite a different matter. 'Maleness' does not presuppose 'manliness', and each culture invents and invests in its own particular requirements for the latter category. One is or is not 'manly' in accordance with essentially relative rules of decorum in social behaviour, whose connection with biological matters is purely formal.

In Elizabethan and Jacobean society, 'rules' at that level seem to have been no less rigid and clear-cut than in our own. 'Men' behaved in one way, women in another. That is to say formal patterns of behaviour were accepted as crudely typifying each set of sexual characteristics. Tears, for example, were 'formally' characteristic of women, courage and bravery of men. But between these two poles the possibility existed, then as now, of a large variety of 'informal' gradations which could include paradoxical 'reversals' of behaviour. Thus, the rebuke suffered by Romeo for his 'womanish' weeping '... Unseemly woman in a seeming man' (III, iii, 110–12), Claudius's accusation that Hamlet's grief is 'unmanly' (I, ii, 94), Coriolanus's fears that 'a woman's tenderness' (V, iii, 129) may betray him, all, in their context, suggest that 'non-manly' characteristics in men can prove not altogether unadmirable (although we are urged, paradoxically in these cases, to disapprove of them). In *All's Well That Ends Well*, Parolles's urging of a crude 'manliness' on Bertram,

> ... To th' wars, my boy, to th' wars!
> He wears his honour in a box unseen
> That hugs his kicky-wicky here at home,
> Spending his manly marrow in her arms,
> Which should sustain the bound and high curvet
> Of Mars's fiery steed.
>
> (II, iii, 271–6)

manifests obvious but effective means by which the 'formal' notions of manliness can undergo probing and questioning when put in the mouth of a dramatic character whom the audience mistrusts. Indeed, on this evidence, the 'informal' idea of manliness contains a number of characteristics that would be classified as 'womanly' on a 'formal' level, and these —Romeo's weeping, Hamlet's grief, Coriolanus's tenderness, Bertram's love, are clearly offered to the audience, in context, as admirable instances of *genuine* manhood, both in the theatre and outside it. To stifle such 'womanly' traits, the plays seem to argue, brings about a kind of dehumanization, a final 'unmanning', a most 'unnatural' man. In fact, the notion that men and women are polar 'opposites' seems to be decidedly a modern one, the product of various social and economic forces whose pressures reached a climax in the late nineteenth and early twentieth centuries. Certainly in the sixteenth century, as in the latter part of the twentieth century, women and men seem naturally to be 'closer', to share more of the same characteristics. In this, as in other matters, Shakespeare's plays seem to be resisting an encroaching 'modernity', perceived as essentially divisive in mode.¹

Genuine manhood, then, proves always to be a notion whose complexity resists facile definition. And, appropriately, its opposite—inhuman 'manliness' such as has been noticed in *Hamlet*—often manifests itself by just that reductive facility; by a grotesque oversimplification of the idea of what makes a 'man'. As Hamlet's bitter eulogy suggests, in its context, the 'peece of worke' could excite disgust as well as admiration, because of its vast potential. Man might be *capax dei*, but he was also capable of a *simpliste* kind of animality that threatened constantly to usurp any higher aspirations. In fact the complexity of his nature springs precisely from this range, this tension. Robert B. Heilman's demonstration that the plays are 'bursting with ideas, of what a man is and what he should be and do'² not only indicates the extent of Shakespeare's concern in the matter, but also the degree to which he avoids easy and oversimple expositions of it. As Heilman says, the plays contain the recognition that 'man must avoid the womanly, but the womanly may be a virtue. Man must avoid the bestial, yet it is always a threat. Man is not a god, but the divine is an indispensable measure of his quality.'

Since the nature of genuine and desirable 'manhood' and 'womanhood' must inevitably be one of the most potent and formative notions held by any group of people, it is not surprising to find it as a central concern of Shakespeare's drama. And it is one which no less inevitably exhibits distinctly linguistic aspects that prove not only interesting in themselves, but also suggestive of dimensions of a play's 'meaning' for its contemporary audience in ways that might otherwise go unnoticed. Language clearly constitutes an area of social behaviour in which 'manliness' (or its absence, or its profession) can be made manifest to other people. In fact in the absence of

[1] See the interesting essay of Leslie Fiedler, 'The New Mutants', *Partisan Review*, Vol. XXXII, No. IV, 1965, pp. 505-25.
[2] Robert B. Heilman, 'Manliness in the Tragedies: Dramatic variations', in Edward A. Bloom (ed.) *Shakespeare 1564-1964* (Providence, R.I., 1964), pp. 19-37.

universally acceptable 'manly' characteristics, its very existence depends on the transmission and reception of congruent signals, for behaviour that is 'manly' in one culture may be simply manic in another. In short, one can speak 'like a man', and speech forms one of the most readily available indications of 'manliness'. Certainly it is a matter with which a serious dramatist must concern himself. There are, as Ben Jonson knew, 'deeds and language such as men do use' (Prologue to *Every Man in His Humour*) which should be distinguished from those which they do not.

If the concept of man without language is impossible, so is the concept of man without men. Man the talking animal is also man the social animal, for language and society interpenetrate. It has been pointed out that the identity of speech-habits and culture, 'way of talking' and 'way of life', is especially marked when the society is a small one, and for most practical and everyday purposes non-literate. And it has been noticed that, like many of his contemporaries, Ben Jonson saw language not only as man's distinctive characteristic but also as the 'Instrument of Society'. Accordingly, in the matter of what constituted the true criterion of responsible manhood in a society such as his own, he had no doubts:

Language most shewes a man; speake that I may see thee.[3]

The function of speech is to permit social communication and so society. And to communicate is to reveal oneself, man-to-man. The genuine 'man' might thus perhaps be said to resemble that 'ideal' figure whom Hamlet extols; who in overcoming the opposition of 'blood' and 'judgement' proves, like Horatio, to be straightforward and revelatory in his communication: 'as just a man/As e'er my conversation coped withal.' (III, ii, 56 ff.): the only one whose speech is capable of telling his tale 'aright'. Like Shakespeare, Jonson may be said to have considered true manhood to reside in 'conversation' of this sort; direct, straight-forward, face-to-face—a necessary activity in a society where methods of recording and scrutinizing speech were scarcely available.[4] In his own words;

[3] *Timber.* See p. 43 above.

Pure and neat Language I love, yet plaine and customary.[5]

Even to one as committed as Jonson was to the idea of drama as literature, plays as 'works' written down for the lengthy perusal of the intelligent few, the chief virtue of a style nevertheless remains '. . . perspicuitie, and nothing so vitious in it as to need an Interpreter'. Shakespeare, whose view of drama was evidently the opposite of Jonson's, would almost certainly have concurred with the sense of decorum in language intended here, and closely linked with Jonson's sense of propriety in human behaviour. Men and women, both dramatists seem to agree, should behave and so speak in a 'pure' and perspicuous manner appropriate to their status as human beings. On such cognate linguistic and biological axes, oral society rests. Hence the force of Jonson's belief that

No glasse renders a mans forme, or likenesse, so true as his speech. Nay, it is likened to a man; and as we consider feature, and composition in a man; so words in language.[6]

A good deal of the Elizabethan culture's response to and expectation of its drama is implied by those lines, and the linguistic principles of characterization together with the notion of 'manliness' involved in them remain tacitly but unmistakably present in the work of its major dramatists. Shakespeare's concern, not with the positive 'manly' ideal so much as with its perversion, or the dangers—even impossibility—of rigid determination in the matter (rules of decorum in human behaviour inevitably invite this dramatic response: they only become capable of realization when broken)[7] seems to focus not unnaturally on language, and especially on the

[4] As Daniel Seltzer points out, 'Elizabethan Acting in *Othello*', *Shakespeare Quarterly*, Vol. X, 1959, pp. 201–10, the 'orthodox idea' of communication to the Elizabethan was that a man ought to show outwardly his inner thoughts and feelings, concealing nothing.
[5] *Timber.*
[6] *Ibid.*
[7] Or as Heilman says, *loc. cit.*, Shakespeare 'might use "man" and "manhood" as if each had a set meaning, but for him they are never clichés seeking stock responses. . . . His wisdom in viewing man emerges as aesthetic resourcefulness; we have not aphorisms, but ideas in action.'

nature of its role in the social order. Oral society depends on revelatory speech. Behaviour which violates this principle must be fundamentally disruptive and unnatural, and thus fundamentally evil—so much has proved demonstrable in *Richard II* and *Hamlet*. It could also by the same token be shown to be 'unmanly' in a deeply serious social and moral sense, though as we have already noticed, one of its most frequent poses is a kind of reductive pseudo-manliness, a hard-boiled muscular assertion of one aspect of man's nature; that animality in physical force and sexual prowess whose unchecked career could only prove socially and morally subversive.

True manhood, Shakespeare seems to argue, lies in true talking and listening which involves the *whole* range of man's potential, not part of it: that direct and complex 'man-to-man' interaction between human beings on which social life—that is, the only real life—depends. False 'manliness', quite simply, involves the reverse. To be less than a man is to avoid communication of that total sort. It is to court deceit, dissimulation, mask-wearing.

II

In *Othello*, as in *Macbeth*, the pattern of the play is one of decline on the protagonist's part from a position of social approval to the reverse; from the status of an admired manhood to that of a creature in some ways 'less than' a man.

Whatever our modern response to Othello's language may be, the play quite clearly indicates that it is communicative at first to a high degree. Indeed, by means of a kind of 'alienation-effect' it draws attention to itself in exactly this regard, both by its ornateness and density on one level, and by a direct self-conscious reference to those qualities on another:

> Most potent, grave, and reverend signiors,
> My very noble and approved good masters,
> That I have ta'en away this old man's daughter,
> It is most true; true I have married her.
> The very head and front of my offending

Hath this extent, no more. Rude am I in my speech,
And little blessed with the soft phrase of peace. . . .
(I, iii, 76–82)

Much critical disagreement about the evident falsity of that statement misses the point that the speech is mainly concerned to establish Othello as 'manly' on all possible grounds. His words are perspicuous. Their 'round unvarnished tale' (I, iii, 90) injects the simple truth into an extremely confused situation. Their apparently ornate character is really a matter of certain adjectives, 'potent', 'grave', 'reverend', 'noble', 'approved' whose purpose it is to suggest a powerfully ordered way of life wholly opposed to the bestiality and riotous disorder implicit in Iago's prior imagery, talk of an 'extravagant[8] and wheeling stranger' (I, i, 133) and Brabantio's accusations of 'spells' and 'witchcraft'. In effect, Othello speaks, he tells us, 'justly' to the Duke's 'grave ears' (I, iii, 124), and his words claim by implication the qualities of bravery and courage (the accused 'standing up to' his accusers), as well as those of simplicity and directness (the 'honest soldier' humbly confronting his devious superiors). They deliver the essence of a man possessed of a serene and powerful confidence in the straightforward 'speaking' qualities of his own presence;

My services, which I have done the Signiory,
Shall out-tongue his complaints. . .

. . . and my demerits
May speak unbonneted to as proud a fortune
As this that I have reached.
(I, ii, 18–23)

His expectation that

My parts, my title, and my perfect soul
Shall manifest me rightly.
(I, ii, 31–2)

is wholly justified. They do. He needs, he knows, but to 'spend

[8] I.e. not permanently attached to a society; peripatetic.

a word here in the house' (I, ii, 48) for the truth to be revealed, and it is this dimension of calm clarity that distinguishes and makes memorable what T. S. Eliot terms the 'irony, dignity, and fearlessness' of the language with which he initially encounters Brabantio:

> Keep up your bright swords, for the dew will rust them.
> Good signior, you shall more command with years
> Than with your weapons.
> (I, ii, 58–60)

Even at the point when Iago begins to plant the first seeds of doubt, Othello's characteristic demand is for open revelatory discussion:

> I prithee speak to me as to thy thinkings,
> As thou dost ruminate, and give thy worst of thoughts
> The worst of words.
> (III, iii, 131–3)

This, surely is the 'language of men' in the play's and the society's terms: the appropriate outward and manifest sign of what even Iago recognises as Othello's 'free and open nature' (I, iii, 393).[9] However, the same words also manage to suggest that language's and that nature's appalling vulnerability in the face of a lesser and reduced notion of 'manliness'. It is this vulnerability which becomes the object of Iago's attack.

The attack takes the form of a total usurpation and obliteration of a man's identity; of his manhood.[10] For *Othello* tells the story of how one man becomes another 'man'; of how Othello gradually begins to see the world, and to respond to it, through the eyes of Iago; to speak, ultimately, with Iago's voice.

---

[9] The notion that true manhood inheres in clear, straightforward and direct use of language lies as an implicit assumption behind such words as those in which Emilia later demands that Iago deny the charges made against him; 'Disprove this villain, if thou be'st a man' (V, ii, 172). Of course, great irony lies in the fact that she makes this demand for genuine 'manly' behaviour from the source of its opposite.

[10] Cf. the arguments of R. B. Heilman in *Magic in the Web: Action and Language in Othello* (Lexington, Kentucky, 1956) pp. 108 ff.

Gradually, the 'language of men' in him is replaced by the language of 'manliness'.

The most noticeable feature of that 'manliness' proves to be its deceitful nature, its concern to hide reality by appearances, and its rejection of the 'free and open' in favour of what Iago calls 'shows' and 'seeming' (I, i, 52–61). Its language, naturally, both reflects and embodies this. Iago swears 'By Janus' (I, ii, 33) the god with two faces. His images of Othello's affair with Desdemona stress dissimulation and animality, rather than communication and humanity:

> Even now, now, very now, an old black ram
> Is tupping your white ewe!
> (I, i, 89–90)

and

> You'll have your daughter covered with a Barbary horse, you'll have your nephews neigh to you, you'll have coursers for cousins and gennets for germans . . . your daughter and the Moor are now making the beast with two backs!
> (I, i, 108 ff.)

Such words obviously intend obfuscation rather than revelation. And as the fundamental mode of the deception, they impose a knowing and reductive 'manliness' on the events they purport to describe. As a result, Othello and Desdemona cease to be human beings who love each other. They become animals which 'tup' and 'cover'. So when Othello demands 'proof' of the charges against Desdemona, Iago deliberately offers it in terms suited more to stud farming than human involvement:

> . . . how satisfied, my lord?
> Would you, the supervisor, grossly gape on,
> Behold her topp'd?
> (III, iii, 398–400)

More than any other character in the play, Iago refers to human beings and their actions in words appropriate to animals. And in return, at the end, such epithets attach themselves to him: 'viper', 'dog', 'monster'. They help to suggest, finally, the extent of his decline from the level of ordinary manhood.

I have argued elsewhere that the voice of Iago is the voice of one kind of very limited reason, and that the play chronicles his application of this faculty and its limitations to the core of Othello's relationship with Desdemona.[11] The process has an obvious linguistic analogue. What ideally might be called a situation of perfect communication, in which the limitations of the body were transcended and Desdemona

> ... saw Othello's visage in his mind
> And to his honours and his valiant parts
> Did I my soul and fortunes consecrate.
>
> (I, iii, 252–4)

becomes in Iago's 'manly' language, 'sanctimony and a frail vow betwixt an erring barbarian and a super-subtle Venetian' (I, iii, 350 ff.). Both Desdemona's account of her love, and Othello's of his wooing, notably stress that it was his talking and her listening which proved the most powerful agency in the encounter. Othello's 'story' made Desdemona 'with a greedy ear/Devour up my discourse' (I, iii, 148–9),

> Wherein of antres vast and deserts idle
> Rough quarries, rocks, and hills whose heads touch heaven,
> It was my hint to speak—such was the process;
> And of the Cannibals that each other eat,
> The Anthropophagi, and men whose heads
> Do grow beneath their shoulders. This to hear
> Would Desdemona seriously incline.
>
> (I, iii, 140–6)

She may coyly have 'wished she had not heard it; yet she wished/That heaven had made her such a man' (I, iii, 161–2), and the Duke himself is moved to comment on such talking and listening's efficacy, 'I think this tale would win my daughter too' (l. 171). Desdemona's plea to the Duke also makes

---

[11] In *Shakespeare and the Reason* (London 1964), pp. 107 ff.

much of her own simple reliance on straightforward oral-aural communication:

> To my unfolding lend your prosperous ear,
> And let me find a charter in your voice
> T'assist my simpleness.
> (I, iii, 240–2)

But Iago's 'manly' version of the relationship reduces all this to 'she first loved the Moor but for bragging and telling her fantastical lies' (II, i, 220–2). The commanding clarity of Othello's early speeches withers under such a scrutiny to

> . . . bombast circumstance,
> Horribly stuffed with epithets of war.
> (I, i, 12–13)

In effect, such 'manliness' boils everything down to a 'known' level at which it can be off-hand and mocking. Even love itself can be reduced thereby to merely '. . . a lust of the blood and a permission of the will' (I, iii, 333). Such a view tallies, predictably, with Iago's small opinion of women. He thinks of them, typically, in animal terms,

> Come on, come on; you are pictures out a-doors, bells in your parlours, wildcats in your kitchens. . . .
> (II, i, 109)

and his repeated urging of the weak Roderigo to 'be a man' (I, iii, 333) as well as his similar prompting of Othello, 'Are you a man? Have you soul or sense?' (III, iii, 371) and

> I mock you not, by heaven,
> Would you would bear your fortune like a man.
> (IV, i, 63–4)

occur in contexts which make it clear that what he means is simple aggressive masculinity. His drinking song in Act II

> And let me the canakin clink, clink
> And let me the canakin clink.
> A soldier's a man,
> O man's life's but a span,
> Why then let a soldier drink.

appropriately has this same flavour.

Roderigo's befuddled rejection of this view, his mild assertion of some vague 'blessed condition' (II, i, 245) in Desdemona that would mitigate such a reduction of her situation meets the full bludgeoning force of hardboiled linguistic 'manliness':

> Blessed fig's end: The wine she drinks is made of grapes.
> If she had been blessed she would never have loved the Moor.
> Blessed pudding!
>
> (II, i, 246 ff.)

Iago's constant use of 'tough' and abusive words; 'knave', 'thief', 'barbarian', 'foul', 'villainous', 'trash', 'fool', ultimately becomes part of the play's felt rhythm, fully informing his plan to 'abuse Othello's ears' (I, iii, 386) about the nature of reality. Whenever he appears, the atmosphere quickly becomes contentious, abusive, uncommunicative. He characteristically 'speaks home' (II, i, 163) to this end, as Cassio says of him, and as the play concludes it seems entirely appropriate that he should finally address his own wife as 'villainous whore' and 'filth' (V, 2, 229 ff.)[12] Certainly, as Cassio discovers to his great cost, Iago's speaking of 'the truth' serves only to inhibit communication between himself and Othello:

> I will ask him for my place again: he shall tell me I am a drunkard. Had I as many mouths as Hydra, such an answer would stop them all.
>
> (II, iii, 302–4)

Appropriately enough, Iago's design for Othello is conceived

---

[12] Cf. R. B. Heilman's valuable account of this process, *Magic in the Web*, pp. 109 ff.

in serpentine, Claudius-like terms. He will 'pour this pestilence into his ear' (II, iii, 356).

As a direct result of the 'vile success' of this sort of 'speech' (III, iii, 223) Othello gradually begins to see the world in fittingly reduced 'manly' terms. What he can at first dismiss as 'exsufflicate and blown surmises' gradually overtake him. He begins to regret 'those soft parts of conversation/That chamberers have' (III, iii, 262–3) denied him by his blackness. His wife, his 'fair warrior', his 'dear love' becomes, in the 'manly' version of that, a 'fair devil' (III, iii, 482), a 'lewd minx' (l. 479), a 'Venetian wife', and a whore. Their relationship accordingly assumes the character of an encounter between a prostitute and her 'manly' customer. Their bedroom becomes a brothel, Emilia its madam, and Desdemona at last appears as

> ... that cunning whore of Venice
> That married with Othello.
> (IV, ii, 90–1)

Terms of abuse and contempt come to dominate Othello's language. He speaks, as Desdemona says, 'startingly and rash' (III, iv, 79), throws

> such despite and heavy terms upon her
> That true hearts cannot bear it.
> (IV, ii, 115–16)

—and, Iago-like, strews terms of animality at large throughout his speech until they begin to obtrude themselves almost involuntarily:

> You are welcome, sir, to Cyprus—Goats and monkeys!
> (IV, i, 263)

As Iago himself later says of him, laconically, 'He is much chang'd' (IV, i, 265).

The mode of the change is largely linguistic. Gone is the 'free and open' quality, the felicity in words to which attention was drawn at the play's beginning, and to which attention is now drawn in other cases, for comparison, as the play progresses:

> *Desdemona:* ... This Lodovico is a proper man.
> *Emilia:* A very handsome man.
> *Desdemona:* He speaks well.
>
> (IV, iii, 36–8)

Othello no longer 'speaks well'. In fact, his speech takes on an opposite character, a tortured, uncommunicative shape from which 'round' and 'unvarnished' characteristics are noticeably absent:

> I think my wife be honest, and think she is not;
> I think that thou art just, and think thou art not;
> I'll have some proof.
>
> (III, iii, 388–90)

and

> Pish! Noses, ears, and lips? Is't possible?
> —Confess?—Handkerchief?—O devil!
>
> (IV, i, 43–5)

The 'rude' and 'straightforward' linguistic qualities of the first Act have become almost the opposite of themselves; repetitious, circular, inward-looking:

> It is the cause, it is the cause, my soul.
>
> Put out the light and then put out the light.
>
> (V, ii, i ff.)

Absurd paradoxes, 'I will kill thee/And love thee after', 'This sorrow's heavenly/It strikes where it doth love' scatter themselves throughout his last major speech, and add to the impression of insanity, unnaturalness, and complete breakdown in language. Words like 'justice' mean in the end only what Othello privately requires them to mean. From being a man talking to other men, he has become a 'man' mouthing to himself. He ceases to be a husband, and becomes a 'judge' pronouncing sentence on a criminal; a madman, as Desdemona sees him, deluded and raving;

> Alas, why gnaw you so your nether lip?
> Some bloody passion shakes your very frame.
>
> (V, ii, 44-5)

It is a picture of a complete failure to communicate, of a monster making noises in a void, totally unmanned.

In this atmosphere, Emilia's horror at the falsehood on which the murder is based communicates the full explicit loathing of an oral community faced with dissimulation in language:

> Emilia: You told a lie, an odious damned lie!
> Upon my soul, a lie! A wicked lie!
> She false with Cassio? Did you say with Cassio?
> Iago   With Cassio, mistress. Go to, charm your tongue.
> Emilia: I will not charm my tongue; I am bound to speak. ...
>
> (V, ii, 177-82)

—and she later determines to

> ... speak as liberal as the north.
> Let heaven and men and devils, let them all,
> All, all, cry shame against me, yet I'll speak.
>
> (V, ii, 218-20)

But even the revelations of the close cannot restore the damage. Iago, the chief subverter of language, finally abandons that distinctive human characteristic altogether with his

> From this time forth, I never will speak word.
>
> (V, ii, 300)

and, as the play ends, all that remains to Othello is a fumbling attempt to reach back to his former identity, his former humanity. He hopes for a kind of redeeming clarity in the relation of 'these unlucky deeds' which the deeds themselves have subverted: 'Speak of me as I am. Nothing extenuate/Nor set down aught in malice' (V, ii, 339). But, in place of clarity, the reiteration of his old triumphs now has only the quality of Iago's spurious and boastful 'manliness':

> And say besides that in Aleppo once,
> Where a malignant and a turban'd Turk
> Beat a Venetian and traduc'd the state,
> I took by the throat the circumcised dog
> And smote him—thus.
>
> (V, ii, 355–9)

Reduced to a level quite below that of genuine humanity, the 'dog' he melodramatically stabs to death is appropriately himself. The irony of such 'manliness' is that its reductive nature finally reduces those who profess it to a level below that of a man. And at the end of such a 'bloody period' as that chronicled by this play, the most telling comment on the language is finally made by Gratiano:

> All that is spoke is marred.
>
> (V, ii, 360)

III

In *Macbeth* a similar pattern of decline informs the play's structure, and follows and reinforces its basic antithetical shape in which, as most critics agree, deceitful appearances gradually take the place of reality. What is interesting is the extent to which 'reality' manifests itself as the genuinely communicative 'language of men', and appearance takes the form of that sort of language whose use has been recognized in Iago.

Put at its simplest, Macbeth's tragedy could be said to result from his belief in certain words. The 'playing' on those words in which the Witches engage brings about his downfall.[13] And, in connection with that downfall, equivocation, juggling with 'meanings', the deployment of ambiguities, all prove to be

---

[13] I have argued this case in a different context in *Shakespeare and the Reason*, pp. 126 ff.

characteristic of false 'manliness' in a sense which the play makes quite clear.[14]

The most obvious feature of the Witches's words is that they communicate little in the way of direct information. The incantatory character of the verses they speak, giving primacy to the rhythmic features of the language and so increasing the unrealizable nature of the horrors thus shadowed forth, virtually ensures that nothing of semantic certainty can emerge:

> Fair is foul, and foul is fair
>
> (I, i, 10)

Such words deal only in devious and uncertain meanings. This is certainly not the 'language of men'.

Yet it is language of this sort in the form of equivocal 'prophecies' that Macbeth chooses to take as meaningful. And he persists in doing so even in the face of the popularly accepted knowledge that the Devil (or his agents, which the Witches are) can never, in the words of Banquo, 'speak true' (I, iii, 108); that their language must be inherently ambiguous.

It is appropriate then that, although nominally female, the Witches should exhibit ambiguously 'manly' characteristics:

> ... You should be women,
> And yet your beards forbid me to interpret
> That you are so.
>
> (I, iii, 45–7)

This epicene quality exactly suits their function as obscurantist dealers in appearances. Truly neither men nor women, they subvert in consequence the matrix of ordinary communal life. They

> ... look not like th' inhabitants o' th' earth
> And yet are on it.
>
> (I, iii, 41–2)

---

[14] See Kenneth Muir's *Introduction* to the *Arden* edition of the play (London, 1951), and my own arguments, *loc. cit.* p. 127. In F. L. Huntley's view, equivocation is a major motif of *Macbeth*: 'Macbeth and the background of Jesuitical Equivocation', *PMLA*, Vol. LXXIX, 1964, pp. 390–9.

and it is fitting that such creatures should be firmly labelled by the community—here, ironically, even by Macbeth himself—as 'imperfect speakers' (I, iii, 70).

A further complexity also operates. Banquo's overt and bewildered response to the Witches's sexual ambiguity meets and articulates part of the audience's own covert response to them, and gives it an established function in the action. The convention that the parts of women were taken by boy actors makes their sexual status also inherently ambiguous in performance. In a situation such as this, the convention suddenly becomes transformed into an element in the play's own statement.

The device recurs in identical form when Lady Macbeth makes deliberate and ironic reference to her own sex. Again, ambiguity results as we hear a boy actor proclaim a desire to change his/her 'female' nature:

> Come, you spirits
> That tend on mortal thoughts, unsex me here,
> And fill me, from the crown to the toe, top-full
> Of direst cruelty. . . .
>   . . . Come to my woman's breasts,
> And take my milk for gall. . .
>
> (I, v, 37 ff.)

—and, later,

> . . . I have given suck, and know
> How tender 'tis to love the babe that milks me—
>
> (I, vii, 54–5)

In both cases the distinction between male and female is deliberately blurred (like that between 'fair' and 'foul') by means of a blurring of the distinction between the 'play-world' and the real world. Women on the stage are made to 'appear' to be what off the stage they are, male. As a result, both Lady Macbeth and the Witches must be considered as more than merely unnaturally masculine on the level of 'character'. In effect, they take on the role of spokesmen for spurious 'manliness' in the play. The irony which derives from their being 'women' in the first instance makes their 'manliness' that much more counterfeit, their violation of social decorum that much more dire.[15]

Viewed in this context, Lady Macbeth's imagery often manifests striking dimensions:

> ... Hie thee hither
> That I may pour my spirits in thine ear
> And chastise with the valour of my tongue
> All that impedes thee from the golden round.
>
> (I, v, 22–5)

The metaphor of pouring spirits into the ear carries connotations of the kind of poisoning at which Claudius and Iago have been noted to be variously proficient, and so it reinforces her connection with other Shakespearean 'men'.

Possibly, too, these words help to substantiate Lady Macbeth as an agent of the devil. The Serpent's seduction of Eve, like Iago's of Othello, was also *via* the ear, by means of words. Appropriately, then, the course of action she goes on to urge involves equivocation, the use of speech in order to deceive, indeed the perversion of every channel of communication:

> Your face, my Thane, is as a book where men
> May read strange matters. To beguile the time,
> Look like the time, bear welcome in your eye,
> Your hand, your tongue; look like the innocent flower,
> But be the serpent under it.
>
> (I, v, 59–63)

If she fulfils the latter function herself, it merely deepens the irony that the serpentine role is a male one also subversive of her 'reality' as a female. As she takes on the 'manly' phallic nature of that seducer, Macbeth's own manhood must be subverted by his growing complementary 'female' role as the one seduced.

---

[15] Cleanth Brooks's essay 'The Naked Babe and the Cloak of Manliness' in *The Well Wrought Urn* (New York 1947), while following another direction, contains a penetrating analysis of this aspect of the play.

In *Coriolanus* a similar attitude to language is promulgated by Volumnia. In Act III of that play, she advises her son,

> ... now it lies on you to speak
> To the people; not by your own instruction,
> Nor by the matter which your heart prompts you,
> But with such words that are but roted in
> Your tongue, though but bastards and syllables
> Of no allowance to your bosom's truth.
>
> (III, ii, 52–7)

As L. C. Knights comments on this passage, 'what Volumnia advocates—the passing of counterfeit coin, the use of words that are but roted in the tongue—is nothing less than an abrogation of those qualities of mutuality and trust on which *any* society must be founded'.[16] When that society is an oral one, the abrogation is the greater. Duncan's complaint in *Macbeth* that

> ... There's no art
> To find the mind's construction in the face.
>
> (I, iv, 12–13)

springs centrally from such a society, where mutuality and trust are integral. Lady Macbeth's formula, on the other hand, incites a fundamental violation of that integrity. When he who abrogates such values would be King, the fault is radical.

When Duncan enters Macbeth's world then, he brings with him that sense of fully communicative order which, after his death, is so powerfully regretted by Malcolm and Macduff. The rhythms and phrases of the verse seem to embody in themselves an accepted scheme of values, an established worldview, an achieved and authenticated community. In this world there is no 'beguiling' of the time, no equivocation, nothing is 'roted' in the tongue. Here the language does most show the man:

[16] L. C. Knights, *Poetry, Politics and the English Tradition* (London, 1954) pp. 13–14.

Lennox: What a haste looks through his eyes! So should he look
That seems to speak things strange.
Ross: God save the King!
(I, ii, 46–7)

Men are what they seem. They are able, as Macbeth himself later says to Banquo, to

...speak
Our free hearts each to other.
(I, iii, 153–4)

Ironically, this 'language of men' speaks initially of Macbeth's own genuine manhood:

Captain: ...brave Macbeth—well he deserves that name—
Disdaining Fortune, with his brandished steel,
Which smoked with bloody execution,
Like valour's minion carved out his passage
Till he faced the slave;
Which ne'er shook hands, nor bade farewell to him,
Till he unseamed him from the nave to th' chops,
And fixed his head upon our battlements.
King: O valiant cousin! Worthy gentleman!
Captain: As whence the sun 'gins his reflection
Shipwracking storms and direful thunders break,
So from that spring whence comfort seemed to come
Discomfort swells. Mark, King of Scotland, mark:
No sooner justice had, with valour armed,
Compelled these skipping kerns to trust their heels
But the Norweyan lord, surveying vantage,
With furbished arms and new supplies of men,
Began a fresh assault.
King: Dismayed not this
Our captains, Macbeth and Banquo?

Captain: Yes;
>As sparrows eagles, or the hare the lion.
>If I say sooth, I must report they were
>As cannons overcharged with double cracks;
>So they doubly redoubled strokes upon the foe.
>Except they meant to bathe in reeking wounds,
>Or memorize another Golgotha,
>I cannot tell—
>But I am faint; my gashes cry for help.

King: So well thy words become thee as thy wounds;
>They smack of honour both. Go get him surgeons.
>
>(I, ii, 16–44)

Words that 'well become' their speaker, and that 'smack of honour', aptly represent those values, that society, that reality in effect, which impedes Macbeth from the golden round. His own early speeches to Duncan carry such values overtly, positively, just as they rest firmly on that assured analogical linking of Duncan's roles as king and father, natural to the world-view of Jacobean society:

>The service and the loyalty I owe,
>In doing it, pays itself. Your Highness' part
>Is to receive our duties: and our duties
>Are to your throne and state children and servants;
>Which do but what they should, by doing everything
>Safe toward your love and honour.
>
>(I, iv, 22–7)

The subsequent linguistic 'reduction' effected by Duncan's murder is signalled at one level by Macbeth's and Lady Macbeth's later, balder references to matters of duty, love and honour;

>You know your own degrees, sit down.
>
>(III, iv, i)

—and, after the appearance of Banquo's ghost—

>   Stand not upon the order of your going
>   But go at once.
>   (III, iv, 120–1)

It is of course wholly appropriate, as was pointed out, that Lady Macbeth should use an Iago-like reductive kind of language in order to urge 'manliness' on her husband. Despite his claim that 'I dare do all that may become a man:/Who dares do more is none' (I, vii, 46–7), she is able to taunt him with the discrepancy between his desire and the act itself which, she says, makes him less than a man. In so doing she can equate murder (an act which by 'real' standards is bestial, and less than the act of a 'real' man) with 'manliness'. Inability to murder becomes, by the same token, something 'unmanly';

>   ... What beast was't then
>   That made you break this enterprise to me?
>   When you durst do it, then you were a man;
>   And to be more than what you were, you would
>   Be so much more the man.
>   (I, vii, 48–52)

Macbeth's own subsequent persuasion of Banquo's murderers that they will find 'manliness' in that deed,

> 1st Murderer: We are men, my liege.
> Macbeth: Ay, in the catalogue ye go for men,
>   As hounds and greyhounds, mongrels, spaniels, curs,
>   Shoughs, water-rugs and demi-wolves are clept
>   All by the name of dogs ...
>   ... and so of men.
>   Now if you have a station in the file
>   Not i' the worst rank of manhood, say't;
>   And I will put that business in your bosoms
>   Whose execution takes your enemy off. ...
>   (III, i, 90–104)

catches the same note. Its fundamental premiss is a notion of 'manliness' which demolishes all scruples, simplifies all complexities, reduces everything to a single dimension, and thus inhibits genuinely responsive interaction. Such manliness, by its very nature, violates the fundamental 'interactive' principle of language, and its most appropriate symbol is the murderer's act: the most uncommunicative deed of all, and the one which most effectively silences speech. In a world where manliness of this sort holds sway, Lady Macbeth is well advised to

> Bring forth men-children only;
> For thy undaunted mettle should compose
> Nothing but males.
>
> (I, vii, 73–5)

—and an intense irony develops after the discovery of the murder when Macduff declines to tell Macbeth's 'gentle' spouse what has happened on the grounds that such 'murdering' language is not suitable for a 'woman's' ear:

> . . . O gentle lady,
> 'Tis not for you to hear what I can speak:
> The repetition, in a woman's ear,
> Would murder as it fell.
>
> (II, iii, 85–8)

But the most immediate casualty of the murder is of course concerned linguistic 'repetition' in the country at large. Duncan's sons realize this almost at once;

> *Malcolm:* Why do we hold our tongues
> That most may claim this argument for ours?
> *Donalbain:* What should be spoken here,
> Where our fate, hid in an auger-hole,
> May rush, and seize us?
>
> (II, iii, 122–6)

And so Macbeth's precipitate call that, in the circumstances, the company should now 'put on manly readiness' (l. 135) sheds its own ironic light on subsequent events in Scotland. It is not until the scene shifts, by contrast, to England that a truer sense of what might now constitute 'manly' behaviour is defined.

The expositor is of course Malcolm, the genuine king who will supplant Macbeth. His pretended confession of his own 'evils' serves paradoxically to remind us of the absence of such free and open colloquy in matters concerning kingship in his own country. And when the news arrives of the murder of Macduff's family, Malcolm's advice significantly links manhood with freedom of utterance:

Malcolm: What, man! Ne'er pull your hat upon your brows;
Give sorrow words. The grief that does not speak
Whispers the o'er fraught heart, and bids it break. . . .

Dispute it like a man.
Macduff: I shall do so;
But I must also feel it as a man.
I cannot but remember such things were,
That were most precious to me. . . .

O I could play the woman with mine eyes,
And braggart with my tongue—But gentle heavens,
Cut short all intermission; front to front
Bring thou this fiend of Scotland and myself;
Within my sword's length set him; if he 'scape,
Heaven forgive him too!
Malcolm: This tune goes manly.
Come, go we to the King.
(IV, iii, 208 ff.)

The 'porter scene' brings the play's theme of 'equivocation' to its culmination and thus constitutes a climactic point in the theme of language and 'manliness'. The setting, in accordance with the Morality-play atmosphere deliberately generated at this point (II, iii,) is at 'hell-gate' itself, whilst the topical references to the well-known 'traitor' Father Garnet (II, iii,

5 ff.) as an 'equivocator' give a 'local habitation' to its significance.

Fittingly, this guardian of Hell speaks of matters which inform the 'devilish' activity of Macbeth and Lady Macbeth, at the very point when their most devilish deed is about to be discovered. So, he speaks of equivocations:

> ... Faith, here's an equivocator, that could swear in both the scales against either scale; who committed treason enough for God's sake, yet could not equivocate to heaven. O, Come in equivocator....
>
> (II, iii, 10 ff.)

That this links Father Garnet with Macbeth as an 'equivocator' and more, one whose equivocation leads to damnation, may now be seen to be an extremely apt comment on this play (especially since James I, whose government had condemned Garnet, was himself watching it). Other dimensions of the play's 'battle' are also hinted at. The deadly conflict between the desire to do something and the performance of the act itself is here given a form of expression deliberately uglier than that which Lady Macbeth had earlier used, with the result that it comments on the essential crudity of her own thinking about the same issue. The difference between 'desire' and 'performance', 'word' and 'deed', of which she makes so much in connection with Duncan's murder is comically linked here with the difference between another kind of 'desire' and another kind of 'performance'. The link occurs in the references to an act of 'equivocation' common to both:

> ... (Drink) provokes the desire, but it takes away the performance. Therefore, much drink may be said to be an equivocator with lechery: it makes him, and it mars him; it sets him on, and it takes him off; it persuades him, and disheartens him; makes him stand to, and not stand to; in conclusion, equivocates him in a sleep, and, giving him the lie, leaves him.
>
> (II, iii, 29 ff.)

Lady Macbeth's gibes at her husband have been centrally concerned with the 'manliness' which the act of murder should have produced in him. The desire for power, she argues, must be matched with the 'manly' performance of the murder which will realize it. The porter here speaks of sexual tumescence, the most literal and limited kind of 'manliness'. His account of the distinction between 'standing to' and 'not standing to' offers a vulgar configuration of the distinction Lady Macbeth had postulated between murdering and not murdering. The presence off-stage of the murdered Duncan weights every word which the porter speaks, and this links what he says with what Macbeth has done. In each case the distinction is said to be the same as that between being 'a man' and being, in Lady Macbeth's words, 'unmann'd'. In Lady Macbeth's case equivocation creates the distinction; in that of the porter 'drink', also an 'equivocator', has the same effect. Her standard of 'manliness', murder, is 'placed' by the porter's standard, sexual potency. Both kinds are said to lead to a sort of 'lechery' which should be repugnant to the real 'man', for only apparent 'manliness' makes lechery of the sexual act, just as only apparent 'manliness' makes murder a prerequisite of ambition, or equivocation the end of speech. Murder is to politics what lechery is to love and equivocation is to language; a fundamental debasement. The implicit equation which exists here between Lady Macbeth's values and the 'lower' values of the porter therefore serves to put her actions on the level of his function at this moment in the play. He guards the gate of Hell, she operates within it.

Like the ghost of *Hamlet*, Banquo's ghost paradoxically brings reality to a world of appearances. And, like Gertrude, Lady Macbeth cannot perceive it, for she sees nothing beyond the fleshly. As she says,

> ... when all's done
> You look but on a stool.
>
> (III, iv, 67–8)

and she is moved only to taunt her husband, with the now familiar gibe; 'are you a man?' (III, iv, 58). In her world, the 'stool' represents reality, and anything else must be unreal; whatever she can see, hear, and touch encloses her completely and she judges 'manliness' by those standards. Anything else can be dismissed as 'a woman's story at a winter's fire'. Macbeth, who finds himself unwillingly in contact with reality of another sort, becomes for her simply . . . 'quite unmann'd in folly' (III, iv, 74). As a result, such 'manliness' becomes the theme of his protest against a reality which lies beyond the evidence of the senses. To 'be a man', by his lights, requires him to live in *this* world, the world of empirical fact:

> What man dare, I dare,
> Approach thou like the rugged Russian bear,
> The arm'd rhinoceros, or th' Hyrcan tiger;
> Take any shape but that, and my firm nerves
> Shall never tremble.
>
> (III, iv, 99–103)

And, indeed, when the ghost retreats, this world easily reasserts itself, laying its claim to 'reality', and to the 'manliness' inherent therein:

> Why so, being gone,
> I am a man again.
>
> (III, iv, 107–8)

Such 'manliness' clearly depends on a seriously diminished notion of the extent of human experience: on the view that all life, 'all that is' in Getrude's words, can be accounted for and 'explained' in rational physical terms. Macbeth's tragedy lies in his discovery that a true 'man' inhabits a world vaster than that of the simple here and now. And of course the discovery comes too late. His attempt to become a 'man' has turned him into a mere 'dwarfish thief' (V, ii, 22). His resolve to be 'bloody, bold and resolute' has generated merely a frightened child, fearing a 'painted devil', whose stolen clothes are too large for him.

The final downfall of his world takes place, appropriately, on a linguistic level. The 'valour's minion' of Duncan's court finds himself facing a life from which the values he once held have long since been eroded, and which now marches only in an arid 'petty pace' to an inexorable 'dusty death'. From the very moment of Duncan's murder, words like 'Amen' have stuck in the throat (II, ii, 31–2). Communicative language has been supplanted by what Lady Macbeth's doctor terms 'Foul whisperings' whereby

> infected minds
> To their deaf pillows will discharge their secrets.
> (V, i, 75–7)

It has become a world in which men 'think but dare not speak' (V, i, 83); one which finally and fittingly seems merely

> ... a tale
> Told by an idiot, full of sound and fury
> Signifying nothing.
> (V, v, 26–8)

As with language, so with culture. Macbeth's 'way of life' has 'fall'n into the sear, the yellow leaf' (V, iii, 23). His very name 'blisters the tongues' of 'good men' (IV, iii, 3, 12), and the traditional manifestations of social interaction, 'honour, love, obedience, troops of friends' he 'must not look to have' (V, iii, 25–6). In their place, his own acts have put the shallow language of 'manliness':

> Curses not loud but deep, mouth-honour, breath,
> Which the poor heart would fain deny, and dare not.
> (27–8)

He has created a world characterized not by oral-aural colloquy so much as by 'sighs and groans, and shrieks that rent the air' (IV, iii, 168), by

> ... words
> That would be howled out in the desert air
> Where hearing should not latch them.
> (IV, iii, 192–4)

In the end, as the full implications of the Witches's prophecies reveal themselves, Macbeth begins for the first time to assess the extent of his linguistic involvement with evil; he begins

> To doubt th' equivocation of the fiend
> That lies like truth.
>
> (V, v, 43–4)

—and the point of his story lies in that. Equivocation, the juggling with words which has been seen to characterize the method by which the powers of evil work, is roundly condemned both in its particular manifestation here, and in a larger sense. As Banquo had realized from the beginning,

> The instruments of darkness tell us truths,
> Win us with honest trifles, to betray's
> In deepest consequence.
>
> (I, iii, 124–6)

Macbeth had sought, by means of such equivocal 'truths', to achieve that 'manliness' to which Lady Macbeth had so forcefully urged him. The irony of his end lies in that the Witches's 'truths' have in fact 'unmann'd' him. He is, and it seems appropriate, killed by a real 'man' whose birth sounds impossible judged by the standards of 'manliness', but whose genuine manhood remains undeniable. True 'men' such as Malcolm, although unrecognized as such by Macbeth (he dismisses him as 'the boy Malcolm' (V, iii, 3)) have nevertheless his measure. In the battle, Siward's son dies 'like a man' (V, viii, 43), and Macduff finds the language of such men simply inappropriate for the purpose of dispatching this 'butcher':

> . . . I have no words:
> My voice is in my sword, thou bloodier villain
> Than terms can give thee out!
>
> (V, viii, 6–8)

In fact, like Iago, Macbeth ceases to be a 'man' at all by the end of the play. He becomes a 'dwarf', a 'bear' (V, vii, 2), a 'hell-hound' (V, viii, 3), finally a 'monster' and a 'coward' (V, viii, 26 ff.). At his death, he seems to recognize the sort of language which has brought him to this pitch:

> Accursed be that tongue that tells me so,
> For it hath cowed my better part of man;
> And be these juggling fiends no more believ'd
> That palter with us in a double sense,
> That keep the word of promise to our ear,
> And break it to our hope:
> (V, viii, 16–21)

IV

Ben Jonson's name was invoked at the beginning of this chapter, and it seems fitting to end it with a note on his own dramatic contribution to its theme.

It is hardly surprising to anyone who reads his *Timber* to find that a notion of legitimate or 'manly' linguistic behaviour runs through Jonson's plays like a moral principle; that language and morality are intertwined in all his writings, and that communication or the lack of it between human beings acquires the status of a moral touchstone—and of a principle of decorum. In *Epicoene, or The Silent Woman* it becomes the subject of the play itself, and draws all other matters under its *ægis*.

If speech is the linguistic 'Instrument of Society' and interaction between human beings its mode, another 'Instrument' proves to be that institution concerned with the biological aspect of human relationships and enshrining another and cognate kind of 'interaction' fundamentally necessary to the society's continued existence: marriage.

In Jonson's society marriage formed the linch-pin of the social order. Not only could the 'family' in the largest sense be said to constitute the society's 'unit'[17] and so provide the basis for its members' identity and social role, but at an early stage of capitalist development, it also provided a context of

[17] See Peter Laslett, *The World We Have Lost, cit.*, pp. 2–21 and *passim*.

'legitimate' inheritance of wealth and position necessary to economic and so political order. Offences against marriage consequently receive in the drama and in real life punishment of (to us) sensational cruelty. Bastardy (a considerable hazard at a time when no effective means of contraception were available) brought with it a burden of guilt and social deprivation sufficient to guarantee the motive of many a stage villain. If the structure of social interaction can be said to be contained in the structure of language, sexual interaction (whose existence is interdependent with that of society) may be said to be 'formalized' by marriage. In Jonson's view both types of 'intercourse' are closely related, and a principle of decorum applies to both 'instruments' of society. The notion of propriety and control, '. . . talking and Eloquence are not the same: to speake, and to speake well, are two things' (*Timber*)—applies to sexual relationships as well as to linguistic ones.

In *Epicoene, or The Silent Woman* 'manliness' and language are considered inevitably and provocatively together, and the qualities which lead to a perversion of the one are seen to be the same as those which lead to a perversion of the other. False manliness, of the type urged by Iago and Lady Macbeth, is equated with a spurious or 'doubtfull' use of language. True manliness, by implication, resides in direct and straightforward communication. The sexual paradoxes which the play comically exploits thus also become linguistic paradoxes. Indeed, the title indicates so much. A 'silent woman' cannot exist; not only on the level of the popular joke (women are not traditionally silent) but also more fundamentally. Silent *people* cannot exist. To be silent is to be less than human. It is to abrogate nature, society, and decorum. It is to be unnatural, as the 'woman's' name, Epicoene (it means having the characteristics of both sexes) suggests.[18] In so far as a male dressed up as a female—the play's central comic situation—is essentially 'unmanly', it is highly appropriate that such a 'woman' should not speak, should remain 'silent', should lack the essential sign of humanity.

---

[18] See the excellent essay on the play in Edward B. Partridge's *The Broken Compass* (London, 1958) pp. 161–77, to which my argument is heavily indebted.

As Partridge notes, 'nearly everyone in the play is epicene in some way'.[19] That is, like Lady Macbeth and the Witches, they are properly neither man nor woman. And it is certainly true that throughout the play those who fall short of full manhood (or womanhood) are seen accordingly to fall short of full social communication. Far from their language being the communicative 'Instrument of Society', in which men and women have clearly defined and complementary roles, these creatures use language to *avoid* communication, to deceive in a manner which befits their 'feigning' sexual status. Thus Clerimont's page-boy—perhaps the same boy-actor who later takes the part of Epicoene—engages in riddling banter about his lack of manhood, 'I am the welcomest thing under a man', which broadly hints at femininity as well as boyhood: an appropriate enough joke in a theatre where women's parts were normally taken by boys in any case.

The same boy (whose relationship with Clerimont, the play hints, is homosexual and far from 'manly') sings the latter's song 'Still to be neat, still to be drest' with its central notion of the deceitful and communication-defeating nature of cosmetics and ornate clothing (the means by which boy-actors would disguise themselves as women) and its praise of 'sweet neglect' as the only antidote to art's 'adulteries'. Indeed, the idea of the Collegiate Ladies as works of this sort of 'feigning' art is explored on many levels: as when Truewit speaks at length of 'their false teeth, their complexion, their eyebrows, their nails' (I, i), their 'dressings' (IV, i) and when Captain Otter complains of his wife that 'All her teeth were made in the Blackfriars, both her eyebrows in the Strand, and her hair in Silverstreet. Every part of the town owns a piece of her' (IV, i). Finally, when Epicoene is unmasked—to the audience's surprise as well as that of the people on the stage—the *coup de théâtre* serves amongst other things to *remind* us that the parts of women in the play were being played by boys.

In this sense, the 'unmasking' of Epicoene plays a kind of double-trick on us in that the actors on the stage suddenly respond to 'her' as the audience in the theatre has done throughout the play, only without the restriction conventionally

[19] *Op. cit.*, p. 162.

imposed on that response. To a greater extent than in *Macbeth* the surprise comes when the convention—our knowledge that the 'woman's' part is being played by a boy—suddenly enters the play's action as part of the overt plot; indeed, as its comic climax. The knowledge which the play 'restricts' to its audience suddenly becomes the 'point' of the play, in a joke which fools everybody in the theatre.

Thus 'women' in this play become symbols of false 'manliness' at every level. Their behaviour proves fundamentally unnatural or indecorous in an almost stylized fashion. Their names, as Partridge points out, typify the play's central theme of 'indefinite' sexual status.[20] Clearly, Jonson seeks to establish them, within the play, as exemplars of that denial of complete 'man' (or 'woman')—making communication, which favours deceit. They seek to avoid fulfilment both as women (they have 'excellent receipts' to avoid conceiving children) and as boy-actors (the audience, knowing the stage convention, 'knows' that they are not what they seem). By turning this convention on its head at the moment of 'unmasking', Jonson demonstrates an ultimate degree of 'feigning' at the play's heart. Both as boys who play women and 'women' whose femininity is in dispute, the ladies are less than men.

And of course the language of the major boy-woman in the play is the reverse of communicative. Not only is Epicoene 'silent' to begin with, but when she does speak her silence is replaced by an uncommunicative torrent of sound. This makes her a fitting member of the Ladies Collegiate, that unnatural 'mankind generation' as Morose calls them, whose chatter deafens, and who, in Truewit's words, hardly communicate any degree of femininity. They 'live from their husbands' and exercise a 'most masculine, or rather hermaphroditical authority'. Mrs. Otter, an 'authentical courtier' rules her husband as her subject. He never 'dares' to speak to her, and their relationship is virtually transposed. She acts as head of the household, and Clerimont calls *her* 'Captain Otter' whilst her husband assumes the role of her 'page'—a mere boy.

Two of the major characters in the play prove to be equally

[20] Partridge, *op. cit.*, pp. 162–5.

unmanly and uncommunicative in a way that suggests these defects are coterminous. Sir John Daw, like the bird his namesake, merely chatters. He is 'The only talking sir in the town', who reckons to 'utter as good things every hour', as Plutarch and Seneca, and considers 'Aristotle, a mere common-place fellow; Plato a discourser; Thucydides and Livy tedious and dry; Tacitus an entire knot; sometimes worth the untying, very seldom'—the very assemblage of names is birdlike. Notably, it is this 'mere talking mole' who writes a poem in praise of 'Silence in woman' (which he considers as 'natural' as 'speech in man').

Sir Amorous La Foole's speech is similarly characterized as mere noise. Boastful, vain and effeminate (Clerimont terms him a 'windsucker'), his long breathless speech on his own lineage,

> They all come out of our house, the La-Fooles of the north, the La-Fooles of the west, the La-Fooles of the east and south —we are as ancient a family as any is in Europe—but I myself am descended lineally of the French La-Fooles. . . .

confirms the aptness of the description. He is properly called a 'precious mannikin'—considerably less than a man.

Significantly, both these non-communicators boast of their exploits in communication, and lay claim to that sort of hard-boiled 'manliness' which Iago extolled. Both offer themselves as 'ladies-men' who have made great conquests—amongst whom, of course, they are easily induced to number Epicoene. However, such claims are quickly disproved. Their swords, their 'naked weapons' (symbols of manliness here as elsewhere in the plays of the period), are easily taken from them, and Clerimont punningly accuses them of 'manslaughter'. When it comes to talk of genuine conquests, both find themselves speechless:

> *Daw:* Why—a—Do you speak, sir Amorous.
> *La-Foole:* No, do you, sir John Daw.
> *Daw:* I' faith, you shall.
> *La-Foole:* I' faith you shall.

But it is in the central character of Morose that the full weight of Jonson's view of language as a social 'instrument' may be said to lie. For in so far as he cannot bear to communicate at all, Morose is presented as uncivilized, anti-social, and finally unnatural and unmanly: the sounds of social life are merely 'noise' to him. Yet, and this is the play's central paradox, although he rejects language, he seeks language's social counterpart, marriage. He does so not, of course, in the spirit of decorum in which Jonson and his society thought of marriage, but for reasons of spite against his nephew Dauphine.

In effect, Morose tries to separate what should be unified; the human activity of communication as evinced both by talking and by marriage. As Truewit puts it 'you would be friends with your wife upon unconscionable terms; her silence.' It is the very 'unconscionable' nature of Morose's divisive demands upon society that place him wholly outside man's nature. And it is notable that when Epicoene is finally 'married' to Morose she usurps his (to the Jacobean) 'natural' male authority and even takes over his name. Haughty tells her 'I'll call you Morose' and does so until the end of the play. In pursuit of a divorce his final plea is that he is impotent, unable to fulfil the man's role in marriage.

Hence, despite language's status as man's *sine qua non*, Morose's life has been dedicated to a search for 'a more compendious method . . . to save my servants the labour of speech and mine ears the discourse of sounds'. Far from involving himself in communicative interaction with his fellow humans, he asserts the principle that 'all discourses but my own afflict me: they seem harsh, impertinent and irksome'. Such self-sufficiency aptly conveys its own wholly divisive quality. The basis of communal life, man-to-man communication, must be subverted as a result.

Morose's divisiveness manifests a further reach when he insists on a thorough-going separation of the normally complementary activities of speech and gesture. His servant (called Mute) may 'speak' only by bodily movement, and must 'answer me not by speech but by silence'. As if to set the final seal of disapproval on him, the Christian Jonson makes Morose admire the heathen in exactly this regard:

The Turk, in this divine discipline, is admirable, exceeding all the potentates of the earth; still waited on by mutes . . . yea, even in the war, as I have heard, and in his marches, most of his charges and directions given by signs and with silence: an exquisite art! And I am heartily ashamed, and angry often times, that the princes of Christendom should suffer a barbarian to transcend them in so high a point of felicity. I will practice it hereafter.

Truly, Morose is made to seem fundamentally uncivilized and thus not a real 'man' as far as Jonson is concerned.

It should be noticed that Morose's objection is not merely to noise; an attitude towards which we in the modern world might have a good deal of sympathy. It is to what he *terms* noise, and this, far from being the simple and, in the circumstances, comic clamour, say, of Otter's drums and trumpets, frequently turns out to be the sound of society in action. Not only does he abhor ordinary speech, but ordinary activity as well:

He cannot endure a costard-monger, he swoons if he hear one. . . . A brasier is not suffer'd to dwell in the parish, nor an armourer. He would have hang'd a pewterer's prentice once. . . .'

Even his complaint against the law-courts that

. . . there is such a noise in this Court, that they have frighted me home with more violence than I went! Such speaking and counter-speaking, with their several voices of citations, appellations, allegations, certificates, attachments, intergatories, references, convictions, and afflictions. . . .

–perhaps justifiable on the level of mild social satire, would, taken more seriously as Morose intends, lead to the proscription of a necessary human activity, fundamental to the rule of law. Indeed, when confronted by Otter (disguised as a divine) and the barber Cutbeard (disguised as a canon lawyer) he not only complains against 'your disputations . . . your court-tumults', but also against what has earlier been referred to as 'phatic communion', the harmless social chit-chat on which every language depends, as a means of smoothing social interaction:

> I had rather do anything than wear out time so unfruitfully sir. I wonder how these common forms, as *God save you* and *You are welcome* are come to be a habit in our lives: or *I am glad to see you* when I cannot see what the profit can be of these words, so long as it is no whit better with him whose affairs are sad and grievous, that he hears this salutation.

It need hardly be said, nevertheless, that such 'common forms' —they refer to hospitality, good-fellowship, the warmth of ordinary interaction between people—are the very stuff of communal life. Morose's inability to see any 'profit' in them suggests on a different scale Lear's inability to see profit in Cordelia's 'nothing'.

With this attitude towards language, we are not surprised to hear Morose condemn himself, as a last resort in his efforts to divorce Epicoene, with the ironic phrase 'I am no man, ladies'. The degrees to which that is true make up a good deal of this play's complexity.

The 'noise' that Morose shuns is the sound of humanity. In shunning it, he denies himself status as a man, and places himself within that category of 'manliness' which, it has been argued, encloses Iago and ultimately Othello; Lady Macbeth and ultimately Macbeth. Quite properly, therefore, Jonson's comedy ends, like *Love's Labour's Lost*, with the thought that its protagonist's final salvation can only lie in involvement with humanity's sounds, with the 'noise' that is its language. It is a notion that *Hamlet*, *Othello* and *Macbeth* themselves reach, as we have seen, and it seems characteristic of Jonson no less than of Shakespeare to locate this sound symbolically within the theatre itself, and amongst the audience which has watched the play. Like *Hamlet* (although less subtly) *The Silent Woman* draws attention to itself at the end, and as the actors leave the stage, Truewit comes forward to speak directly to us:

> Spectators, if you like this comedy, rise cheerfully, and now Morose is gone in, clap your hands. It may be, that noise will cure him, at least please him.

Certainly to playwrights like Jonson and Shakespeare, for whom life was play-like, the world a stage, acting a formalization of the interacting that is the stamp of humanity, the sound of clapping hands would signal a degree of communication and fulfilment, whose therapeutic and civilizing social effects they would recognize and approve, not only as dramatists, but as human beings. For them, there is a sense in which such a sound most aptly celebrates the true language of men.

10
King Lear and Antony and Cleopatra:
the language of love

Language may be man's distinctive means of communication, yet traditionally it is surpassed by love. Love's goal is utter communion: the merging of two human beings into one. Such unity makes language redundant. To the outside world, lovers are blind, deaf and dumb.

No doubt this presents an idealized and unrealistic picture, and the extent to which actuality fails to match it provides a constant theme for art. Lovers who betray each other, love itself which falls short of total physical and spiritual merging, the alienating demands of lust, all offer large subjects of concern.

If man can be regarded as a creature 'designed' to communicate with others, one for whom 'reality' resides only in that activity, then a deficiency in the capacity to love must prove seriously diminishing. To resist the ultimate 'merging' with others, to retain singularity, to remain inviolable, is finally to reject communication itself, and so community.

For an oral society, with its vested interest in reciprocation at all levels, this represents a serious subversion. And a special odium remains traditionally reserved for those who abrogate mutuality in this sphere; who offer trust in order to betray, 'love' that they may satisfy lust. Traditionally the acts of villains, these also rank as less than human.

In respect of the reciprocities of love itself, the nature of the debasement takes classic form in the imposition on them of the standards of another 'lower' kind of human interaction.

The exchange of money, buying, selling, and negotiating, is a human activity of a communicative sort. Indeed, it acts as a kind of 'language' in which counters, coins, notes, goods, are interchanged on the basis of set conventions, to enable a society to apportion and divide the work requisite for its existence. The language of money is as necessary to society (and thus to human life) as the language of love. Both can claim involvement at their different levels in the procreation of life which ensures the society's continued existence. Yet our scale of values is such that we place these activities at opposite extremes, in the sense that we require them to inhabit areas whose moral assumptions we judge to be mutually exclusive. And although financial interaction is as 'natural' to human beings as the sort of interaction we term 'love', any activity which connects them incurs a deep distaste. Money and love are traditionally 'opposed' in our culture. One can marry for love, or for money, never for both.

If love represents the highest point of interaction, prostitution—in its largest sense, with reference to a range of human behaviour far beyond that of the girl on the streets—represents the lowest. And the odium it incurs is the greater because its *modus operandi* is spuriously to invoke its opposite. 'Love' of one kind poses as love of another; the least good pretends to be the best. When the values of money obtrude on those of love, the process seems deeply inappropriate, mocking, and reductive. The Faustus legend gains much of its permanent applicability from the fact that its protagonist puts a price on that which is priceless.

If we now turn to those two mature plays of Shakespeare's most concerned with human interaction in the form of love, it will be seen that they naturally tend to explore the situation in terms of the gigantic 'interactive' instrument of language; in particular in terms of the language of 'love' itself.

I

The first scene of *King Lear* has been described as improbable. Lear's disturbing question 'How much do you love me?' has been called imponderable and improper. And his proffered 'equation'—so much love 'equals' so much land—probably ranks as immoral. Yet somehow these negative epithets, 'improbable', 'imponderable', 'improper', 'immoral' fail to capture the scene's immense positivity, the sense that its concern is with matters fundamental to human existence. Lear's 'darker purpose' evokes a complex response in performance. It is as if his question probed us to the core.

In fact the first scene of the play probes nothing less than the nature of love. And it does so by means of a simple, stark confrontation between the language of love and the language of money.

Of course a similar confrontation also occupies the play at the level of character and theme, with the spiritual quality of Cordelia's love pitted against the material gains for which Goneril and Regan vie, as well as at a symbolic level where the divisive forces of ambition tear asunder the unity of family and kingdom. But the subtlest probing of the issue seems initially to take place in terms of the actual words used by the participants in this first scene; particularly the word *love* itself. The two distinct, almost opposite meanings which this word could carry at the time the play was written suggest, in miniature, the movement of the whole piece.

The *Oxford English Dictionary* gives as a developed meaning of *Love*, v.² (OE. *lofian* 'praise') 'to appraise, estimate or state the price or value of'. This is an entirely different word in origin and phonetic history from *Love*, v.¹ (OE. *lufian*), and was not originally a homophone of it. Its normal development to [lɔːv] is shown by the sixteenth-century spelling *loave*; but there are fourteenth- and fifteenth-century spellings, *louve*, and *lowf*, which indicate a raising of the vowel as may be found before v in several words.[1] The apparent development of *Love*, v.² into a homophone of *Love*, v.¹ by this process—whether or not followed by shortening—would make possible the punning use quoted by the *Dictionary* from the *Towneley Mysteries*, in which the meaning of 'to estimate the value of' is made to intrude on the more usual 'to feel affection for'. The pun as used in this particular situation might be said to acquire something of an archetypal nature, for it is Judas who is asked how

---

[1] See E. J. Dobson, *English Pronunciation 1500–1700* (Oxford, 1957), § 151 and n. 2.

much he *loves* Jesus Christ. In the punning sense his answer is inevitable:

> *Pilatus:* Now, Iudas, sen he shalbe sold,
> how *lowfes* thou hym? belyfe let se.
> *Iudas:* ffor thretty pennys truly told
> or els may not that bargan be
>
> (xx, 238 ff.)

As late as 1530 this use of *love* is recognized in John Palsgrave's *Lesclaircissement de la Langue Francoyse*, in the English-to-French section of a 'Table of Verbes':

> I love, as a chapman loveth his ware that he wyll sell. *Je fais.* Come of, howe moche love you it at: *sus, combien le faictiez vous?* I love you it nat so dere as it coste me: . . . I wolde be gladde to bye some ware of you, but you love all thynges to dere . . .[2]

This sense does not appear in any dictionary after 1530, but seems to have been singled out for close attention here. It seems fair to say, then, that this other verb *to love*, with its clearly defined meaning, was well known at this time, and probably for some time afterwards.

In his book *Words and Sounds in English and French* (Oxford, 1953), Professor John Orr writes of a homonymic 'collision' which took place between the Old French verbs *esmer* and *aimer*. In the evolution of the French language, says Orr, *esmer* 'to reckon, calculate', although later replaced by the modern *priser*, nevertheless tended, in the final stages before *priser* supplanted it, to invade the 'psychological field' of *aimer* 'to love'. To illustrate his point he quotes from the *Roman de Brut* by Wace (one of the sources of the *Lear* story and significantly very like Holinshed's version).[3] Cordelia, disgusted at her sister's flattery, answers, when asked by her father how much she loves him:

[2] Quoted from the Paris edition of 1852, p. 614.
[3] See W. Perrett, *The Story of King Lear* (Berlin, 1904).

> Mes peres iés, jo aim tant tei
> Com jo mun pere amer dei.
> E pur faire tei plus certein,
> Tant as, tant vals e jo tant t'aim.
>
> (1739 ff.)

The apparent translation of this last line is 'so much you have, so much you are worth, and so much I love you'. But Orr goes on to show that the line has the status of a recognizable proverbial saying, in the manner of a pun, where the equivocation is between *aimer* 'to love' and the similarly pronounced *esmer* 'to estimate the value of'. So the punning translation of this line becomes 'So much you have, so much you are worth, *of such a price (or value) you are to me*'.

Thus the fact that there was a homonymic intrusion of *esmer* into the psychological field of *aimer* is established. It persists in the use of *aimer cher* in the Old and Middle French period, cognate with English 'to love dearly'. Palsgrave and the other evidence of *O.E.D.* shows that a similar intrusion, of the sense of *lofian* into the field of *lufian*, was possible in English at this time.[4]

It is generally accepted that Holinshed's *Chronicles* were among Shakespeare's sources for *King Lear*. Holinshed's version of Cordelia's reply to Lear in the 'division' scene is almost exactly taken from Wace:

> ... I protest vnto you that I haue loued you euer, and will continuallie (while I liue) loue you as my naturall father. And if you would more vnderstand of the loue that I beare

---

[4] The existence of a punning connection of the two meanings of *love* for a length of time cannot be conclusively demonstrated, but it would be ridiculous to suppose that immediately after the publication of *Lesclaircissement* the verb *Love*[2] fell out of use. Often examples of the equivocation crop up unexpectedly, such as in Marvell's *To His Coy Mistress*:

> An hundred years should go to praise
> Thine eyes, and on thy forehead gaze. ...

> For lady you deserve this state,
> *Nor would I love at lower rate.*

The connection of *love* and *rate* fairly invites the equivocal interpretation of *love* as 'value'.

you, assertaine your selfe, that *so much as you haue, so much you are worth, and so much I loue you and no more.*[5]

Whether the pun is intended in this version of the line mentioned above is not apparent. But linguistically it is implicit in the two senses of *love* whether Holinshed meant it to be there or not.

Shakespeare's grasping of the potentialities of the pun upon *love*, whether or not from Holinshed, can be detected without doubt in *King Lear*. Not surprisingly, Goneril's *love* presents a fairly precise, tabulated catalogue in the manner of an 'estimate':

> Sir, I love you more than word can wield the matter,
> Dearer than eyesight, space, and liberty;
> Beyond what can be valued rich or rare;
> No less than life, with grace, health, beauty, honour;
> As much as child e'er loved or father found;
> A love that makes breath poor and speech unable;
> Beyond all manner of so much I love you.
>
> (I, i, 56 ff.)

It is left to Regan to colour this estimate in terms of money, which she does with an image of coinage:

> I am made of that self metal as my sister,
> And prize me at her worth. . . .
>
> (I, i, 68 ff.)

Cordelia's remark at a very early stage in the proceedings has indicated her absolute rejection of the concept of *love* as an expressible 'value'. She seizes on the notion that the largest and truest sense of *love* implies something impossible to conceive of and 'estimate or state the value of' in any terms. Discarding the punning use of the other verb *to love* which her sisters have offered to Lear, she says 'What shall Cordelia speak? Love, and be silent' (I, i, 63). Her reply to the king comes with all the force of Wace's play:

---

[5] Everyman edn. (London, 1927), p. 226.

> ... I love your majesty
> According to my bond; no more nor less.
>
> (I, i, 93)

If we now turn to the beginning of the play we notice that love of one sort or another permeates the language from the start, and that the significance of these two opposed punning meanings thus takes on a kind of centrality in the action.[6] In fact a bewilderment about Lear's 'loving' and its vagaries prompts Kent's observation to Gloucester, which is the play's first line:

> I thought the King had more affected the Duke of Albany than Cornwall.
>
> (I, i, 1)

Lear's 'affection' and its nature remain of crucial importance throughout, and Gloucester's reply hints at its most alarming quality:

> It did always seem so to us; but now in the division of the kingdom, it appears not which of the dukes he values most, for equalities are so weighed that curiosity in neither can make choice of either's moiety.
>
> (I, i, 3 ff.)

Lear's 'valuing' of the dukes is an instance of his 'affection' at its most divisive, his 'love' at its most 'estimating'. He has 'loved' them, Gloucester is saying, at equal weight. Each has been assigned a 'moiety' of land and money in accordance with Lear's assessment. His subsequent attempt to gauge the 'love' of his daughters is here prefigured as an attempt to impose the values of one sort of love on those of another: to set a price on that which should be priceless.

---

[6] Cf. Alfred Harbage's essay on *Lear*, 'The Fierce Dispute', in his *Conceptions of Shakespeare* (Harvard, 1966) pp. 77–98, which places 'love' as the central concern of the play, and concludes that 'no greater symbols have been offered anywhere of man's capacity for love, and need to love and be loved' (pp. 95–6).

At this point, Kent suddenly appears to change the subject. He notices Edmund:

> Is not this your son, my Lord?
> (I, i, 8)

Of course the subject has not been changed so much as ironically reinforced in another key. For Edmund is a child of love; at least, of the act which bears that name. And Gloucester's attitude towards him, and towards the circumstances of his birth, reveals a good deal:

> His breeding, sir, hath been at my charge. I have so often blushed to acknowledge him that now I am brazed to it.
> (I, i, 9 ff.)

It reveals an attitude towards love at once no less reprehensible than that of Lear, and cognate with it. If Lear imposes an improper linguistic 'shrinking' upon love, making it a matter of money and land, Gloucester imposes on it the equally improper reductions of mere lust and levity. As he says, 'though this knave came something saucily to the world before he was sent for, yet was his mother fair, there was good sport at his making, and the whoreson must be acknowledged' (1, i, 21 ff.).

Both Gloucester and Lear thus deny love its full range of demands and they rank as unmoved, unresponsive, single individuals in a society which requires them above others to be the opposite. Both apply to their respective situations a reduced notion of human relationships which proves literally, as well as metaphorically, illegitimate. Edmund, the 'natural' in the sense of 'illegitimate' child, dedicates himself thereafter to an unredeemed Nature whose compulsions prove as positively destructive in respect of human community as the actions of Lear's 'unnatural' daughters. Both Lear and Gloucester are shown from the beginning to be merely 'users' and 'assessors' of people for their own pleasure. Such 'use' or 'assessment' stands condemned in this play as 'love' of one very limited kind.

And it is not until both Gloucester and Lear are purged of

this 'estimating' kind of love that they can admit the existence of another sort. For Gloucester, this involves a rejection of worldly, material values, symbolized first by the loss of the sight which formerly made him 'blind', and later by a complete renunciation of the 'assessable' visual world:

> This world I do renounce, and in your sight
> Shake patiently my great affliction off.
>
> (IV, vi, 35–6)

His 'fall' from the cliff results in a new life, as well as a new concept of love ushered in by his meeting with Lear in the fourth Act.

Lear's irrationality in this scene (IV, vi), itself a liberation from a hitherto excessively rational, 'measuring' state of mind, gives his language a width of reference far beyond the events he actually encounters on the stage. Significantly, his words centre on love, offering to Gloucester, as to all men, a broad and all-embracing acceptance:

> What was thy cause?
> Adultery?
> Thou shalt not die: die for adultery! No!
>
> (IV, vi, 111–13)

The 'pardon' comes, notably, not because the sin is now condoned, but because Lear's new 'loving' refuses to assess or measure it, recognizing in it a common compulsion, and so a matter for large compassion:

> The wren goes to 't and the small gilded fly
> Does lecher in my sight.
> Let copulation thrive; for Gloucester's bastard son
> Was kinder to his father than my daughters
> Got 'tween the lawful sheets.
>
> (IV, vi, 114–18)

The observation is wry, not bitter, in its refusal to distinguish between 'legitimate' and 'illegitimate' loving, and it suggests a much more expanded response to life than that of the play's first scene. Noting Gloucester's blindness, Lear sees in it both the image of the sin whose punishment it represents, and the complementary image of its possible redemption:

> I remember thine eyes well enough. Dost thou squiny at me? No, do thy worst, blind Cupid. . . .
> (IV, vi, 138 ff.)

The figure of 'blind Cupid' juxtaposes instantaneously the sin, its consequence, and the means of redemption appropriate to it. For Gloucester has sinned against love of one sort in the name of 'love' of another sort, and the reference is not only to the painted sign of 'blind cupid' traditionally said to be hung outside brothels—and so to Gloucester's own fornication—but also to the punishment of his own 'blindness' and ultimately to the God of Love which his redeemed person now suggests. As Edgar says to Edmund at the end of the play:

> The Gods are just, and of our pleasant vices
> Make instruments to plague us:
> The dark and vicious place where thee he got
> Cost him his eyes.
> (V, iii, 172–5)

By means of that purgation, Gloucester has moved from the realm of one sort of Cupid to that of another; from a false, merely visual, and so 'painted' love, to its real 'seeing' counterpart which in his blindness he paradoxically embodies. He stumbled when he saw.

Lear, too, has changed. His hand now 'smells of mortality', and he assures Gloucester that 'I'll not love' (IV, vi, 140). He refers to his former way of 'loving'—associated here as before with Gloucester's physical lust—which involved simple measurement in physical terms so reductive that they could diminish the complexities of an oral culture to the merely visual dimension of a map crudely divided into three parts.

Of course, by this time Lear has undergone a purgative, literally maddening experience in which such 'loving' has been applied to himself. His 'needs' in respect of the body of knights necessary for him to retain his 'kingly' way of life have been assessed by his daughters much as he formerly assessed theirs, in terms of calculable number. And as their 'loving' has progressively diminished that number, he has experienced the bitterness evidenced in his shattering comment to Goneril about Regan:

> Thy fifty yet doth double five and twenty
> And thou art twice her love.
>
> (II, iv, 258–9)

Now love of that 'estimating' sort has been replaced in him by love of a larger kind. His super-rational 'madness', cognate with Gloucester's 'seeing' blindness, represents the price Lear has had to pay for that love in a world where sanity and sight and the sort of 'loving' in which they deal are very restricted and restricting affairs indeed.

That world, of course, derives from and relates to the post-Renaissance world experienced by Shakespeare himself. It is one in which, as Karl Mannheim describes it, 'quantity and calculation' inexorably became the basis of a 'new ideal of knowledge' wholly dissociated from 'personalities and concrete communities':

> This 'quantitative' rationalist form of thought was possible because it arose as part of a new spiritual attitude and experience of things which may be described as 'abstract'. . . . A symptom of this change is the . . . tendency to 'quantify' nature. . . . With the substitution of a system of commodity production for a subsistence economy there takes place a similar change in the attitude towards things as in the change-over from qualitative to quantitative thinking about nature. Here too the quantitative conception of exchange value replaces the qualitative conception of use value. In both cases therefore the abstract attitude of which we have been speaking prevails. It is an attitude which gradually comes to include all forms of human experience. In the end, even the 'other man' is experienced abstractly. In a patri-

archal or feudal world the 'other man' is somehow regarded as a self-contained unit, or at least as a member of an organic community. In a society based on commodity production, he too is a commodity, his labour-power a calculable magnitude with which one reckons as with all other quantities. The result is that as capitalist organization expands, man is increasingly treated as an abstract calculable magnitude, and tends more and more to experience the outside world in terms of these abstract relations.[7]

It is a world easily recognizable as the forerunner of our own. Nevertheless, in the teeth of it, and as a comment on it, Lear's new-found love proves one in which the 'other man's' concrete reality finds full affirmation. It is a love, at last, which refuses to assess, to measure, to apportion praise or blame in any abstract mode:

> None does offend, none, I say, none.
> (IV, vi, 170)

The argument of the play seems finally to affirm a faith in this kind of 'loving' negation. Both Cordelia's 'Nothing' and Lear's 'None' represent, in the end, the same refusal to take part in that inhuman process of division, that improper degree of 'assessment', that impertinent and preposterous form of 'loving' which formerly characterized Lear's way of life. Such negativity represents perhaps the only proper rejoinder to the abstract quantifying of a world whose most fitting epigraph, then as now, is Lear's own earlier calculation: 'Nothing will come of nothing' (I, i, 92). Rejection of that mechanistic prospect, and deliverance from the aridity of its equations, can only come about, *King Lear* seems to say, through an ultimate compassionate recognition of the unity of human life and of the interdependence of the language, the culture, and the kingdom which then comprised it.

The sort of love which reinforces the faith that something *can* come of nothing, and which refuses to be divided, 'esti-

[7] Paul Kecskemeti (ed.), Karl Mannheim, *Essays on Sociology and Social Psychology* (London, 1953) pp. 86–7.

mated' and assessed in accordance with a merely 'visual' quantification of land and money-values, may itself be said to be divinely blind in the way of those who genuinely 'see'. And its 'blindness' must serve to reinforce its mutuality with the non-visual nature of the words in which it is expressed.

For if mechanistic thinking is rejected, so is mechanistic language, abstracted by a false 'objectivity' and 'clarity' from its speaker's living being. It is replaced by the kind of unity in which speech itself inherently deals, particularly in the form of the homonym. To establish an argument, as poets of this period characteristically do, by pun and by analogy, is endemic in an oral society. The pun on 'love' manifests and resolves, orally and aurally, the division *King Lear* probes. In so doing it sheds its own valuable light on the nature both of the art form itself and of the audience towards which it is directed.

II

The relationship between *King Lear* and *Antony and Cleopatra* is often misconceived because of certain critical presuppositions about the nature of the latter play. Most of these find themselves crystallized in Dryden's version of the same subject, *All for Love or The World Well Lost*. The title itself gives a sense of the degree of sentimentality generated in that play by the trite distinction it proposes between 'all' on the one hand, and 'love' on the other. And it may, not unfairly, exemplify the kind of unthinking preconception that a casual reading of *Antony and Cleopatra* often involves. Happily, Shakespeare's play is of a subtler order.

In fact, it proves a work of high complexity, probing and testing the values and the language of love in a variety of ways to reach a more complex view of the world we live in, and of the intricacies of those communicative means which serve us both to shape and to apprehend it.

Antony's tragedy derives, like Dryden's, from an assumption that a choice has to be made between mutually exclusive opposites. In this, he resembles Lear.

But the action of *Shakespeare's* play provides a clear illustration of the falsity of that imagined choice by virtue of the very mode in which it casts Antony's perception of the proposed central distinction between Egypt and Rome. It is not that 'love' resides in Egypt, 'all' in Rome, or some such sentimental disposition of the demands of existence, but that the distinction itself is a false one, because too readily reductive of the complications of human experience. Life demands no uncompounded choice between Egypt and Rome, 'love' and 'all'. It would be simple if it did.

It has been argued that man is the talking animal. But nobody just talks. Man does not communicate by words alone, and complex combinations of voice and body, sounds and gestures, contrive to form in us a total multi-stranded apparatus finally inclusive of a wide range of activities. Over-simple 'divisions' of this communicative structure serve only to mislead and confuse.

And yet the distinction maintained in *Antony and Cleopatra* between Egypt and Rome seems to be precisely of this order. It ascribes to each location a simplistic notion of the nature of human language, and, cognately, bestows on each a simplistic concept of the nature of love itself. If man's communicative system depends, finally, on two interdependent units, voice and body, the play assigns voice alone to Rome, body alone to Egypt. Rome is a place of words, Egypt a place of actions. Rome is where love is talked of, Egypt is where love is made.

A powerful sense of 'reduction' can thus be felt to haunt even Cleopatra's first words in the play, particularly when we realize that her apparently lighthearted question is the selfsame chilling demand that Lear put to his daughters:

> If it be love indeed, tell me how much.
> (I, i, 14)

Antony's response—and his first words in the play too—recalls Cordelia's:

> There's beggary in the love that can be reckoned
> (I, i, 15)

The spectres concerning the nature of loving explored in *King Lear* also stalk this play. And in the succeeding interchange

> *Cleopatra:* I'll set a bourn how far to be beloved.
> *Antony:* Then must thou needs find out new heaven, new earth.
>
> (I, i, 16–17)

the crude 'assessing' limitations she proposes, the grandiosely immeasurable nature of his rejoinder, both point to the same tragic withering of genuine human proportion in matters of communication that has manifested itself conspicuously in *Hamlet*, *Othello*, *Lear* and *Macbeth*.

The 'bourns' Cleopatra imposes on love will prove very confining indeed. They extend, in the event, to only half of what we are, for their limits are those of the body. And Antony finds himself accordingly committed to a way of life in which the body predominates; where, to use his own memorable phrase,

> ... The nobleness of life
> Is to do thus.
>
> (I, i, 36–7)

At this, he embraces Cleopatra.

Many critics have commented on the play's sense of universality. Una Ellis-Fermor felt this to be a matter of the pervading feeling of 'space', and Granville-Barker termed it 'the most spacious of the plays'.[8] A kind of encircling amplitude certainly seems to inform the action. In its vivid *montage* of places and people, love and death, the play appears to embrace the whole known world. To go beyond its limits would indeed apparently require a new heaven and a new earth.

But on another level, that same sense of 'embracing', of encircling in close physical contact, may be said to give rise to an opposite, claustrophobic effect. It is as if, despite the play's

---

[8] Una Ellis-Fermor, 'The Nature of Plot in Drama', *Essays and Studies*, Vol. 13, 1960, pp. 65–81. H. Granville-Barker, *Prefaces to Shakespeare, Second Series* (London 1930), p. 111.

clamour, we and it remain no less obstinately tied down to this old earth and its older heaven. *Antony and Cleopatra*'s amplitude does not prevent it from looking inward as much as outward.

Philo's opening words have already pointed out that Antony's eyes, formerly famed as overt, outward-directed emblems of hostility, which

> . . . o'er the files and musters of the war
> Have glowed like plated Mars.
>
> (I, i, 3–4)

now 'bend, now turn' embracingly on Cleopatra. His 'captain's heart', inured to violent physical combat, and the 'scuffles of great fights' (l. 8) has also 'turned' to take up a smaller, circular, repetitive function as the bellows and the fan to heat and to cool a gypsy's lust. In Egypt, we quickly discover, close physical, tactile, 'embracing' contact constitutes the mode of everyday existence. Space there may be, but it exists to be constantly encircled and filled by willing flesh.

In effect, Antony's embrace of Cleopatra turns out to be paradigmatic. At that moment when their bodies unite on the stage, the word 'thus' and its concomitant gesture stand for, 'embrace', the totality of the Egyptian way of life. For the rest—

> Kingdoms are clay; our dungy earth alike
> Feeds beast as man.
>
> (I, i, 35–6)

The reduction is staggering. Animals can 'do thus' as well as man, and unless man is to be accounted merely a beast, there must be more to him than 'thus' allows. To embrace is also to enclose, to restrict. Even Cleopatra recognizes the depth of the implied degradation. But it is an 'excellent falsehood!' (I, i, 40), and if life were really of this order, it would be wonderfully simple.

In fact, every effort is made to *make* life that simple in Egypt; a simple matter of the body alone, of sexual coupling, of doing 'thus' and little else. The beds in the east are soft. There, 'the love of Love and her soft hours' clashes only with the 'conference harsh' of Rome (I, i, 45–6). There, the intensest kind of bodily communion prevails. Antony's blush (I, i, 30) 'speaks' volumes. Hands, not words, are 'read' (I, ii). The tactile potential of figs, 'oily' palms and 'inches' is idly and lengthily discussed (I, ii, 32 ff.), and the senses are drugged with mandragora (I, v, 3). In fact, Cleopatra and her attendants tend to use language itself not so much as a vehicle for rational discourse, but rather as a physically luxurious thing, part of a totality of sensuous indulgence in which all events rank as potential sources of bodily pleasure. Thus even a messenger charged with the office of simple verbal communication is urged alarmingly to

> Ram thou thy fruitful tidings in mine ears,
> That long time have been barren.
>
> (II, v, 23–4)

In short, in Egypt, Cleopatra seems to inhabit a virtually 'non-verbal' sphere more closely connected with unredeemed Nature than with its civilized human analogue:

> We cannot call her winds and waters sighs and tears; they are greater storms and tempests than almanacs can report.
>
> (I, ii, 150 ff.)

It is a world in which spatial, gestural relationships 'speak' potently, however silently:

> *Cleopatra:* Pray you, stand farther from me.
> *Antony:* What's the matter?
> *Cleopatra:* I know by that same eye there's some good news....
>
> (I, iii, 18–20)

—a world of tastes, textures and perfumes where the visitor finds

> ... Epicurean cooks
> Sharpen with cloyless sauce his appetite.
>
> (II, i, 24–5)

and what Pompey slyly calls 'your fine Egyptian cookery' on which Julius Caesar 'Grew fat with feasting' (II, vi, 62–4). Mere discourse, promises, 'mouth-made vows/Which break themselves in swearing' (I, iii, 30–1) count for little in an atmosphere in which the body deals in its own language-disdaining futurity, where lovers find that

> Eternity was in our lips and eyes,
> Bliss in our brows' bent, none our parts so poor
> But was a race of heaven.
>
> (I, iii, 35–7)

In short, the language of love in Egypt is the silent language of the body, whose covert meanings softly usurp overt utterance, however exotic. In performance, the spatial relationship between the actors' bodies must be a good deal closer in the Egyptian scenes than in those set in Rome. Significant and suggestive groupings, gestures, winks and nods are obviously called for to communicate their full ambience.[9] How else could Cleopatra's account of Antony,

> His delights
> Were dolphin-like, they showed his back above
> The element they lived in.
>
> (V, ii, 88–90)

aptly deliver its meaning? Words alone are held in little regard: discursive speech seems to be a Roman vice. As Cleopatra curses when Enobarbus alleges that her presence 'puzzles' Antony:

> Sink Rome, and their tongues rot
> That speak against us.
>
> (III, vii, 15–16)

As the messenger discovers, a normal talking-listening inter-

---

[9] John Russell Brown's remarks on the use of gestures and 'business' in this play support this point of view, and contribute an excellent commentary. *Shakespeare's Plays in Performance*, cit., pp. 40 ff.

change is out of the question in this atmosphere. Cleopatra's 'conversation' proves almost entirely a matter of physical, not verbal, encounter, with blows being struck, knives drawn, hands kissed, and a haling up and down. Her obsession with Octavia's physical appearance, her size, shape, posture and gait (see also III, iii, 14 ff.) overrides any other consideration:

> Bring me word how tall she is.—Pity me Charmian,
> But do not speak to me.
>
> (II, v, 118-19)

Even at the edge of disaster, Antony grandiloquently 'rates' tears and kisses beyond all military losses,

> Fall not a tear, I say; one of them rates
> All that is won and lost. Give me a kiss;
> Even this repays me.
>
> (III, xi, 69-71)

And later, in pursuit of the final 'gaudy night' which presages defeat, his gestures must 'speak' as much as the words in lines like these:

> Come on, my queen
> There's sap in't yet! The next time I do fight
> I'll make death love me for I will contend
> Even with his pestilent scythe.
>
> (Exeunt)
> (III, xiii, 191-4)

Antony's body, his 'inches', thus carry more weight in Egypt than his protestations. His words of sorrow at Fulvia's death (in the face of Cleopatra's cynical sexual pun, 'Can Fulvia die?') only meet demands for physical signals as proof that such sorrow exists:

> O most false love!
> Where be the sacred vials thou shouldst fill
> With sorrowful water?
>
> (I, iii, 63-4)

And when he wishes to leave her, Cleopatra catches him in one of her embraces, and pursues her argument with positive bodily movements:

> *Cleopatra:* Good now, play one scene
> Of excellent dissembling, and let it look
> Like perfect honour.
> *Antony:* You'll heat my blood: no more.
> *Cleopatra:* You can do better yet; but this is meetly.
> *Antony:* Now by my sword—
> *Cleopatra:* And target. Still he mends. . . .
> (I, iii, 78 ff.)

The physical gestures which must accompany this interchange suggest themselves. Their importance to the play's theme can be gauged from the risk that this self-consciously takes of embarrassing or distracting the audience in a theatre in which women's parts were played by boys. Like most of the contemporary dramatists, Shakespeare rarely permits much physical contact between men and 'women' on the stage for this reason. Moreover, the 'theatrical' references to 'playing' a sexual 'scene' draw covert attention to Cleopatra's actual maleness just when her virtual 'female' wiles are seen at their overt height. The 'reminder' here that 'she' is a boy focuses an 'alienated' and so powerfully reiterated attention on the physical nature of her relationship with Antony.

This scene ends, incidentally, with Antony's breaking away from Cleopatra's attempt to make him 'do thus', and her archly botched effort, as a last resort, to use words to reach him:

> Courteous lord, one word,
> Sir, you and I must part, but that's not it:
> Sir, you and I have loved, but there's not it:
> That you know well. Something it is I would—
> O my oblivion is a very Antony,
> And I am all forgotten.
> (I, iii, 86–91)

Mere words, she seems to argue with contrived pathos, are not her medium.

Of course, she is right. Enobarbus's famous evocation of her rests on that premiss. She embodies the senses, and 'embracing', nothing discursive:

> . . . the poop was beaten gold;
> Purple the sails, and so perfumed that
> The winds were lovesick with them; the oars were silver
> Which, to the tune of flutes kept stroke and made
> The water which they beat to follow faster,
> As amorous of their strokes. . . .
>
> (II, ii, 198–203)

Perhaps the 'beggary' that inheres in 'the love that can be reckoned' finds itself mirrored in her word-defeating person which 'beggared all description'. Even her colour (she is 'with Phoebus' amorous pinches black' (I, v, 28)) suggests 'embracing', and her gustatory qualities receive constant mention:

> . . . other women cloy
> The appetites they feed, but she makes hungry
> Where most she satisfies.
>
> (II, ii, 242–4)

She is a 'morsel for a monarch' (I, v, 31) 'Salt Cleopatra' (II, i, 21) Antony's 'Egyptian dish' (II, vi, 126), her proper tribute a wordless admiration:

> great Pompey
> Would stand and make his eyes grow in my brow;
> There would he anchor his aspect, and die
> With looking on his life.
>
> (I, v, 31–4)

Unfortunately, the play strongly hints, just as 'death' (in its punning meaning of sexual climax) ends embracing, so (in its ordinary meaning) does it end a life based on that limited and limiting activity. The play exploits the pun on death at length, to make this point. Of a way of life whose 'nobleness' resides in 'doing thus' with such frequency Enobarbus can rightly say

I do think there is mettle in death, which commits some
loving act upon her, she hath such a celerity in dying.
(I, ii, 143 ff.)

There his meaning was overtly sexual. At the play's end, after
a last drawn-out and ultimately ludicrous 'embrace' from
Antony, to achieve which he has been heaved 'aloft' to her side
with cries of 'Here's sport' and 'How heavy weighs my lord'
and 'O come, come come. . . . Die where thou hast lived' (IV,
xv, 33 ff.), she finds 'Immortal longings' in her own body,
discovers that

> The stroke of death is as a lover's pinch,
> Which hurts, and is desired.
> (V, ii, 295–6)

—and the pun's final irony becomes explicit. A life based on the
body alone, on physical love-making, on doing 'thus' as its sole
end, finds nothing at its conclusion but a grimmer version of
the 'death' it has punningly sought many times. Embracing,
as a way of life, proves ultimately sterile, meaningless, only half
human. So Cleopatra's physical death mocks her many sexual
'deaths'. She dies fondling the phallic asp, whose vulgar
symbolism has been fully exploited by the Clown. Many
women have indeed 'died' of this worm. So her death fittingly
takes on an orgasmic dimension:

> As sweet as balm, as soft as air, as gentle—
> O Antony! . . .
> (V, ii, 311–12)

It is not insignificant that Antony, enveloped in this atmosphere, should seal his projected alliance with Caesar with an
embrace and a phrase that ironically recalls it:

> . . . Tis spoken well.
> Were we before our armies, and to fight,
> I should do thus.
> (II, ii, 25–7)

He meets his own death, not surprisingly, in sexual terms, resolving to be

> A bridegroom in my death, and run into't
> As to a lover's bed.
>
> (IV, xiv, 100–1)

And he falls in suggestive mockery of the sexual 'embrace' on his sword, symbol of his potency, claiming, to the aptly named Eros that

> ... To do thus
> I learned of thee.
>
> (102–3)

He has been one kind of love's apt pupil, but its life of 'embracing' and of orgasmic 'dying' has brought about a course of disaster which leads inevitably to death of a more final sort. And it leads, conclusively, to Caesar's apt epitaph which draws its irony from the finality, and grisly quality, of the very last 'embrace' the lovers enjoy:

> No grave upon the earth shall clip in it
> A pair so famous.
>
> (V, ii, 358–9)

Rome is Egypt's direct opposite in every way. If Egypt emphasizes the body, one level of language, one sort of 'love', and the concomitant womanly powers of Cleopatra, Rome is a place of words, another level of language, another kind of love, and of a self-confident 'manly' prowess. Our first sight of Octavius Caesar (I, iv) shows him very much concerned with discursive verbal matters (he is reading a letter) and complaining of Antony's unmanly behaviour. He finds him

> ... not more manlike
> Than Cleopatra, nor the queen of Ptolemy
> More womanly than he. ...
>
> (I, iv, 5–7)

KING LEAR AND ANTONY AND CLEOPATRA   189

Rome is a place where precise distinctions are preferred, where men are men and women are women, each accorded a distinct role in the community. In fact Caesar evokes Antony's former 'manliness' in terms of his ability to stomach much more starkly unadulterated food than the exotic 'dishes', the 'lascivious wassails' he now encounters:

> ... Thy palate then did deign
> The roughest berry on the rudest hedge. ...
> (I, iv, 63–4)

The scene in which Antony, Octavius, and Lepidus meet together to resolve their differences (II, ii) perhaps has the most distinctive Roman flavour. Formal spatial relationships prevail between them. They sit (and so remain in fixed positions throughout) and talk. They speak of relationships between politicians. The question of relationships between men and women only arises in connection with arrangements for a politically convenient marriage between Antony and Octavia. Interchanges such as this suggest the prevailing atmosphere:

> *Caesar:* Speak, Agrippa.
> *Agrippa:* Thou hast a sister by the mother's side,
> Admired Octavia: great Mark Antony
> Is now a widower.
> *Caesar:*   Say not so, Agrippa:
> If Cleopatra heard you, your reproof
> Were well deserved of rashness.
> *Antony:* I am not married, Caesar: let me hear
> Agrippa further speak.
>
> *Agrippa:*   ... Pardon what I have spoke;
> For 'tis a studied, not a present thought,
> By duty ruminated.
> *Antony:* Will Caesar speak?
> *Caesar:* Not till he hears how Antony is touched
> With what is spoke already.
> (II, ii, 123–46)

'Speaking' not only dominates the communicative process of the seated men, but imposes its discursive mode of communication, perhaps, on an area of experience which Antony normally encounters by means of non-discursive action and bodily gesture. To speak of the institution of marriage in Rome, for reasons of policy, is the exact opposite of doing 'thus', illicitly in Egypt, for no 'reason' at all. In Rome, words 'speak' louder than actions, where the reverse is true of Egypt. In Rome, love is a word; in Egypt, love is a deed. And if Antony's 'Egyptian dish' offers love as sustenance for the body, his wife, we learn ominously, has opposite Roman virtues. As Enobarbus perhaps unkindly reminds us, she manifests 'a holy, cold, and still conversation' (II, vi, 122). Indeed, for both Antony and Cleopatra Rome is a place where life as they know it can only be parodied: where Antony would be 'windowed'

> ... with pleached arms, bending down
> His corrigible neck, his face subdued
> To penetrative shame, whilst the wheeled seat
> Of fortunate Caesar, drawn before him, branded
> His baseness that ensued.
>
> (IV, xiv, 72–6)

and Cleopatra would see

> Some squeaking Cleopatra boy my greatness
> I' th' posture of a whore.
>
> (V, ii, 220–1)

The ironic reference these lines make to the maleness of the painted boy-actor who himself utters them on the stage, again induces a powerful 'alienation effect' at a crucial point in the play, which casts its own sardonic light on the limiting sexuality of the 'greatness' to which she lays claim. If death seems preferable to life in such circumstances, it clearly does so in the way that 'death' of a sexual sort provides release from the Roman world of words. Cleopatra surely speaks of both sorts of 'dying' when she recognizes that 'Tis paltry to be Caesar' and therefore 'great'

> To do that thing that ends all other deeds,
> Which shackles accidents and bolts up change;
> (V, ii, 5–6)

Since 'that thing' finally makes cognate the act of love and the act of death, it can only claim to be as much, and so as little, as 'to do thus'.

III

Love and death perhaps represent opposite extremes of human experience. Where love implies the absolute and virtually complete union of two formerly separate persons, death implies the reverse. Its essence is loss of communication, and the experience itself, though common to all humans, remains incommunicable. The act of love creates life. Death literally defeats man's nature, and its victory can be regarded either as fulfilment, or at another extreme, as violation. In any event, it finally prevents man from being himself, where love, perhaps, enables him to be most himself.

A good deal of the 'universality' which can be sensed in *King Lear* and *Antony and Cleopatra* perhaps springs from the fact that both love and death are fundamental concerns of both plays. Like all great works of art, they span the range of human experience. And they do so through the central image of man as the talking animal. In *King Lear* the notion of man's communicative relationship with other men proves fundamental to the play. As Maynard Mack remarks,

> Existence is tragic in *King Lear* because existence is inseparable from relation; we are born from and to it; it envelops us in our loves and lives as parents, children, sisters, brothers, husbands, wives, servants, masters, rulers, subjects—the web is seamless and unending. . . . There is no human action, Shakespeare shows us, that does not affect it and that it does not affect. Old, we begin our play with the need to impose relation—to divide our kingdom, set our rest on someone's kind nursery, and crawl toward our death. Young, we

begin it with the need to respond to relation—to define it, resist it even in order to protect it, honor it, or destroy it. Man's tragic fate, as *King Lear* presents it, comes into being with his entry into relatedness, which is his entry into humanity.[10]

A particular concern with the language of love, and especially the word 'love' itself, focuses attention on an aspect of that issue which the body of *King Lear* develops fully. What, it asks, is the nature of the relationship between human beings with regard to love? What duties does it impose, what responses are required? By means of a careful juxtaposition of overt and covert 'meanings' of the word, dimensions of these questions are revealed, so that the play's larger action can explore them. The fundamental question, lying at the play's heart, can thus be approached: can love be measured? What can one reply to 'how much do you love me?' The simplest, and most honest reply must be Cordelia's 'nothing', and it is *King Lear*'s wonderfully fulfilled task to justify the apparent harshness it contains: to point out that such negation is the only reply worthy of love itself.

Antony and Cleopatra begins, in a sense, where *King Lear* ends. Death, which seemed so inexplicable and even unnecessary in the earlier play, here undergoes the same kind of probing that was formerly given to love and, significantly, in the same oral manner. Where *King Lear* explored a pun on 'love', *Antony and Cleopatra* explores a pun on 'death'. The two extremes, love and death, unite in speech. To 'die' becomes, punningly, to love. Conversely, to love is also to 'die', sexually in terms of the pun, psychologically in the sense that one 'loses' one's individual existence in another, and finally—almost as a 'natural' consequence—physically, in terms of the word's literal meaning: the lover's embrace prefigures that of the grave.

Thus the logic of these plays seems to locate 'loving'—the ultimate communicative activity as it has been argued—as central to man's nature, and requiring death in both senses to complete both that activity and that nature. Death, and its

[10] Maynard Mack, *King Lear in Our Time* (Berkeley, Calif., 1965) pp. 110-11.

counterpart 'death', become the climax, the purpose, the focal point of a human existence whose mode is—must be—love. Love affirms reciprocation, and guarantees community. It lies at the heart of all societies, and is in the forefront of those which are oral. Antony's tragedy springs from his mistaken response to such a metaphor. In effect, he proves unable to grasp its unity, and improperly separates the elements of which it is composed. He remains unable to see, in the play's oral terms, that the two 'sides' of the pun on death are complementary, not opposed, in utterance. Like Dryden, Antony conceives of Egypt's 'love' as an 'all' that necessarily opposes Roman demands, and he ignores the complementary function of both places. Thus, like Lear, he violates the complex nature of language by means of reductive objectification and a simplistic and divisive insistence on unitary 'meaning'.

In short, if a 'tragic flaw' exists in Antony and Lear, it could be characterized as an inability—or refusal—to respond to the full social and moral complexity of oral language; especially the language of love. Shortcomings in this respect must inevitably rank as tragic. Where Lear insists on a narrow and exclusive meaning of the word 'love' itself, Antony bases a 'way of life', or joins a culture whose way of life is based on an equally narrow and exclusive meaning of the complementary word 'death'. Ultimately, what Lear means by 'love'—as essment—and what Antony means by 'death'—sexual climax—become coterminous as betrayals and diminutions of the larger 'meanings' of those words which circumstances inevitably thrust on them.

Where overt and covert usages of words themselves interact in a version of the oral-aural colloquy of the human beings who use and are shaped by them, Shakespeare's mature dramatic skill is literally heard at its most powerful. Life, these plays seem to say, is language; language life. Drama may often say less than that. It can say no more.

11

The Tempest:
speaking your language

> Thus shall we make it appear that Truth is the daughter of Time, and that men ought not to deny everything which is not subject to their own sense. . . .[1]

There is an apocryphal scene of the American cinema of the last thirty years which has worked its way into popular consciousness rather more than most. It features an inscrutable oriental face, its supercilious smile reinforcing an evidently unjustified *hauteur*, confronted by an ingenuous White Anglo-Saxon Protestant face, attractively puzzled by the presence in this world of deceitful cunning. The oriental face delivers itself of the observation 'Ha-ha, Amellican, you surplised I speak your language!'—and adds in explanation a brief, ill-accented *curriculum vitae*, detailing its owner's ungrateful attendance at some Anglo-American seat of learning.

The point of the scene is its emphasis on 'surprise'. Why should the fact that a self-evident foreigner can speak 'our' language be an occasion for it? The reason lies, presumably, in the larger social context in which such a film is made, and seen by its audience. It is war-time. The oriental face represents the enemy. And the enemy is not simply 'foreign', but feral; emphatically *not* human.

The surprise comes about because of our sense that, despite this, to speak is to be human. Man is the talking animal; language is his distinctive feature. It is what makes him different from the other animals. To speak another man's

[1] William Strachey, *A True Reportory of the Wrack and Redemption of Sir Thomas Gates . . . upon and from the Islands of the Bermudas*, 1610.

language is to manifest one's humanity to him in the most obvious and direct fashion. Language and 'way of life', it has been argued, are so closely connected as to be virtually coterminous. If I 'speak your language', it follows that I am human *in the same way that you are.* It means that we share assumptions about the way the world is. When that language is spoken by a creature who in all other respects manifestly lacks our sort of humanity and who forcibly resists our assumptions about the world, a paradox results. Hence we are, or are meant to be, or think we would be 'surplised'.

One of the most obvious examples of such 'surplise' ought to be provided by Shakespeare's plays. He speaks our language. Yet he does so from the centre of a way of life whose assumptions about the nature of the world probably lie much further from our own than those which might reasonably be imputed to the owner of the Hollywood oriental face. And yet we are not really surprised. It seems 'natural' to us that the language he spoke has developed so that it can just as easily embody our own very different world.

Our lack of surprise, our sense of a 'natural' connection between his language and our own, our sense that his plays are in some way fundamentally *important* to us, because of the way in which they speak to us, comes about, perhaps, because of a series of events that took place in Shakespeare's lifetime. They were, after all, events which were to ensure, not only that he speaks our language, but that we still speak his.

The events had to do with colonization. In the face of a Europe economically, politically, religiously, linguistically hostile, this meant an expansion to the West, and the planting of a little-known language and culture, for profit, in the New World that was to be found there. The plantation was ultimately successful. The minor European tongue became in the fullness of time a major world language. That apparently inevitable, 'natural' process has by now no capacity to surprise. Yet at the time it was a wild surmise, the wilder perhaps for the nonchalant confidence with which it was often amazingly expressed:

> And who in time knowes whither we may vent

> The treasure of our tongue, to what strange shores
> This gaine of our best glorie shal be sent,
> T' inrich unknowing Nations with our stores?
> What worlds in th' yet unformèd Occident
> May come refin'd with th' accents that are ours?
> Or who can tell for what greate worke in hand
> The greatness of our stile is now ordain'd?
> What powres it shall bring in, what spirits comand,
> What thoughts let out, what humours keep restrain'd?
> What mischiefe it may powrefully withstand,
> And what faire ends may thereby be attain'd?

wrote Samuel Daniel calmly in his *Musophilus* (1599, 957–68).[2] The genuinely surprising aspect of the situation is not perhaps that a similar notion may be found in Shakespeare's last play, but that we find it at the play's heart.

There are many levels at which *The Tempest* addresses itself to the issues confronting voyagers to the 'yet unformèd Occident' that was Britain's (and has become Europe's) future. One of the most important of these concerns the matter of an appropriate language, and an appropriate drama fit to embody a new way of life: the stuff of a new 'Globe', perhaps, for a new world. And, in fact, the two ideas of playmaking and of colonization seem to become radically linked and centrally active together in *The Tempest*.

The sense of 'theatricality', of the play as a dramatic construct, lies unusually close to the surface, and a concern with the 'mechanics' of playmaking makes itself evident throughout. All critics notice the unusually full and elaborate stage-directions ('A tempestuous noise of thunder and lightning heard. . . . Enter Mariners wet. . . .') which perhaps indicate that Shakespeare wrote the play in semi-retirement at Stratford (1610–12), whilst unable personally to be involved in the production. To an almost unique extent in the Shakespeare canon, *The Tempest* adheres rigorously to the 'unities' of time,

---

[2] See also the massive evidence collected in J. L. Moore's *Tudor-Stuart Views on the Growth, Status and Destiny of the English Language*, Studien zur Englischen Philologie, XLI, 1910, and Richard Foster Jones, *The Triumph of the English Language* (Stanford, California, 1953) pp. 168–213.

place, and action. Tableaux, culminating in a masque, proliferate. The play draws upon all the available modes and machinery of the contemporary stage, from the realism of the opening scene, with its Mariners literally 'wet', to scenes in which, as the stage direction has it,

> Enter certain Reapers, properly habited. They join with the Nymphs in a graceful dance, towards the end whereof, Prospero starts suddenly and speaks; after which, to a strange, hollow, and confused noise, they heavily vanish.
>
> (IV, i, 138 ff.)

And finally, overseeing all the action, and indeed *contriving* it, we find the figure of Prospero whose involvement with all the events depicted on the island, from the shipwreck to the masque, has the quality of that of a dramatist actively creating and moulding situations to his own design.

The group of contemporary notions generated by the colonization of the American continent, in particular the colony of Virginia, also acts as an obvious source of inspiration for the play. The story of the wreck and subsequent miraculous preservation of Sir Thomas Gates, Sir George Somers, and the company of the *Sea Venture* in the Bermudas in 1609 was well-known. William Strachey's 'A True Reportory of the Wrack and Redemption of Sir Thomas Gates' was possibly studied in manuscript by Shakespeare, and further details were readily available in Silvester Jourdain's *A Discovery of the Bermudas, Otherwise Called the Isle of Devils* (1610).[3]

But beyond the physical details of the shipwreck there lies the larger symbolic role played by America in the colonizing European psyche, and evident in those writings; the sense, deeply and popularly felt, of the New World as another Eden, replete with an infinity of good things, a Terrestrial Paradise, a place of redemption, of everybody's second chance.[4] The wreck of the *Sea Venture* quickly acquired the dimensions of a 'fortunate misfortune', rather like the archetypal *felix culpa* of

---

[3] Selections from Strachey and Jourdain are included in Louis B. Wright ed., *The Elizabethan's America* (London, 1965) pp. 188–201.
[4] See Louis B. Wright (ed.) *op. cit.*, pp. 9–10.

Christian doctrine whereby the original fault might be restored, the original loss be recouped, man's original 'Wrack' be saved by a providential 'Redemption'.[5] The modern American map abounds with names, Providence, New Haven, New England, which commemorate, and perhaps now mock at these assumptions.

So *The Tempest* naturally includes some of the stock Jacobean visions of the New World, the fault-free 'earthly paradise', made popular by the travel-books of the time. Sir John Mandeville's and Sir Walter Ralegh's beliefs in semi-human monsters of strange horrific shape find themselves literally embodied, perhaps, in the 'savage and deformed slave' which is Caliban. Philip Amadas's and Arthur Barlow's report to Ralegh on a voyage of reconnaissance along the coast of what is now North Carolina, with its claim that 'We found the people most gentle, louing, and faithfull, voide of all guile and treason and such as lived after the maner of the Golden Age. The earth bringeth forth all things in abundance as in the first creation, without toil or labour' (printed in Richard Hakluyt's *Principal Navigations*, 1589[6]) is itself echoed in works such as Drayton's *Ode to the Virginian Voyage* (1606) which speaks of

> VIRGINIA,
> Earth's onely Paradise.
> Where Nature hath in store
> Fowle, Venison, and Fish,
>   And the fruitfull'st Soyle,
>   Without your Toyle,
> Three Harvests more,
> All greater then your Wish . . .
>
> To whose, the golden Age
> Still Nature's lawes doth give
>
> (23–38)

These and many other similar accounts[7] clearly lie behind

---

[5] See Louis B. Wright (ed.) *op. cit.*, p. 196.
[6] *Cit.* Louis B. Wright (ed.), *op. cit.*, p. 109.
[7] E.g. the First Canto of Waller's 'The Battle of the Summer Islands'.

Gonzalo's musings on the sort of society that would pertain were he king and had 'plantation' of the island:

> I' th' commonwealth I would by contraries
> Execute all things. For no kind of traffic
> Would I admit, no name of magistrate.
> Letters should not be known. Riches, poverty,
> And use of service, none. Contract, succession,
> Bourn, bound of land, tilth, vineyard, none.
> No use of metal, corn, or wine, or oil.
> No occupation: all men idle, all,
> And women too, but innocent and pure.
> No sovereignty—
>
> All things in common nature should produce
> Without sweat or endeavour. Treason, felony,
> Sword, pike, knife, gun, or need of any engine
> Would I not have; but nature should bring forth
> Of its own kind all foison, all abundance,
> To feed my innocent people.
>
> I would with such perfection govern, sir,
> T' excel the Golden Age.
>
> (II, i, 150–73)

However, as subsequent events on the island make abundantly clear, the Golden Age remains, in the concluding words of E. M. Forster's *A Passage to India*, 'not yet . . . not there'. A deflating commentary on the part of the all too human Sebastian and Antonio punctuates Gonzalo's words in performance and offers directly to the audience the real frailties which characterize real people in any real world. Against Gonzalo's ideal of 'No sovreignty', Sebastian astutely sets the plain fact 'Yet he would be king on't' (II, i, 159). Against the absence of formal and legal compunction leading, as Sebastian puts it, to 'No marrying 'mong his subjects' (II, 168–9), Antonio sets the inevitable (to the Elizabethans) result; 'None, man, all idle—whores and knaves' (ll. 170–71). The audience is invited, in short, to agree with Antonio's verdict 'The latter end of his commonwealth forgets the beginning' (II, i, 160–1), and to pass it in the name of fallible humanity upon all such Utopian fantasy. It might, of course, by now, also be the verdict of history.

The play, in short, invites its real and corruptible audience to venture beyond the popular traveller's tales of the time. It invites consideration of what colonization of the New World might *really* be like; how it might genuinely be made to operate, and on what basis a human society might properly and fruitfully be constructed there. Certainly, if it was to be a recognizably human society, an extension into the future of that British one from which the audience was drawn, one which, in the words of John Donne, would make 'this island, which is but as the suburbs of the old world, a bridge, a gallery to the new, to join all to that world that shall never grow old, the Kingdom of Heaven',[8] then it would surely have to be based upon that distinctive feature from which such humanity is permanently derived: the English language.

The Tempest manifests this concern throughout, even in its opening scene of shipwreck where it shows the inability of Gonzalo's words, peremptorily expressive of his puny and abstract 'authority', to deal with the more solidly based elemental forces surrounding the ship. In this situation, the concrete personalized 'professional' language of the seamen seems more closely appropriate:

> Down with the topmast! Yare! Lower, lower! Bring her to try with main-course.
>
> (I, i, 34-5)

—and the Boatswain's sarcastic comment to Gonzalo comments precisely on the ineffectiveness of Court language, and the pretensions embodied in it:

> You are a councillor. If you can command these elements to silence, and work the peace of the present, we will not hand a rope more. Use your authority.
>
> (I, i, 20-3)

---

[8] John Donne, *Sermon upon the 8th Verse of the 1st Chapter of the Acts of the Apostles*, cit. Louis B. Wright (ed.) *op. cit.*, p. 14.

Unless and until he learns that 'these roarers' care nothing 'for the name of king' (I, i, 16) Gonzalo, and the depersonalized 'authority' represented by his language will find great difficulty in adapting to the demands of the new world into which they are about to be cast. That world, like all worlds, as we were reminded in *Love's Labour's Lost*, must be as it is. And human language, as well as human life, must embrace and reflect it, or they founder.

The structural design of *The Tempest* follows this pattern. Human pretensions must be brought to a human scale. The 'second chance' offered on Prospero's island, as in the new world, is the chance to become, not godlike, but human once again. The 'wrack' offers the gateway to 'redemption'. And the ultimate discovery made by the explorers will be themselves, pristine and aboriginal.

True to the play's contrived 'theatricality', the developed situation on the island manifests overtly the traditional tensions of a traditional form: the pastoral. Thus the theme of Nature *versus* Art, and its analogues Country *versus* Court, love *versus* lust, and so on, stand clearly in evidence, and attention has been drawn to them many times.[9] The clash between Caliban and Prospero, the central element of the action, has positive aspects which make these terms appropriate. However, it would take an exceptionally reductive reading of the play to leave the matter there.

Prospero makes it quite clear from the first that his downfall as Duke of Milan originally came about as a result of his withdrawal from a proper involvement with his people and their affairs, into an enclosed and private literary world. As a result, he 'grew stranger' to government 'being transported/ And rapt in secret studies' (I, ii, 73 ff.). And consequently,

> I, thus neglecting worldly ends, all dedicated
> To closeness and the bettering of my mind
> With that which, but by being so retired,
> O'er prized all popular rate, in my false brother
> Awaked an evil nature. . . .
>
> (I, ii, 89–93)

[9] E.g. Frank Kermode, Introduction to the Arden edition of *The Tempest* (London, 1954), pp. xxxiv–lxxi.

The fault lies clearly in his obsessive study as much as in his brother's 'evil nature'; the two factors have contributed equally to his present exile:

> ... he needs will be
> Absolute Milan. Me, poor man, my library
> Was dukedom large enough.
> (I, ii, 108–10)

Like the 'bookmen' of *Love's Labour's Lost,* Prospero has subsequently discovered that the silent world of study offers little defence against subversion from without, and the play reinforces this theme again and again. 'Knowing I loved my books' Gonzalo furnished Prospero before his journey 'From mine own library with volumes that/I prize above my dukedom' (I, ii, 166–8)—and these seem to have formed the basis of his life on the island hitherto. 'Remember', Caliban advises Stephano and Trinculo,

> First to possess his books, for without them
> He's but a sot as I am, nor hath not
> One spirit to command. They all do hate him
> As rootedly as I. Burn but his books.
> (III, ii, 93–6)

However, as part of the redemptive, 'humanizing' pattern of the play, the Prospero we now encounter seems anxious to re-involve himself in the resonant world of talking and listening. In a scene often interpreted in production as wholly comic, he recounts the history of their arrival on the island to Miranda, constantly urging her to *listen* carefully as he speaks:

Prospero: Dost thou attend me?
Miranda: Sir, most heedfully.
(I, ii, 77–8)

Prospero: Thou attend'st not!
Miranda: O, good sir, I do!
(86–7)

Prospero: Dost thou hear?
Miranda: Your tale, sir, would cure deafness.
(ll. 106–7)

Whatever the humour of these interchanges, their purpose has the entirely serious end of enjoining her participation in the human activity of talking and listening, itself the basis of human affairs and their government, in which Prospero has once more resolved to take part. The world of books will be rejected at last for the world of human colloquy. And at the end of the play, his redemption together with that of the others involved complete, he resolves notably that

> ... deeper than did ever plummet sound
> I'll drown my book.
> (V, i, 56–7)

Caliban, it seems clear, must rank less as Prospero's opposite, than as the other side of the same coin. He stands as far removed from involvement in talking and listening as Prospero originally did, and his barbarity, although the opposite of Prospero's condition, thus represents perhaps a sophisticated enough comment on his master's and Gonzalo's Milanese 'civilization', in the spirit of Montaigne's trenchant views on cultural relativity given in his essay on cannibals.

It has been pointed out that the Elizabethan–Jacobean civilization had a clear-cut view of the nature and function of the spoken language in social life. The prime, and most forcefully expressed notion was of speech as a unifying and civilizing force amongst men. In the *Leviathan,* Hobbes argues that language actually *confers* manhood, and keeps bestiality at bay. Without it '. . . there had been amongst men neither Commonwealth, nor Society, nor Contract, nor Peace, no more than amongst Lyons, Bears and Wolves.'[10] Earlier writers concurred. George Puttenham, for instance, was in no doubt that

> Utterance also and language is given by nature to man for

[10] *Leviathan* I, IV.

perswasion of others, and aid of them selves, I meane the first abilite to speake.

Such ends were helped by an intensification of language's essential characteristics in the 'artificiall' form of Poesie, the 'profession and use' of which can be traced back

> ... before any civil society was among men. For it is written, that Poesie was th' originall cause and occasion of their first assemblies, when before the people remained in the woods and mountains, vagrant and dispersed like the wild beasts, lawlesse and naked, or verie ill clad, and of all good and necessarie provision for harbour or sustenance utterly unfurnished: so as they little differed for their maner of life, from the very brute beasts of the field.[11]

Certainly, in the concern of those who wrote of language at the time, the voice of Cicero and Isocrates is plain to hear. Thomas Wilson sees in language the basis of man's construction of social forms:

> Where as Menne lived Brutyshlye in open feldes, having neither house to shroude them in, nor attyre to clothe their backes, nor yet any regarde to seeke their best auayle: these appoynted of God called them together by vtterance of speache, and perswaded with them what was good, what was badde, and what was gainefull for mankynde.[12]

In fact writers of the sixteenth century often cite Orpheus, son of Apollo (the god of speech), as a major example of language's creative power as a persuasive to civilized life. Just as his song tamed wild beasts, so (the analogy went) by the power of his language he was able to charm men from bestiality to civilization, and to persuade them to form human communities. In this, he was also sometimes identified with Christ, in Puttenham's words

[11] *The Art of English Poesie*, 1589 Bk. I.
[12] *The Arte of Rhetorique*, 1553.

implying thereby, how by his discreete and wholesome lessons . . . he brought the rude and savage people to a more civill and orderly life.[13]

Orpheus's descent into Hades, like Christ's harrowing of Hell, ranks as a standard metaphor of language's power, even over death.[14]

The later sixteenth century in England stresses this 'Orphic' view of language, with its Christian analogues, as an educational ideal. For example, Stephen Guazzo's widely read *Civile Conversation* (1586), bases its precepts for behaviour wholly on the social art of speech, and the concept of 'civil conversation' as the ultimate goal of language amongst men seems to develop naturally from such a view.[15]

Of course 'civil conversation' is exactly what the unredeemed Caliban lacks. The dimension of reciprocity essential to the act of conversing is entirely absent from his speech. He never 'Yields us kind answer' (I, ii, 307) and, animal-like, has rejected those attempts to 'civilize' him which, notably, have taken the predominant form of teaching him language. In Miranda's words,

> . . . I pitied thee
> Took pains to make thee speak, taught thee each hour
> One thing or other. When thou didst not, savage,
> Know thine own meaning, but wouldst gabble like
> A thing most brutish, I endowed thy purposes
> With words that made them known. But thy vile race,

---

[13] *The Art of English Poesie*, 1589, Bk. I.
[14] See the comments of George Steiner in his essay 'Linguistics and Literature' in Noel Minnis (ed.) *Linguistics at Large* (London, 1971), pp. 134–5.
[15] See Kirsty Cochrane, 'Orpheus Applied: Some Instances of his importance in the Humanist view of Language', *Review of English Studies*, Vol. XIX, No. 73, 1968, pp.1–13. Like Guazzo, Puttenham in his *Arte of English Poesie* saw speech as fully integrated into social behaviour, and not able to be abstracted from it. He includes sections on decorum in areas such as comportment, manner of speech, dress, and manner of styling and length of hair (Bk. III, Chapter XXIV), which obviously, for him, form part of 'conversation'.

Though thou didst learn, had that in 't which good natures
Could not abide to be with.

(I, ii, 354–61)

The biological analogue of linguistic interchange might be said to be the act of sex. The word 'intercourse' legitimately applies to both activities, and both clearly have a fundamental role to play in the structure of any society. The analogical relationship between conversing and coupling was lightheartedly explored, it was noticed, in *Love's Labour's Lost*. There, linguistic intercourse was seen to precede and prefigure its sexual counterpart, the 'fruitfulness' of both being necessary to the preservation of a healthy community.

Marriage traditionally stands as one of the manifest signs of 'civilized' human society in European terms. Men and women are said to be redeemed from bestiality, indeed to *become* fully men and women by its means. The Elizabethan horror of sexual licence, and the felt need to contain its drive by means of the institution of marriage needs no exposition. Absence of marriage, or its abrogation, seemed a sure sign of savagery, of decline from human status. The linguistic analogue of 'married' sex might thus be said to be 'civil' conversation. Both act as a socially sanctioned means of fruitful intercourse between humans, on which the health and future of society depends.

An interesting link between Caliban and Prospero, which again emphasizes that they represent not opposites, so much as differing degrees of the same situation, lies in their deficiencies in these fundamentally related respects. Caliban's resistance to language constitutes a basic part of his wholly unredeemed nature which 'any print of goodness wilt not take' (I, ii, 353). His reply to Miranda is explicit:

You taught me language, and my profit on 't
Is, I know how to curse. The red plague rid you
For learning me your language!

(I, ii, 363–5)

Appropriately, and analogously, his sexual interest in Miranda proves equally unredeemed. The institution of marriage never enters into it. Nor does the sense of the fruitful generation of those 'civilized' human beings on which successful colonization (and potentially disastrous under-population at home) depends. On the contrary, Caliban's lust concerns only himself, and his own gratification. Miranda is reduced in his eyes to an object by whose means he might have 'peopled. . . . This isle with Calibans' (I, ii, 350–1). The absence of reciprocity, of the ability to venture beyond himself noticed in his language, thus also characterizes him on this level, and serves to define his lust, and to distinguish it—in our eyes perhaps no less than in those of the Elizabethans—from its opposite, love.

In the case of Prospero we are confronted not by sexual, but by a kind of intellectual lust, manifested in his earlier, almost narcotic dependency upon books. The printed page naturally tends to generate, not a sense of community, of others and their needs, and their existence, but a mirror-image of the self. Books do not converse. And they may feed a self-concerned, self-obsessed abstraction from reality. In fact Prospero recognizes this as the cause of his own deposition. He has peopled his Milanese kingdom with Prosperos.

True love, true reciprocity, true humanity, finds its aptest representation in the play in the relationship between Ferdinand and Miranda. The innate nobility of each will, we are told, result in the breeding of noble (i.e. 'non-vile') offspring which will guarantee the future of the race (and the colony). Of course, this can only take place within the institution of marriage, and the virtues of restraint and chastity—the opposite of the qualities represented by the unredeemed Caliban and Prospero—are frequently enjoined upon the lovers, and readily acceeded to by them (IV, i, 16 ff.: 52 ff.). The game of chess at which Prospero later 'discovers' them (V, i, 171 ff.) traditionally symbolizes a sexual or linguistic encounter. The *formality* of the game, and its insistence on carefully defined interrelationships, and the prohibition of 'false' play are emphasized. Fittingly

> All sanctimonious ceremonies . . .
> With full and holy rite
>
> (IV, i, 17–18)

will, we are told, constitute the appropriate 'civile' stamp on this 'conversation'.[16] And so it is not without significance that at their first meeting Ferdinand responds traditionally to the unmistakable sign of common humanity that Miranda gives him. He asks

> My prime request
> Which I do last pronounce, is—O you wonder!—
> If you be maid or no?

She replies, confirming the virginity that both manifests her restrained and 'civilized' status, and links her with the innocent newness, and promise, of the colonial Eden named for England's virgin Queen,

> No wonder, sir,
> But certainly a maid.

—and he responds

> My language? Heavens!
>
> (I, ii, 425 ff.)

She speaks his language, she is human, like him.

We may contrast Ferdinand's surprise that Miranda speaks his language, with that of Stephano when confronted by Caliban:

> This is some monster of the isle with four legs, who hath got, as I take it, an ague. Where the devil should he learn our language?
>
> (II, ii, 64–6)

---

[16] Cf. Edmund Leach on the subject of 'Conversation as a Game': 'The players make moves alternately—as they do in a conversation—and again as in a conversation, each move is a response to the other player's last move.... The other player then responds not in a narrowly defined mechanical way but by assessing the overall situation in the light of the rules of the game ... the players are responding to one another in much the same way as in an ordinary conversation.... The point I am trying to make is simply this: although the tree diagrams which bespatter the pages of the transformational grammarians of the Chomsky school are not 100 per cent convertible into descriptions of the strategies of a game of chess, there are very significant similarities between the two types of pattern.' 'Language and Anthropology' in Noel Minnis (ed.), *Linguistics at Large, cit.* pp. 139–58. See pp. 143–5.

However, it quickly becomes clear that Caliban's command of the language may easily be overcome—and by a traditional colonial stratagem: the use of alcohol. Significantly, the drink given to Caliban to 'humanize' him

> Open your mouth. Here is that which will give language to you. . . .
> (II, ii, 81–2)

acquires the metaphorical dimension of the written version of the language;

> *Stephano:* Here, kiss the book (*He gives him wine*)
> (II, ii, 127)

The 'kissing' of this 'book', far from affirming Caliban's human status, serves only to make him the besotted slave of Stephano and Trinculo. As literally in the case of Prospero, so metaphorically in the case of Caliban, 'books' constitute a means of alienation and subjugation. Caliban's role as the duped aboriginal here excites our sympathy, and perhaps sorts oddly with his function elsewhere in the play. It serves, none the less, to link him significantly with Prospero in the capacity of one whose language and humanity are sapped by contact with a corrupting, though apparently 'civilizing' force. Wine becomes to Caliban what books were to Prospero: a drug.

In a sense, Prospero's act of repentance for his former way of life could be said to take the form of the play which we have just witnessed, and the various other 'plays' it has contained. Most critics agree that Prospero represents art; man's exertion of power over nature. As an artist, he has moved from the world of books to the world of language; from abstraction to involvement. Language, it has been said, is man's distinctive feature, the 'central fact' of his nature. And the only art which wholly derives from and exploits this central fact is drama. Drama celebrates, and manifests, the reality of man as the talking animal. If language is man's distinctive feature, drama is his distinctive art. Prospero has become involved in that art. He has moved, that is to say, from the library to the theatre. His creation of *The Tempest*'s first scene is explicit: he creates the masque in IV, i, and is responsible for the fundamental structure of the action, as recognized and memorably described by Gonzalo:

> In one voyage
> Did Claribel her husband find at Tunis,
> And Ferdinand her brother found a wife
> Where he himself was lost; Prospero his dukedom
> In a poor isle, and all of us ourselves
> When no man was his own.
> (V, i, 208–13)

Prospero has created that pattern of events. The sense that 'all of us' (and in performance, the phrase and accompanying gesture would include the audience) have 'found ourselves' in this new world provides a final confirmation of Shakespeare's notion of the revelatory, 'enabling' function of drama in society that we have noticed elsewhere in his plays.

Since language and culture, or 'way of life', are closely linked—a sense particularly strongly felt in a fundamentally non-literate community—so drama and way of life must be closely involved. In a sense, drama represents a formal 'enactment' of a culture's language. It mirrors the culture, and becomes a 'second' nature for its members. And it is on this close relationship of the world in the theatre to the 'real' world beyond it that Prospero insists as the action reaches its climax, and as it becomes apparent that both worlds, *all* worlds in effect, turn out to have been 'created' by the 'dramatizing' language of those that live in them. We are all dramatists, all actors, those in the audience as much as those on the stage, united by our 'talking' nature, and drama's 'talking' art. We 'talk' our world into existence. And in this world, plays themselves must be as ephemeral as the utterances which in performance comprise them. And their ephemerality should be approved, embraced:

> Be cheerful, sir.
> Our revels now are ended. These our actors,
> As I foretold you, were all spirits, and

Are melted into air, into thin air;
And, like the baseless fabric of this vision,
The cloud-capped towers, the gorgeous palaces,
The solemn temples, the great globe itself,
Yea, all which it inherit, shall dissolve,
And, like this insubstantial pageant faded,
Leave not a rack behind.
(IV, i, 147–56)

Yet the question remains: what will the great Globe (Prospero's gesture must include the theatre) inherit? If plays are ephemeral, what of the greater 'play' in the greater 'Globe' outside the theatre? What future lies ahead for the culture the lesser Globe contained, enacted, and helped, by its 'talking', to reinforce and create? Shakespeare's last play looks to a new world.

Indeed, Prospero's government of his island has many analogues—so the contemporary pamphlets indicate—in the principles of 'good' government established by the British colonies in America.[17] The basic principle involves the redemptive grafting of the 'nurture' of civilization on to the 'nature' confronting the colonist. Prospero's role as the representative of nurture in the form of 'art', particularly of the art of drama in the play, suggests a link between the activities of 'governing' a colony and of 'dramatizing' an action which would have excited the imagination of a professional playwright. A colonist acts essentially as a dramatist. He imposes the 'shape' of his own culture, *embodied in his speech*, on the new world, and makes that world recognizable, habitable, 'natural', able to speak his language. Like the gardener, he redeems untouched landscape by imprinting on it a humanizing art; he brings nurture to nature. Like Adam in Eden, he names things. Like Orpheus, he replaces savagery by 'civil conversation'. Like Shakespeare, like Prospero, he imposes the Globe on the globe, so that the new world acquires the dimensions of

[17] See the excellent essay by J. P. Brockbank, '*The Tempest*, Conventions of Art and Empire' in John Russell Brown and Bernard Harris (eds.), *Later Shakespeare* (Stratford-upon-Avon Studies 8, London 1966) pp. 183–201, where this and many other relevant ideas are explored.

a stage whereon a new society can be 'dramatized'. Marvell, writing in the middle of the seventeenth century, perhaps punningly hints at some such notion in the song that rises from the 'English boat' as it nears the new coastline;

> He lands us on a grassy stage
> Safe from the storm's, and prelat's rage.[18]

Similarly, the dramatist is metaphorically a colonist. His art penetrates new areas of experience, his language expands the boundaries of our culture, and makes the new territory over in its own image. His 'raids on the inarticulate' open up new worlds for the imagination.

It is not insignificant that, in 1610–12, with English still a little-known European tongue, Shakespeare should imaginatively link the future of both language and culture with the colonization of North America, and with the sense of a new English 'play' to be enacted there, and a new English-speaking society both to generate and respond to it; a new lease of the 'permanence-in-ephemerality' that is life itself.

At the end of *The Tempest* Prospero steps forward, a mere actor now, and asks, in an Epilogue, for applause. The sound of clapping hands—as in *Epicoene* the ultimate 'completing' indication of approval in the ephemeral 'language' of the theatre—probably constitutes the only memorial Shakespeare would have considered fitting for a dramatist. The warning of *Love's Labour's Lost* against 'book-men' remains constant. We, inheritors of an enabling and enlarging dimension of experience in the form of a new world that speaks the language of our old one, as we speak his, might rather conclude that the power of his drama has still no more appropriate, or more permanent monument than the English tongue itself.

[18] *Bermudas*, 11–12.

Part III
Conclusions: New Languages for Old

> Truth sayes, of old, the art of making plaies
> Was to content the people; and their praise
> Was to the Poet money, wine, and bayes.
> But in this age, a sect of writers are
> That, onely, for particular likings care,
> And will taste nothing that is populare.
> With such we mingle neither braines, nor brests:
> Our wishes, like to those make publique feasts
> Are not to please the cookes tastes, but the guests.
> <div align="right">Ben Jonson, Prologue to <i>Epicoene</i></div>

> *Stage-Director:* ... I was speaking of the theatre as an asset of the nation.
> *Playgoer:* Yes? Well, we are going to have a National Theatre in England.
> *Stage-Director:* Not at all. We are going to have a Society Theatre.
> <div align="right">Edward Gordon Craig, <i>On the Art of the Theatre</i></div>

> If the age turns away from the theatre, in which it is no longer interested, it is because the theatre has ceased to represent it. It no longer hopes to be provided by the theatre with Myths on which it can sustain itself.
> <div align="right">Antonin Artaud, <i>The Theatre and its Double</i></div>

> ... whether one deplores or rejoices in the fact, there are still zones in which savage thought, like savage species, is relatively protected. This is the case of art, to which our civilization accords the status of a national park, with all the advantages and inconveniences attending so artificial a formula.
> <div align="right">Claude Lévi-Strauss, <i>The Savage Mind</i></div>

12
Drama versus Theatre

(i) *Stamp Out Live Theatre*

A good deal of sentimentality propels the notion of the supposed 'universal' and 'permanent' appeal of great plays. We can learn a lot from Prospero. Of all art forms in fact the most ephemeral, drama's true permanence may be said ultimately to derive from that of its raw material, language itself. And language's permanence resides less in the ephemerality of individual utterance than in the permanent and distinctive fact of man's talking and listening. If words fly away, language remains. Like individual utterances, individual plays must be as ephemeral as their individual performances. It is drama itself, like language, that is permanent and universal.

We are Shakespeare's inheritors. But our inheritance, as *The Tempest* seems to suggest, might be said to lie not so much in the 'insubstantial pageant' of his plays as in the language these found, reinforced, amplified and fostered.

And so it seemed fitting, at the beginning of this book, that an investigation of the ideas about language embodied in the plays should start from notions about such matters current in the daily life of our own society. Those ideas about language were seen to lead, inevitably, to issues concerning drama itself and its relationship to a community's total way of life, which seemed to be particularly firmly formulated in Elizabethan culture. The scope of their implications now seems to make it no less appropriate that the investigation should conclude by returning to its point of departure. In short, it seems proper that, as inheritors, we should look at the relationship of drama to society in our own time, in the light of what we might now claim to know about that relationship in Shakespeare's.

There is, following Prospero, a sense in which this could reasonably be judged one of the more fruitful uses to which the plays might be put. Their essential ephemerality subverts the claims mere performance might make to a living link between past and present. And in any case, few modern productions aim to take us much beyond the banality of their directors' 'insights' into areas of character and motivation wholly alien to the world-view from which the plays spring. Events at any of our contemporary Stratfords unwittingly reveal more about our own world's preoccupations than about Shakespeare's. His plays, when glimpsed, seem to plead, like Ariel, for their release.

The point is not that the past is unreachable through its plays, but that the plays provide us with unexpected information about the past which proves relevant to the present in an unexpected way. As was argued earlier, in the Elizabethan theatre a predominantly oral culture enacted its own 'shape' through a drama which constituted a formal realization of its own language. In that drama, the unity of language and way of life was both manifested and reinforced by dramatic argument. So the Elizabethan play in the Elizabethan theatre seems characteristically not merely to mirror but to guarantee and underwrite the society from which its audience was drawn.

We inherit a society in which such a relationship of way of life, language, drama and theatre is inherently and damagingly inconceivable. If Shakespeare's drama enables us to conceive it, this does not ultimately result from an analysis of the *content* of individual plays, but from knowledge of the social function of the drama of which they form part. Unique information about the past may thus uniquely be found less in the abstractions of character and motivation than in concrete knowledge of the nature of the social institutions which that kind of drama shapes or brings into being. In short, the means by which the plays relate to the society that generates them turn out to be uniquely revelatory of that society.

The value of such revelation ultimately lies, of course, in the light it sheds on our own unacknowledged presuppositions about contemporary society. The notions about language, way of life, drama and theatre implicit in Shakespeare's plays offer us a unique purchase on the past which in turn offers to view a revealing dimension of the present. His Globe forces us to face our own.

In the first chapter of this book it was argued that, as man's most distinctive characteristic, his *sine qua non*, language involved a range of everyday experiences and responses not only wider and more comprehensive than those of writing, but in circumstances fostered and upheld by our educational system and its presuppositions, almost opposed to them. Drama was seen as the art-form which springs centrally from man's communicative nature, and which thus celebrates, reinforces, and finally perhaps establishes his role and status as the 'talking animal'. However, in our society, drama seems to have been removed from the area of 'talking' altogether, and restricted to that of 'reading', even when plays are 'performed'. Indeed, most 'performances' underline the paradox by the response they generate in their audiences. Drama has become part of literature.

Carried to an extreme—one which the baldness of this summary perhaps suggests—such an argument risks, and possibly sustains, absurdity. Literature, it might be replied, can by now claim to be as 'natural' to man as language, at least in the Western world. Moreover, although none of us reads 'by nature', neither do we talk so. Speech like most things has to be learned.

Nevertheless, such replies miss a central point. Man speaks before he writes, and speech is his distinctive feature, writing a shadow of it. We can learn as much from *Love's Labour's Lost*. Speech and writing are not the same activity, and the conflict between the presuppositions of each needs, as that play tells us, to be resolved. The persistent confusion about these matters inherited by our society might be said to be partly responsible for a certain debilitating tension between language and literature which it exhibits. In more particular terms, it might be argued that that tension by now prefigures and incites a cognate and wholly un-Shakespearean conflict between drama on the one hand and the theatre on the other.

'The theatre is dying!' 'Support the live theatre!'—the slogans prove durable, even in the face of facts. Worse, the half-truths they embody nurture cherished illusions, offer desirable roles, provide a simple shibboleth for membership of that most agreeable of social groups, the 'discerning few' nobly and actively pitted against the inert and stupid many. Ultimately they even serve to buttress the infinitely comforting notion that the democratic experiment has failed in a notable case; that an aristocracy of taste exists to which one can demonstrably belong; that all men, thankfully, are not born equal; that God is not mocked.

And so the first problem any interested observer has to face is that numbers of people have invested quite large amounts of emotional capital in the theatre's permanently 'dying' state, and have an interest in so preserving it. The situation naturally reflects aspects of a way of life dominated by the presuppositions of near-universal literacy. We notice and reward skills in this field above all others. As a result our theatre has long been inextricably associated and involved with the sort of response that an educated audience accords to works designated as 'literature'. This perhaps most distinctly marks the difference between our society and that for which Shakespeare and Jonson wrote. As a result of it, we tend unthinkingly to classify plays as 'literature' on syllabuses and in the class-rooms, to examine them as such, discuss them as such, and in general assume them to be such usually without question, or at the most with a standard caveat advising that we should remember that the play was 'written for the stage'; a way of putting the matter which, it will be noticed, emphasizes the primary importance of writing, of the literary element which is assumed to be dominant.[1]

As 'literature', drama can be neatly compartmentalized in our culture as something out of the ordinary. In a virtually universally literate society, it ranks, paradoxically, as the preserve of a minority. However, to assume that that minority constitutes an *élite*, in some way 'better' or 'more responsive' or more 'sensitive' than the majority is to mistake the nature of the paradox. That only relatively few people can respond

[1] Cf. Artaud, *op. cit.*, p. 68.

adequately and appropriately to great works of literature has to do with the nature of literature, not of people, and with the nature of the demands its particular mode of communication must make. Literature, after all, is not a 'social' or 'communal' medium. Writing and reading, the means by which literature communicates, are solitary activities. And, by being 'solitary', they pull against what might be termed man's more 'natural' inclination towards community. They demand skills which have to be laboriously acquired 'against the grain' as it were, and those who have the propensity so to acquire them find themselves favoured by a society whose investment in these skills is considerable.

'Literature' is literacy's creature; the highest, most impressive and important achievement of those skills. But drama properly forms no part of 'literature' in this sense, nor has it much to do with literacy, and its solitary demands. For all those involved, actors and audience, drama is a *social*, a *communal* medium. It depends on and results from interaction 'face to face' between people on the stage, people in the audience, and between stage and audience as well. Without such interaction, itself a version of the interaction of ordinary social life, drama cannot and does not exist. So the difference between the act of going to a play and that of reading a book appropriately receives its full Elizabethan weighting when Shakespeare makes Julius Caesar formulate the momentous distinction between Cassius and Antony precisely in those terms. 'Spare Cassius', we learn,

> ... reads much.
> He is a great observer, and he looks
> Quite through the deeds of men: he loves no plays
> As thou dost, Antony.
> (*Julius Caesar*, I, ii, 200–3)

'Drama', as Edward Gordon Craig aptly put it, 'is for the people if ever an art was for the people.'[2]

It follows that to impose on drama the demands of another, alien and arguably opposite medium, is indeed to kill it. And

[2] *Op. cit.*, p. 282.

if the theatre is dying, it is for this reason. We have required it to fulfil a function in our society for which it is fundamentally unfitted, and for which another medium, that of the written word, is better fitted. In the event, the real enemy of the theatre turns out to be not so much literacy itself as an education system which tests and rewards only literate skills. We are all 'book-men' now. The highest marks in an examination will always go to the candidate with a good *reading* knowledge of the text of the play (who 'knows the text' as his teachers will have urged him)—and who can *write* fluently about it. And the same candidate will go to the theatre (possibly he will even be one of those who 'support the live theatre') with certain presuppositions which, for exacerbated fiscal reasons, become demands that the theatre must fulfil.

These consist, in sum, of an involvement with the stage in the singular, solitary, and 'reduced' mode appropriate to literacy. It is not accidental that modern theatres in general darken the auditorium in performance, light up a page-like stage as a cynosure, encourage total 'reading' absorption in it on the part of each member of the audience, and consequently, and by the same token, discourage awareness of others assisting at the occasion (their presence, signalled by coughing, the rustling of paper, etc., becomes a 'distraction' to be frowned on).

The 'singleness' of the modern response of course has many complex roots which go beyond the seeming banalities of everyday unanalysed experience. For instance, the apparently simple fact that in our society most people's sight has been subjected to a series of normative tests, and accordingly 'corrected', by spectacles, to a relative standard of 'normal' vision (in which the ability to read written letters on a card has played an important role) means that an arbitrary 'singleness' of response has been silently 'built into' our visual relationship with our world. As a result, and regardless of the intentions of nature, we each of us physically see more or less the same single picture of reality that everyone else sees.

The presence of this factor alone makes going to the theatre now a very different proposition from what was involved in Shakespeare's day, since the modern dramatist and producer, like the modern author of a book, can assume and rely on an invariant visual presentation of his art being available to each member of the audience. Since each of us, reader or theatregoer, now 'sees' much the same as everyone else, our books and our plays tend to expect and to count on this uniformity of response. They also permit and encourage its transference to levels other than that of the visual. As a result, we tend to look for and to recognize distinctive uncomplicated structures elsewhere in our art, possibly in part because they meet responses formed paradigmatically on the visual level. We *expect* to see what everyone else can see, and so we look for that and for that alone. We look, that is, for a reduced 'singleness' in art that we perceive in the world around us. The Elizabethan theatre and its drama could and did make no such assumption.

Indeed, the most appropriate term to describe the perceptual mode of an Elizabethan audience remains 'multi-consciousness', or the capacity and the willingness *not* to bother about singularity, but to respond at more than one emotional, moral, or any attentive level simultaneously, and without gratuitous analysis, separation, or division of the response, however apparently 'contradictory' its elements might seem to be. The term was first used and defined by S. L. Bethell:

> This is the core of my present thesis: that a popular audience, uncontaminated by abstract and tendentious dramatic theory, will attend to several diverse aspects of a situation, simultaneously, yet without confusion.[3]

Hence the characteristic Elizabethan 'mixing' of *genres*, of comedy and tragedy, of conventionalism and naturalism, which the modern mind finds difficult to accept but which, in terms of contemporary 'playhouse psychology' represents simply 'the plasticity of unselfconscious art'.

Support for Bethell's ideas have recently come from somewhat unexpected quarters. In his book *The Savage Mind*, Claude Lévi-Strauss suggests the term *bricolage* as a description of the means by which the non-literate, non-technological mind of so-called 'primitive' man responds to the world around

[3] S. L. Bethell, *Shakespeare and the Popular Dramatic Tradition* (London, 1944), p. 28.

him. The process constitutes a 'science of the concrete' (as opposed to the 'civilized' science of the 'abstract') which carefully and precisely orders, classifies and arranges into structures (i.e. myths) the *minutiae* of the physical world in all their profusion. The myth-structures, 'improvised' or 'made-up' (these are rough translations of the process of *bricoler*) as *ad hoc* responses to an environment, then serve to establish homologies and analogies between the ordering of nature and that of society, and so satisfactorily 'explain' the world and make it able to be lived in. 'Nature' and 'culture' are thus caused to mirror each other.[4]

A significant feature of *bricolage* is clearly the ease with which it enables the non-civilized *bricoleur* to establish satisfactory analogical relationships between his own life and the life of nature instantaneously and without puzzlement or hesitation:

> The mythical system and the modes of representation it employs serve to establish homologies between natural and social conditions or, more accurately, it makes it possible to equate significant contrasts found on different planes: the geographical, meteorological, zoological, botanical, technical, economic, social, ritual, religious and philosophical.[5]

In other words, the 'savage' mind has its own 'socio-logic' which operates by means of an immense number of possible analogical 'transformations' in a 'totemic' mode (the totem providing the means of transcending the oppositions between nature and culture). That is, it is a 'multi-conscious' mind, able and willing to respond to an environment on more than one level simultaneously, and constructing in the process an elaborate and to us a bewilderingly complex 'world picture':

> The savage mind deepens its knowledge with the help of *imagines mundi*. It builds mental structures which facilitate

---

[4] I have made the same point, with particular reference to the process of *bricolage* and the work of Lévi-Strauss, in *Metaphor, cit.*, pp. 83–4. There the material forms part of a larger argument (pp. 78 ff.) concerning the relationship of language to reality. See above pp. 11–14.

[5] Lévi-Strauss, *The Savage Mind* (London, 1966), p. 93.

an understanding of the world in as much as they resemble it. In this sense savage thought can be defined as analogical thought.[6]

By this token, Shakespeare's audience might be termed 'savage' in the sense that its culture could in essence be considered non-literate and pre-technological, its 'world-picture' appropriately concrete, complex, and all-embracing. In fact it seems feasible to characterize the 'crisis' which afflicted it as involving a relatively sudden change from that mode to its opposite; from a 'savage' mode to a 'civilized' one, from non-literacy to literacy, or from multi-consciousness to the 'single' consciousness that we have tended to presuppose the necessary mode of life outside as well as inside the theatre. Marshall McLuhan's account, in *The Gutenberg Galaxy*, of the reductive effect of print on otherwise multifarious human responses provides supportive evidence here:

> ... the increasing separation of the visual faculty from the interplay with the other senses leads to the rejection from consciousness of most of our experience.
>
> (p. 255–6)

The Elizabethan theatre could be said to have demanded a complexity of response from its audience whose perceptive mode was, in Bethell's term 'multi-conscious', in Lévi-Strauss's term, that of *bricolage*, and in McLuhan's sense 'non-literate'. In terms which I have elaborated elsewhere, such a response also presupposes a notion of the faculty of reason much wider than that commonly held today, and embracing a good deal that we would now think of as 'non-rational'.[7] And, as with reason, so with language. The 'language' of the Elizabethan theatre involved much more than mere words on a page. It utilized all the levels and complexities of communication that pertained outside the theatre, in real life. In this central respect, 'real' life and the theatre, the *imago mundi* and the

[6] *Op. cit.*, p. 263.
[7] See *Shakespeare and the Reason*, pp. 1–38.

theatrum mundi, were one, and the audience would have responded to the play with the same degree of 'multi-consciousness' that, as human beings, they responded to real life.

On the other hand, real life stays firmly outside the modern theatre, together with what McLuhan calls 'most of our experience'. The totality of 'language', something of whose structure I have tried to outline in Part One of this book, is replaced by written words demanding a much less complex and much more narrowly 'rational' response. The concrete practical communicative mode of *bricolage*, essentially visual and oral-aural in character, has been replaced by the 'abstract' mode of a technological civilization in which knowledge is transmitted non-practically, by books.

The modern audience's singular 'solitary' response has of course been reinforced dramatically, by a hitherto predominantly 'naturalistic' style of acting and of setting which seeks to iron out ambiguity, to 'involve' the spectator as an emotional participant, and to discourage any awareness of an obtrusive 'medium' (that is, the play) lying between him and the 'story'. Modern attempts to reverse this situation in the theatre (Brecht's 'alienation-effect', Artaud's 'theatre of cruelty' represent frontal assaults on it) can hardly compete against an educational (and so social) system which encourages the treatment of plays—even those of Shakespeare—as quasi-novels in which realistic 'characters' come 'alive' in cause-and-effect dominated 'plots' whose sequence mimics that of 'real life'. In any case, in a literate society like our own, such attempts must rank as occasional and sporadic; exceptions which prove the existence of a rule and which too often, as in the case of Artaud, fly so far in an opposite direction as to initiate the very response they intend to avoid—a kind of sophisticated *literary* pigeon-holing (as in the designation 'theatre of cruelty') which provides a ready-made and non-disconcerting response for an audience which in any case is a minority one.

Action on the stage, too, tends to have a 'uniform' quality, and to demand a singleness of response more appropriate to the medium of print than to the 'live' situation which ought to characterize the theatre. Characters have a wholly unreal 'consistency' forced on them as a result, and the rage for singularity extends far into the play itself. The Elizabethan clown, for example, was part of the regular theatre company. His counterpart, the modern comedian, has, on the contrary, become separated from the theatre, and 'hived off' into another form of stage show. Music-hall or 'variety' entertainment—which we think of as quite distinct from the 'legitimate theatre'—was very much part of the Elizabethan audience's expectation in it. The clowns, even those who have roles in the great tragedies, were professional 'star' comedians; the very people we banish from the 'legitimate' stage, and require to amuse us with an art quite divorced now from that of acting, and in a medium which we place as 'lower' in a scale of artistic value. Clowns' parts in Shakespearean plays are normally taken by classically trained actors these days. They are, as one might expect, usually as unfunny as if any modern comedian's 'script' were read by a 'straight' actor. Yet the text of the part has approximately the status of such a 'script'. That is, the words would have been designed to be interspersed with comic 'business', or delivered in comic fashion, or 'placed' as comic by various means such as vocal pitch or bodily gesture, or the use of paralinguistic items, like pauses, coughs, spluttering or whatever, capable of a high degree of innuendo.[9] One can imagine the disparity between written 'script' and actual performance that would pertain in the case of a modern comedian like, say, Frankie Howerd. Yet that 'script' finds itself reverenced as the 'text' on which the performance is built, in a modern production of Shakespeare. If a modern popular comedian (such as Frankie Howerd) were to appear as the Porter in *Macbeth*, supplementing the words in the play with his own asides, interjections, innuendo, and 'business'—a situation that could perhaps capture the disturbing and complex range of experience offered by that play to its own audience (the part would probably have been played by Robert Armin, a well-known comic 'star' in his day)[10]—the modern audience would find itself somewhat bewildered. For whilst we are just about prepared to allow the introduction of disturbing contra-

---
[9] See John Russell Brown, *Shakespeare's Plays in Performance* (London, 1966), pp. 91–112.
[10] See A. M. Nagler, *Shakespeare's Stage* (New Haven, 1958) p. 74.

dictions of conventional expectation into an 'ultra-modern' play as a means of 'expanding' momentarily an audience's awareness (as in the plays of Artaud's followers, such as Ionesco's *The Bald Primadonna*), the notion of it in 'ordinary' or 'classical' plays is unthinkable.[11] A tragedy, we believe, is a play whose atmosphere is *uniformly* tragic. Comedian's performances on the other hand should form part of a *uniformly* comic context. Yet such 'alchemical' juxtapositioning of the genuinely comic and tragic as *Macbeth*, or *Lear* evince is a stock-in-trade of the theatre of the Elizabethan period, and should come as no surprise to anyone aware of its potentialities, or indeed of the capabilities of the poetic minds which worked in it: minds whose nature it was, as T. S. Eliot says, to be 'constantly amalgamating disparate experience'.

Perhaps most seriously in this respect, the social and psychological role played by the theatre in our society also has a considerable influence on the audience's response. This, as has been pointed out earlier, involves the notion of going to the theatre as something 'special' and out of the ordinary, yet, perhaps for that reason, also meritorious; the sense of belonging to a virtuous minority-*élite* engaged valiantly in keeping something 'alive' by positive acts of 'support'; in short exactly the atmosphere in which some modern literary critics argue the case for the importance of great *literature*. To go to the theatre today seems deliberately to 'step outside' the ordinary experience of life, like going to Church on an occasional Sunday. A reverential, dutiful, self-approving atmosphere prevails. Each member of the audience can feel an earned right to the desirable role of hero, as much as anyone on the stage. At the final curtain, the audience applauds itself along with the other actors.

Finally, the 'serious' theatre in the twentieth century is almost exclusively patronized by a single section of the community. Or, to put it another way, a very large section of the community in the areas in which serious theatres exist do not patronize them. The theatre simply forms no part of the lives of the bulk of our people and what goes on in the theatre usually

---

[11] See Artaud, *op. cit.*, pp. 43 ff.

goes on in front of (and so concerns) a predominantly middle-class audience. This has arguably been the case since 1660.

At all events, a theatre like that for which Shakespeare wrote, whose audience was a reasonable cross-section of the community[12] no longer seems sociologically possible. It is not necessarily a question of money. The artisan is as financially capable of visiting the theatre as anybody else. It is simply a social fact that he does not; or rather that the range of experience which characterized Shakespeare's theatre has been divided, and the section of it which now attracts certain groups within the community is that which we label 'music-hall' or 'variety'. In Shakespeare's theatre no such division existed, and places for 'variety' acts, 'music-hall' turns were found in serious tragedy. Starved of material as fundamental to a theatrical experience as comedians and song-and-dance and tumbling acts, a decline in the attendance of theatre audiences becomes almost predictable. By definition going to the theatre is a communal activity. In the modern world a large segment of the community has cut itself off from that activity. As Alfred Harbage memorably puts it: 'If an accidental collision at the Globe would have brought us face to face with a grocer, an accidental collision in a theatre today would bring us face to face with a schoolteacher.'[13] The theatre is no longer 'communal', and a 'minority' theatre cannot *a fortiori* be an institution in which the full potentialities of drama can be realized, if these potentialities are in essence *social* in character, not solitary; dramatic, not 'literary'.

The theatre's financial plight partly indicates the situation's social dimension. Stage productions have become so lavish that, even if the theatres were full at every performance, they could not pay their way, and would require subsidy. Money and art, we are brought up to believe, have little to do with each other, and this is perhaps true of most of the arts, and especially those connected with literacy. But drama is a social, communal art, and has its roots in that social interaction which

---

[12] Harbage, *Shakespeare's Audience*, p. 11, says the Elizabethan theatre '... was a democratic institution in an intensely undemocratic age'. See also p. 83.
[13] *Shakespeare's Audience*, p. 166.

money mirrors. A play's relationship with its audience is of a 'negotiable' kind, and money in this case provides a valuable signal concerning a situation whose roots are societal and have to do with social interchange.

The signal indicates that little interaction exists in respect of modern theatre between what goes on on the stage and the values of the society in which it goes on. The theatre has become a director's medium, not that of an actor and playwright. Not only is there no interaction, there cannot be any. To extend the money metaphor, the theatre is bankrupt.

Now under ordinary conditions, the matter would settle itself. The theatre would 'die' for perfectly good social, economic (and these, as has been argued, constitute in this case *artistic*) reasons, and it would be replaced by something else. Man is a dramatic animal. Drama will never cease to exist, but it has never been an art form that necessarily limits itself to one medium. The death of any *theatre* has never meant the death of *drama*, and a perfectly natural process of decay and change can be discerned in theatre history. One form of 'container' for drama decays, another grows up in response to changing social conditions. Shakespeare's theatre, we should remember, was a fairly new venture when he wrote for it, and had been raised (against not inconsiderable opposition) on the ashes of a decayed, and subsequently transmuted, tradition. In this sense money, as a metaphor of society, provides a perfectly healthy signalling device. Certain aspects of crude market-place standards must be applicable to an art which, like the market-place, is communal, social, crudely interactivist in mode.

The final reason for the present state of the theatre must be sought at this level. For instead of letting the theatre die (an event that would normally have happened some time ago) it has been kept, not alive, but gratifyingly 'dying' by means of subsidy from public funds. The normal and traditional social machinery of change, one which a 'social' art must find healthy and sustaining if it is itself in a healthy state (it produced, after all, the finest plays of Shakespeare, Ben Jonson, and others), has been suspended. On the contrary, artificial and massive support has been given in an attempt to *avoid* fundamental social change. Such a situation can only encourage lavish and ludicrous productions for minority audiences who thereby indulge the unhealthy luxury of seeing themselves as upholders of a sacred tradition. The theatre's death can be partly laid at their door: it has been killed by kindness. The pity of it is that that same kindness refuses to let it lie down, to 'dissolve' as Prospero said it would, and thus obstructs the rise of another kind of theatre which would inevitably take its place.

(ii) *Drama in Camera*

Probably more covert guilt has been aroused by television than by any other medium of communication in the history of our society. Those who began by saying that they 'wouldn't have it in the house', or, later, by restricting themselves to only one channel, and later still to only two, have found themselves in a position of steady retreat; one which their guilt forces them to regard as a process of equally steady decline. A life of quiet degradation stretches comfortably ahead.

The guilt exists usually in the context of other, prior and more worthwhile pursuits that television is presumed to overwhelm. Of these, two predominate: reading and conversation. Television apparently extirpates both, or reduces them to a shallow, and worthless level. On it we heap the odium reserved for barbarity, triviality, and in the long run, perhaps, commonality in our culture.

To defend the medium against these charges in particular instances would not be difficult. But it seems more to the point to suggest that the time has come to remove the blanket and generalized charges lying behind them: that television destroys valuable elements in our community and its way of life simply by its predominance over other media; that, although mitigated by 'some good programmes', its fundamental influence subverts the true and the good in our heritage; that when we watch television (or find ourselves 'under its influence'—the medium attracts the metaphors of drug addiction) we betray our better natures, our culture, our society.

Some obvious anomalies can be immediately disposed of. First, most of these charges put the same case that was levelled against books when print began to be widely used, and against the theatre, when it first began to distract Shakespeare's

Londoners from their daily work. Most new media have to compete with the prejudices occasioned by the old, and these usually take the same form. Much that is now said of television was, in its day, also said of radio. Second, the prejudices are those of a society committed to literacy and the skill of reading. In this connection, it might be noticed that reading and conversation are in any case mutually exclusive activities. One can hardly talk and read effectively at the same time. In fact books have, not insignificantly, many of the characteristics imputed to television. Reading, after all, is genuinely anti-social in its effect, and destructive of communal activity (to read, one has to isolate oneself effectively). And there can be no doubt that the bulk of reading material available in the bookshops and the local libraries could be classified as undemanding and mindless, if not degrading, trash. Those who decry television for keeping children from reading should ask themselves what sort of material children may be likely to read as an alternative. Printed trash has been with us for far longer, and with an effect far more likely to be deleterious than television. Indeed, television can hardly be said to have destroyed anything of value that existed before it. It has simply filled a vacuum that was already there in most people's lives.

Nor does television kill conversation, as a few moments' unprejudiced observation will establish. It is, as Marshall McLuhan argues, a *social* medium, one which invites *group* participation. He points out how much less satisfactory it is to watch television alone than as a member of a group, usually in a family group. If reading 'breaks up' families, television literally brings them together, encourages inter-communication about itself and because of itself.[14] The medium does not encourage silent ingestion in front of the screen, although this is the popular guilt-dominated image; the stupified viewer hypnotized into silence by a malevolent magic box. On the contrary, it does encourage a kind of group involvement and participation, vocal and positive which, again significantly,

[14] Jackson and Marsden, *Education and the Working Class* (London, 1962), note that when a television set was placed in the otherwise sacrosanct 'front room' of working-class homes, '. . . then the special function of that place was much altered. The television drew it into the living space of the household', p. 63.

reverses the popular image of itself. And this kind of participation, it should be noted, is of the same order as that which formed a distinctive part of the traditional theatrical experience in Shakespeare's theatre. The interjected comments of the audience on a play, and their 'participation' in it became common enough practice for this to be included as part of plays themselves; e.g. *A Midsummer Night's Dream*, *Hamlet*, *The Taming of the Shrew*, and others. In effect, 'the theatre' for most of the community has become television. And a theatre which is not 'for most of the community' (in a sense which has nothing to do with the *number* of people in the audience and everything to do with the *kind* of people they are) cannot by definition satisfy a larger national and cultural need for dramatic experience. That is now satisfied outside the 'official' theatre.

In most respects this represents a distinct improvement. The heart of the argument against the theatre was its exclusion, in the manner of 'literature', from the realm of most people's experience. Drama is a communal art, and the plain fact is that the theatre in modern society simply does not form part of the communal experience. A 'minority' theatre (a perfectly worthy thing in itself) has neither the scale nor the scope of a theatre like Shakespeare's. This is not to speak of the Elizabethan theatre in unduly rosy terms, or to think of it as a 'people's theatre' in any crude numerical sense. Only a small percentage of the population ever patronized it. Nevertheless, its audience, and its plays, were genuinely 'popular'; the result of an amalgam of the elements of the culture, and an artistically honest 'projection' of it. When that amalgam disintegrated, the 'universality' which can be felt in the plays vanished (and even at the time, the private theatres, in terms of the plays written especially for them and their 'special' audiences, never produced anything matching the quality of those current in the public theatres). Its absence forcefully imposes itself when we place the plays of the Restoration beside those of the Elizabethan and Jacobean theatre. That theatre can never be reproduced, but its true heir in our culture can only be television. Television constitutes the only really 'national' theatre our society is likely to have.

For in the first place, the actual theatrical experience it

offers differs qualitatively from that presently available in the theatre itself, and, in its way, proves arguably 'larger', more 'universal' in potential. Indeed, it may not be impertinent here to suggest that the television coverage (in Britain) of the 1966 and 1970 World Cup soccer matches provided millions of people of all kinds and levels of 'intelligence' with their first really memorable experiences that could be called 'theatrical' as well as literally national. Without being pompous, it seems reasonable to suggest that many people were moved at the time by crudely 'theatrical' situations to a degree that surprised and disturbed them, since they had never encountered such sensations in the 'official' theatre.

An important factor in the matter must be that it is normally in no way 'special' or 'unusual' for most people to watch television. It forms part of everyday experience, meets everyday responses, and little physical separation exists between art on the television set and life in the living-room. Unlike the theatre, its art hardly requires the abandonment of everyday important things like ordinary clothes, ordinary food, ordinary involvement with others, in order fully to savour it. One doesn't 'go out' to watch television ordinarily, to an 'unusual' place, in an 'unusual' way, and only very rarely on 'special' occasions. Television happens every day in the same way. It forms part of 'real' life, and merges with it in the way that drama most effectively does.

This is not to suggest that the play does not constitute a special experience of its own. Of course the Elizabethans who went to their theatres put on their finest clothes and made special arrangements to do so. But the *mode* of that theatre was different, in that it was positively *theatrical* and not 'literary'. It rejoiced in its own theatricality. The action of its plays took place in daylight, before an audience which knew it was an audience, and whose members were not encouraged to think of what they saw as anything but a play. That is, not as a 'special' or 'artistic' event requiring a special 'artistic' set of responses distinct from those of everyday, and thus separable from everyday experience; able to be pigeon-holed, as most modern theatrical experiences can be, as 'unusual'.

Indeed, drama in those days was hardly classified as 'art' at all, and to go to a play was a normal enough thing to do, albeit not altogether respectable. Most of the audience would respond unselfconsciously to what they saw, without steeling themselves for the 'special' sort of response which a modern audience tends—ironically enough—to accord to Shakespeare. The 'atmosphere' if nothing else was by all accounts as undemanding in one sense as that of a modern cinema. And the plays themselves, stories of palaces, kings and princes, consisted of the stuff of everyday life in so far as the doings of kings and princes had an immediate and telling effect on the life of everyone in that small society. The political issues of Shakespeare's history plays formed part of ordinary experience to the man in the audience, and affected his day-to-day life. They concerned men talking to men, as *Richard II* has shown. Few plays of our day command this level of immediacy, and no theatre can compete with television in this respect.

Technically, too, television manages to avoid certain of the pitfalls facing the theatre. Its mode is far from 'literary' and only rarely that of the film. In the theatre a misleading 'unity' imposes itself on events on the stage because of the effects of lighting, audience response, and the physical, psychological, and social pressures already described. But a similar unit of time, an 'evening', say, spent watching television will have a quality of multifariousness within a much larger and more significant unity; that of the home, the known surroundings, the family or other 'setting' in which the response to television usually takes place. An isolated picture-frame 'cynosure' does not monopolize the attention, because the screen itself sheds light on, and draws *to* itself a known and literally 'inhabited' environment. Such an environment encourages audience participation, reinforced by the fact that the members of the audience usually constitute a group who know each other intimately. Such knowledge, such responses, serve to discourage the hypnotized absorption in an enveloping dream-like 'plot' or situation characteristic of the theatre's mode, and that of the cinema. (Films designed for the cinema of course fail to communicate in this mode on television. They appear odd, artificial, in a way which has nothing to do with the size of the screen. Again, a few moments' unprejudiced personal observation can easily verify this—especially if it concerns a film which has previously been seen in the cinema.) Conversely, a more critical, astringent, and *communal* response is encouraged. In fact, as Marshall McLuhan has noticed, television has an implosive effect on a culture: a nation watching television 'shares' experience much as a village community, and its 'drama' does not limit itself to events called 'plays'.

A unit of time spent watching television usually reveals the medium's considerable inclusiveness. In direct contrast to the theatre, where 'legitimate' and 'music-hall' modes of dramatic communication have long been artificially separated, television offers an almost Elizabethan comprehension of the world. It is the new *theatrum mundi*, the 'Globe' as Shakespeare's theatre had it. For the television experience will yield, not only plays about whatever aspect of human behaviour concerns the dramatist, but also news bulletins, comedy shows, music, and other diverse activities, *in the same unit*. Of course, the unity is imposed by the medium and its programmers, not by the writers who supply the scripts for the plays or whatever. But that is precisely the point—the *medium itself* makes for unity, for cohesion, or for disconcerting juxtaposition; that is, for the essence of the genuine dramatic experience. The play written for television gains from the surrounding events *on* the screen, whether apparently congruent with it or not, and it gains similarly from the surrounding events and objects *not* on the screen, that is, the 'home' background.

In fact, it might be said that the medium tends in this accurately to reflect the condition of real life, and that here may be found its most positive characteristic. For if one were to set out to establish a 'grammar' of television, it would be necessary at the outset to postulate that the basic and irreducible constituent of the medium is *not* the discrete and individual programme fed into the camera, but the much larger unit (which includes that programme) and so the much more complex kind of congruity, that emerges from the receiving set.

Children's responses (that is, those of the first genuinely 'televisual' generation) prove revealing in their manifestation of an unwillingness to impose what obviously seems an arbitrary division between one programme and the 'next', or between a programme and the advertisements which intersperse it. This suggests that the medium demands—as 'real life' does—a non-singular, 'multiconscious' response on different but unanalysed levels. Only the presuppositions of an older, print-dominated generation urge us to think of an experience as 'finished' and 'closed off' when the particular programme which embodies it ends; this in spite of the difficulty we all experience in performing the actual physical counterpart of this notion in the form of 'switching off' the set when the discrete programme we wanted to watch has finished.

If we admit the 'difficulty' as symptomatic of a *genuine* response to the medium's nature, we can cease to feel guilty and recognize it for what it is; a natural unease in the face of an unjustifiable attempt to impose the alien structures of one medium on another, and consequently to violate the essential nature of the new medium. In this sense, to 'switch off' at the end of a programme 'feels' like stopping reading in the middle of a sentence, and the notion that each particular programme must offer a unique separate set of experiences, able to be switched 'on' or 'off' at will, represents an unwillingness to recognize the 'inclusive' nature of television, and embodies virtual denial of the complexity of the life it reflects. In effect, it represents an attempt to *isolate* experiences by confining them, in the mode of the theatre, to a special 'place' to be encountered on a special evening, under special circumstances kept in a separate compartment from the circumstances of 'ordinary' life.[15]

A good example of such a response reveals itself in this statement by Muriel Telford, Headmistress of Leek High School for Girls:

> Television can transmit to us an unbroken succession of sounds and visual impressions which, taken individually, would each demand a different kind of expectation and response from the viewer, but which are given a spurious homogeneity by the sameness of the room and atmosphere in

[15] See the essay 'The New Languages' by Edmund Carpenter in *Explorations in Communication cit.*, pp. 162–79.

which we view, the sameness of the box from which the impressions come and the kind of physical effort we have to make to receive them. They are also given a spurious continuity because on neither channel is a moment of space or silence permitted between one programme and the next ... we obligingly 'keep watching' and in moods of idleness accept a programme we would never have turned on for its own sake because we were led straight into it from one we had chosen. Unless and until we train ourselves to switch off smartly, no opportunity occurs for assimilation of the programme just finished, for criticism or discussion of it, or even simply for pleasurable recollection. More important, we have not the time or opportunity for adjustment to a different type of programme or a different level of realism.... Too often we expect just 'the telly' rather than a specific kind of programme.[16]

Such a response to television differs only in degree from that nineteenth century response to Shakespeare's plays which, imposing on them the presuppositions of the currently dominant medium, tried to make them into linear narratives, each with a beginning, a middle, and an end, featuring the psychological 'development' of involved 'characters'; that is, quasi-novels. In this case, it might well be asked why sameness of room and atmosphere (that is, a 'home' background) should result in a homogeneity of experience that, whilst usually considered valuable and genuine in other emotional contexts, necessarily becomes 'spurious' in respect of television. Such thinking clearly presupposes that the actor–audience situation, as 'art', should be removed from 'home' and 'real life' contamination. No less interesting is the presupposition that programmes *ought to be* such discrete units that their individuality requires signalling by 'a moment of space or silence': that is, by a kind of 'paragraph' or 'end of chapter' pause appropriate to the responses of literacy. That such in fact may not be the relevant response to the medium has never been questioned. In fact the 'natural' response to television finds itself here dismissed

[16] *Screen Education*, No. 11, December 1961. Quoted in A. P. Higgins, *Talking about Television*, British Film Institute, London 1966, p. 4.

as 'moods of idleness' which require that we rigorously 'train ourselves' to 'switch off smartly' to avoid contaminating one programme by another. It is perhaps unfair to comment that such a 'compartmentalizing' response to life itself would be disastrous if it were not impossible, and that it makes of a popular medium rigid and unquestioned requirements that would quickly push it into the frigid and exclusive realms of 'art' or 'theatre'. Rather more revealing is the entirely literary presupposition that 'art' of any deserving kind requires deliberate poring-over, analysis, time for 'assimilation', for the always necessary 'criticism or discussion' and subsequent 'adjustment to a different programme'. Television, by comparison, exhibits an ephemeral nature, its programmes usually 'one shot' in character, rarely repeated, lamentably incapable of detailed mulling-over.

We might remind ourselves that detailed analysis of a 'text', however appropriate to literature, must prove, in a sense that I hope is now clear, not altogether appropriate in the same way to 'dramatic' experience, or to the oral and visual language which constitutes its raw material. *Hamlet*, after all, was a 'one shot' and ephemeral oral-visual experience for most of its non-literate audience in its own day. It is at least open to question whether the contemporary audience enjoyed it less for that reason than the modern one does. What cannot be doubted is that the experience hardly proved inhibiting in any major respect for artist or audience. In fact the reverse proved true, for the play was followed by the no less 'one shot' masterpieces of *Othello*, *Macbeth*, and *King Lear* amongst others. And in any case, the literate notion that anything that is not written down must be 'transitory', that *verba volant, scripta manent,* is fundamentally misleading as I hope to have shown.

Television's ephemerality in fact forms part of its nature, as an element in its 'grammar' that relates directly to the structure of its 'units'. Since these are not discrete programmes, but entirely larger groupings of events on the screen and off it, the individual programme (which appears to literate experience to be the basic unit) will certainly appear as distressingly transitory. But in the medium's *own* terms (the only relevant ones) this is no more distressing than the fact that Iago's 'character' does not genuinely seem to 'develop' in *Othello*, or that Hamlet offers no convincing 'reason' for his delay in killing his uncle. The ephemerality of television programmes, properly understood and exploited by artists and audience, offers a considerable new dimension to be explored. Doubtless Prospero would concur. And in any event the notion that, once having been moved by an experience, we immediately revert back to our previous state unless we continually and literally re-experience it, is so far from the truth that we might in that light reappraise our notion of what ephemerality really involves. Life itself is totally ephemeral after all. So is utterance. If television is ephemeral it is lifelike, like utterance, and it demands from us, as life and speech do, a totality of response, a multi-conscious 'wholeness' of involvement, no less worthy for being normally effortless, since our natures prompt us to respond so. Confronted by television, we have less need to 'train ourselves' to act 'smartly' than to force ourselves to forget a good deal of our previous 'training' which the new medium renders inappropriate.

Naturally, no one reality is the true reality, and no single medium has unique access to it. Nevertheless, for our particular way of life, television seems to rank as the major, because most sufficient, medium. As a 'language', it 'fits' our culture perfectly. Its programmes are ephemeral, and the opposite of discrete; they 'bleed' one into the other, as events in our 'real' world do. The centrality, on any evening, of the 'news' programme ensures not only that the uncertainty or total 'potentiality' of real life will be reflected within the boundaries of that particular programme (we can't know beforehand what it will be 'about', and events will 'change' the programme almost whilst it is taking place) but also that the same unpredictable potentiality will merge into other programmes as a major or minor formative element. A B.B.C. programme such as *The Black and White Minstrel Show* followed immediately by a news programme whose main story is of race rioting in the U.S.A. or Britain, the war in Vietnam, or Belfast, generates a kind of irony in the responses of the viewer parallelled only by the 'real life' which it reflects. Such a situation might even cause us to reappraise some of our notions about art in the sense that it manifests what might well be thought of as 'drama' without using the traditional form of a 'play'. Both programmes, 'news' no less than Minstrel Show, are artefacts after all; they 'shape' life rather than merely 'present' it. Whether the irony of their juxtaposition is intended or not hardly matters, any more than it does in a play. For both programmes, the situation represents a tremendous gain of a new, dramatic and disturbing dimension of universality and inclusiveness: exactly that dimension which we most admire in the plays of Shakespeare and his contemporaries.

Ultimately, too, television removes drama from its 'minority' one-class audience, and places it before an audience similar to Shakespeare's in that it draws upon a cross-section of the community. Its size, much dwelt on by critics, remains its least significant aspect, merely a relative factor. The *effective* size of the television audience, the one involved as an element in that audience's response, is normally small, limited to the family or other similar groups. But, and this constitutes a major distinction, the writer and everybody involved in producing the programme has to bear in mind the audience's *scope*. The finished product (like those of Shakespeare) has to have a wide appeal, and not just on that mythical level of 'putting jokes in for the groundlings'. The good television play has a universal appeal 'built in' to it for sound artistic (and, let this be said again, these are in the case of a society's drama going to be equally *financial*) reasons. The parallel with Shakespeare's theatre proves almost exact, and Alfred Harbage's complaint, made thirty years ago, that by comparison with Shakespeare's theatre 'a universal audience' for the drama may belong to conditions impossible to recover[17] could not be made today, in the era of television. As Ben Jonson knew, under the right conditions, the 'people generally are very acceptive and apt to applaud any meritable work'.[18]

[17] *Op. cit.*, p. 167.
[18] Cf. Brian Jackson, '. . . the middle class with its background of good schooling over several generations, and its strong pull towards London, has easy access to the dramatic heritage of western civilisation. But the arrival of television into almost every home in Dewsbury, Warrington or Swindon is often the first sustained encounter with what "drama" can offer as an entry into other experience: a leap of the imagination so common to many

Finally, to take a broader view, television serves, as all communal art does, to confront a society with itself. That may be said to be the ultimate purpose of drama. It is a purpose which the modern theatre does not and cannot now fulfil. Indeed, perhaps no medium other than television could do so. For our society, in contrast to that of Elizabethan England, is a dispersed and diffracted one, in which unity tends rarely to be a felt actuality. The effect of television on such a society proves at once diagnostic and remedial.

For instance, part of the experience of modern Britain, until a few years ago, was that to live outside London and its environs was to inhabit a kind of destitute limbo. Manchester, Cardiff, Liverpool, these were places in which nothing much happened of interest to a London-centred national press, and in which nothing much could happen as far as a London-based intelligentsia was (and indeed is) concerned. Given this situation, programmes as otherwise banal as *Z Cars*, *Coronation Street*, and *Softly, Softly* served and serve on one level the purpose of unifying and knitting together our national life, much as radio did in wartime, with its vivid welding of apparently diverse national predilections into a memorable whole. Today the average child in Britain spends as long in front of a television set as he does in front of a teacher. For many of them this is longer than is spent in contact with all other arts and forms of communication.[19] Amongst adults, audiences of 15 to 20 million for one performance are not uncommon.

Television's most significant quality, then, is also the one for which our society has most need. It manifests itself as the general ability to bring otherwise disparate entities together; to create unity; to impose wholeness on life. Thus, not only does the medium bring people, regions, and even continents together in a unity of place; it can also, by various techniques, juxtapose past events with present ones, create simultaneity, to achieve an equally satisfying unity of time. And by enabling us to see disparate incidents—on the other side of the world

---

well-educated middle-class citizens, and so fundamental to their most serious culture, that they may be inclined to accept it as being open to all.' *Working Class Community* (London, 1968), p. 10.

[19] See A. P. Higgins, *op. cit.*, p. 1.

perhaps—happening together (this occurs in most news bulletins), it can impose the final unity of action. Television is truly unifying, truly communal, because ultimately, so far as its unities are concerned, it is truly dramatic. The theatre struggles under the net of literature. Meanwhile, its worthy successor has become Prospero's new Globe; the major modern embodiment, it seems, of the art of the talking animal.

Index

Abel, 100
Abercrombie, David, 18 n., 19 n., 20 n.
Acting, 27, 116–26 *passim.*, 185, 210–12, 219, 224, 233
 Elizabethan acting, 30 n., 117 ff.
Adamov, Arthur, 29
Adamson, J. W., 43, 44 n.
Agricola, 39
All's Well That Ends Well, 128
Altick, Richard D., 83
Amadas, Philip, 198
America, 197 ff., 212
Anthropology, 1, 16, 18
Antony and Cleopatra, **178–91,** 191–3; complexity of, 178, 191–3; Antony's choice, 178–9; distinction between Egypt and Rome, 178–9, 190; communication in Egypt, 181–8; in Rome, 188–90; gesture, 182–8 *passim.*; 'manliness', 188–9; notions of language, 179, 193; of 'love', 179–80, 188, 190–3; of 'death', 184, 186–8, 190–3; of 'playing' 185; boy-actors, 185, 190; comparison with *King Lear*, 191–3
Apollo, 69–72, 204
Aquinas, St. Thomas, 41 n.
Argyle, Michael, 19 n.
Aristotle, 9, 37, 50, 161
Armin, Robert, 225
Artaud, Antonin, 27–30, 31, 32–3, 213, 218 n., 224, 226
Audience, 2, 4, 31–3 *passim.*, 37, 49, 73, 92, 116 ff., 124–6, 164–5, 210–12, 218–41 *passim.*; Elizabethan audience, 221–9, 232–3; modern audience, 226–9, 232–3; television audience, 233–41 *passim.*

Barlow, Arthur, 198
Barthes, Roland, 16 n.
Bateson, Mary Catherine, 16 n.

Beckett, Samuel, 29
Bentley, G. E., 71
Bernstein, Basil, 10, 11
Berry, Ralph, 55 n.
Bethell, S. L., 221, 223
Bible, The, 39, 104
Birdwhistell, Ray, 19 n., 20 n.
Bloom, Edward A., 129 n.
Bodleian Library, 47 n.
Books, nature of, 3, 25, 26, 40, 48, 54ff., 73–4, 103, 201–29 *passim.*; number of, 46–7; and knowledge, 46–7, 220 ff.
Bradbrook, M. C., 41, 49–50, 54 n., 59 n.
Bradley, A. C., 26
Brecht, Bertolt, 224
Brockbank, J. P., 211 n.
Brooks, Cleanth, 145 n.
Brown, John Russell, 30 n., 77 n., 183 n., 211 n., 225 n.
Bush, Douglas, 47 n.

Cain, 100, 111
Calderwood, James L. 104 n.
Campbell, O. J., 26 n.
Carpenter, Edmund, 14 n., 19 n., 235 n.
Ceremonies, 31
Chambers, E. K., 69
Chambers, L. R., 27 n., 29 n.
Chapman, Gerald W., 101 n.
Characterization, 25–6, 30, 131–2, 236
Charney, Maurice, 126 n.
'Chinook Jargon', 19
Cicero, 9, 204
Cipolla, Carlo M., 42 n.
Clowns and comedians, 225–6
Cochrane, Kirsty, 205 n.
Commedia dell'Arte, 56
Coriolanus, 128, 146
Coughing, 17, 20, 225

243

INDEX

Craig, Edward Gordon, 26, 28 n., 29–30, 213, 219
Culture, and drama, 2, 9–33 *passim.*, 51–2, 73–5, 215–41 *passim.*; and language, 2, 9–14 *passim.*, 23, 31–3, 37–52 *passim.*, 73–5, 104, 130, 195 ff., 210–12, 216–29, 238–41; and printed book, 25–6, 48, 53 ff.

Daniel, Samuel, 196
David, Richard, 69
Dobson, E. J., 168 n.
Donne, John, 200
Drama, nature of, 1–2, 3, 9–33 *passim.*, 117–18, 215–41 *passim.*; and language, 24–30, 31–3 *passim.*, 37–52 *passim.*, 193, 195, 209–12, 217 ff.; as an oral art, 3, 27, 32, 37 ff., 41–2, 51–2, 71–4, 105–6, 117–18, 209, 218, 232; oriental drama, 27; drama and society, 3–4, 26 ff., 31–3, 37–52 *passim.*, 215–41 *passim.*; and literature, 26 ff., 41, 218 ff., 224, 226, 231–32, 237–8; and culture, 31–3, 37–52 *passim.*, 209–12, 215–41 *passim.*; and theatre, 215–29 *passim.*, 231; as symbol of communication, 4, 27, 105–6, 124–6; popular tradition, 4–5, 45, 75, 215–29, 231; poetic drama, 30
Drayton, Michael, 198–9
Dryden, John, 72
All for Love, 178–9, 193
Dullin, Charles, 27
Durkheim, Emile, 10

Education, 3, 13, 123, 217–24 *passim.* Elizabethan education, 3, 38, 41–2 n., 46–9 *passim.*, 125, 205; ramist influence on, 40–41
Eliot, T. S., 29, 134, 226
Ellis-Fermor, Una, 180
Ephemerality, 4, 5, 38ff., 210–12, 215–16, 237–41
Evans, Malcolm, vii, 69

Faustus, Dr., 167
Fiedler, Leslie, 129 n.
First Folio, The, 71, 72, 126 n.
Firth, J. R., 11 n.
Forster, E. M., 199
Frye, Northrop, 67

Galbraith, V. H., 46
Galloway, David, 71 n.
Garnet, Fr., 151–2
Gates, Sir Thomas, 197
Genet, Jean, 29
Gesture, 15–23 *passim.*, 27–31 *passim.*, 51, 53, 107–120 *passim.*, 162–3, 182 ff., 225; facial expression, 15, 16; posture 15, 16; bodily movement, 2, 15, 16 ff., 24, 29, 162–3, 225
Goffman, Erving, 19 n.
Goody, Jack, 39 n., 75 n.
Granville-Barker, Harley, 180
Guazzo, Stephen, 205
Guthrie, Tyrone, 70

Hackforth, R., 54 n.
Hakluyt, Richard, 198
Hale, Horatio, 19
Hall, Edward T., 21, 22 n.
Hamlet, **105–26.** 127, 132, 153, 164, 231, 237, 238; 'reality' in, 105–6; notions of drama and theatre in, 105–6, 116–26; Hamlet and the players, 19, 118, 119; drama and language, 117–18, 124–6; the court's abuse of language, 106–13, 119–22; the ghost's language, 106–7, 114 ff.; Hamlet's language, 51, 106, 113–15, 124–6; Hamlet and the aural faculties, 114–19, 123–6; the court and the aural faculties, 115–19; 'cosmetic' language, 119–22; acting, 'manliness' and language, 122–3, 124, 128–30; memory and language, 125–6; spying, 112–13, 115, 120; fathers and sons, 107, 108, 110, 113–14, 120; play and audience, 124–6
Harbage, Alfred, 44 n., 48, 51 n., 172 n., 227, 239
Hardison, O. B., 32 n.
Harriot, Thomas, 56
Harris, Bernard, 211 n.
Havelock, E. A., 125 n.
Hayes, Alfred S., 16 n.
Heilman, Robert B., 129, 131 n., 134 n., 138 n.
Heywood, Thomas, 72
Higgins, A. P., 236 n., 240 n.
Hill, Archibald A., 22 n.
History plays world-view, 74–5
Hobbes, Thomas, 203
Hoggart, Richard, 47
Holinshed, Raphael, 169, 170, 171
Holloway, John, 26 n.
Hopi Indians, 11
Howerd, Frankie, 225
Humanism, 50
Huntley, F. L., 143 n.
Hymes, Dell, 10 n., 17 n.

Intonation, 16, 27
Ionesco, Eugene, 29, 226
Isocrates, 9, 204

Jackson, Brian, 230 n., 239 n.

INDEX

James I, King, 152
James, Henry, 26
Johnson, Saumel, 51
Jones, Richard Foster, 196 n.
Jonson, Ben, 3, 9, 42–3, 51, 59 n., 69, 71, 130, 131, 213, 218, 228, 239; *Epicoene*, **157–65,** 212; boy-actors 159–60; cosmetic art, 159; role of 'women', 160; 'manliness' and language, 158–61; marriage and language, 157–8, 162; Epicoene and language, 160; Daw and La Foole and language, 161; Morose and language, 162–5; 'phatic' communion, 163–4; play and audience, 164–5
Joseph, B. L., 30 n.
Jourdain, Silvester, 197
Joyce, James, 52 n.
Julius Caesar, 219

Kecskemeti, Paul, 177 n.
Kees, Weldon, 19 n.
Kermode, Frank, 201 n.
Kinesics, 19
King Lear, 164, **167–78,** 191–3, 226, 237; 'love' in, 167–72, 177–8, 192–3; Lear's 'love', 167, 172–8; his 'madness', 176–8; Goneril and Regan's language, 171; their 'love', 175–6; Cordelia's language, 171–2, 177; Gloucester's 'love' 172–8; his blindness, 175–6; Edmund, 173; 'calculable magnitudes' 176–7; comparison with *Antony and Cleopatra*, 191–3
Kingship, 75, 79, 85–7 *passim.*, 100–104, 146
Kitchin, Lawrence, 32 n.
Knights, L. C., 45, 146
Knowledge, its 'forms', 40, 46–52 *passim.*, 54–5, 63–4
Kutenai Indians, 20

Landar, Herbert, 10 n.
Language, 1–2, 11, 22–3, 24 ff., 73, 76 ff., 224; as man's distinctive feature, 9, 27–33 *passim.*, 51, 76, 105–30 *passim.*, 166, 179, 191, 194, 209, 215–18 *passim.*; and reality, 10–14 *passim.*, 29, 61, 64, 105, 166, 222; and gesture, 15–23; and reason, 54–72 *passim.*; and knowledge, 46–7; and literature, 1, 25 ff., 31–3, 51–2, 56 ff., 217–24 *passim.*; Elizabethan notions of, 37–52 *passim.*, 71–3 *passim.*, 195–6, 203–5, 215; language of men 127–32; see Culture, Drama.
Laslett, Peter, 44, 47, 49, 157 n.

Lavers, Annette, 16 n.
Leach, Edmund, 208 n.
Leavis, F. R., 45, 52
Lee, Dorothy, 12–13
Levin, Harry, 25, 26, 101 n.
Lévi-Strauss, Claude, 33, 213, 221–3
Lévy-Bruhl, Lucien, 49
Linguistics, 1, 10, 11, 15, 25, 205 n., 208 n.
Literacy, 2–3, 24–5, 26, 46–7, 51, 56 ff., 217–29 *passim.*, 230, 237–8; and knowledge, 46–7, 123 ff., 220 ff.; Elizabethan illiteracy, 2–3, 37–52 *passim.*, 73–5, 223; percentages, 41–2, 43–4, 123–6; non-literacy, 53 ff.
Logic, 37–41 *passim.*, 54–5, 95 ff.
Lord, Albert B. 25 n.
Love's Labour's Lost, **53–72,** 164, 201, 202, 206, 212, 217; impact of books, 3; and the *Phaedrus*, 53–4, 69; the 'bookmen', 54–5, 65–6, 67, 70; rhyme and reason, dialectic and rhetoric, 54–5, 61–2, 64, 66–8; writing and speech, 53 ff., 61–2, 64, 66–8; Berowne and language, 55–6, 60, 61–2, 63–5, 68, 71; Armado and Holofernes, 56–61 *passim.*, 69; Costard, 56–61 *passim.*, Dull, 59–60; 'cosmetic' language, 58, 61, 64; orthography, 59, sexuality and language, 62–3; 'knowledge', 63–5; 'playing' 68–9; 'Mercury' and 'Apollo', 69–72; contemporary allusions, 56

Macbeth, 132, **142–57,** 164, 225, 226, 237; appearance and reality, 142, 153–4; the Witches's language and 'manliness', 143–4, 156–7, 159; Lady Macbeth's language, 145–6, 149, 152–3, 164; her 'manliness', 144–5, 149, 153–4, 157, 159, 164; Macbeth's language, 147–8, 149–51, 155–7, 164; his 'manliness', 154–7; Duncan's language, 146–8; Malcolm's language and 'manhood', 150–51, 156; the porter scene, 151–3, 225; equivocation, 142–3, 145, 151–3, 156
Mack, Maynard, 191–2
Mahood, M. M., 51, 84 n. 85 n., 93 n., 95, 96 n., 101 n., 126 n.
Malinowski, Bronislaw, 18
Mandelbaum, David G., 12
Mandeville, Sir John, 198
'Manliness', 122–4 *passim.*, 127–32, 133–65 *passim.*, 188–9
Mannheim, Karl, 176–7
Marsden, Dennis, 230 n.
Marvell, Andrew, 170 n., 212

INDEX

McLuhan, Marshall, 14, 19 n., 48 n., 49 n., 50, 123 n., 223, 224, 230, 234
Mead, Margaret, 12, 25
Memory, 37, 38, 41 n., 44, 53-4, 74-5, 116 ff., 125
Mercury (Hermes), 43, 55 n., 69-72
Midsummer Night's Dream, A, 231
Miller, Arthur, 26
Miller, Jonathan, 48
Miller, Perry, 38, 42 n., 50, 51 n.
Mime, 29
Minnis, Noel, 205 n., 208 n.
Miracle and Morality plays, 73
Montaigne, Michel de, 203
Moore, J. L., 196 n.
More, Sir Thomas, 43, 44
Muir, Kenneth, 143 n.
Mulcaster, Richard, 59 n.
Music-Hall, 225, 227
Myth, 33, 75, 222-3

Nagler, A. M., 225 n.
Nashe, Thomas, 56, 70
Nature, 12, 182, 201-12 *passim.,* 220, 222; 'second' nature, 31-2, 210
Noises, 17, 20, 24, 28 n., 31, 51

Ong, Walter J., 37, 38-9, 39-40, 42, 49, 50, 95, 104 n., 109 n., 115, 116
Oral tradition, 2, 3, 41-52 *passim.,* 125; oral style, 51, 131-2, 137; oral culture, 53-5, 65-75 *passim.,* 86, 95, 103, 105, 123-32 *passim.,* 146, 166, 209-29 *passim.;* oral view of history, 74-5, 104
Orpheus, 204, 205, 211
Orr, John, 169, 170
Orthography, debate about, 59, 61
Ostwald, Peter F., 20 n.
Othello, **132-42,** 164, 237, 238, play's pattern, 132, 327-8; Othello's language, 132-4, 139-42, 164; Iago's language, 134-6, 137-9, 141, 145, 161, 164; Desdemona and Othello, 136-7; Emilia's language, 141
Owst, G. R., 45, 73-4

Palsgrave, John, 169, 170
Paralanguage, 16-18, 22-31 *passim.,* 53, 225
Partridge, Edward B., 158 n., 159, 160
Perrett, W., 169
'Phatic communion', 18, 163-4
Pike, Kenneth L., 15 n.
Pittenger, Robert E., 15 n.
Plato, 53-4, 69, 161
Preaching, 73-5
Prince Hal (Henry V), 79, 99, 104

Printing, 3, 38, 40, 45-7, *passim.,* 73
Pronunciation, 59 n.
Protestants, 39, 40
Puritans, 38
Puttenham, George, 42, 43, 203-5 *passim.*

Quiller-Couch, Sir Arthur, 69
Quinn, E. G., 26 n.

Ralegh, Sir Walter, 56, 198
Ramus, Peter, and Ramism, 37-41 *passim.,* 53, 95-6, 109 n., 115, 116
Reynolds, Edward, 42
Rhetoric, 37-42 *passim.,* 51-62 *passim.,* 95-6
Richard II, **73-104,** 105, 110, 111, 132, 233; Richard as King, 76-83, 85-7; Richard's language, 76, 78-9, 81-93 *passim.;* his 'deafness', 82; his identity, 85-9; as Christ, 90; as 'actor', 91-2; his 'reality', 77-97 *passim.;* Bolingbroke and Mowbray, 76-83 *passim.;* Bolingbroke as king, 97-101; Bolingbroke's language, 77-78, 85, 93-9 *passim.;* Bolingbroke as 'actor', 92; Gaunt's language, 82-3, 85, 93-4, 101-3; rhetoric and dialectic, 95-6; attitudes to reality, 83-85, 93-7, 100-102; kingship, 75, 79, 85-7, 100-104 *passim.;* names and nature, 84-5, 89-91, 95, 97 ff., 101-2
Richards, Mary Caroline, 28
Righter, Ann, 117; see Roesen
Robertson, D. A., 67
Romeo and Juliet, 128
Roesen, Bobbyann, 63 n.
Ruesch, Jurgen, 19 n.

Sapir, Edward, 11-12
Saunders, J. W., 72 n.
Sebeok, Thomas A., 15 n.
Seltzer, Daniel, 131 n.
Shuswap Indians, 20
Simon, Joan, 46-7
Smith, Alfred G., 15 n.
Smith, Colin, 16 n.
Smith, Henry Lee, 15 n., 22 n.
Socrates, 69
Somers, Sir George, 197
Space and spatial relationships, 17, 21, 22, 28, 39-40, 51, 53, 74, 114, 182-9
Speech, 1-29 *passim.;* 38-54 *passim.,* 61, 73-6 *passim.,* 95, 104, 116, 189-90, 202-3, 215 ff., 233
Spencer, T. J. B., 71
Steiner, George, 55, 205 n.

INDEX

Stephanus, Robert, 70
Stone, Lawrence, 41 n., 44 n.
Strachey, William, 194, 197
Swetnam, Joseph, 46

Taming of the Shrew, The, 231
Television, 4–5, 46 n., **229–41,** and reading, 229–30; and conversation, 230–31; and theatre, 231–41 *passim.*; and reality, 232, 236–7, 238–41 *passim.*; appropriate 'unit' and response, 233–41 *passim.*; unity of experience, 234, 240–41; film on, 233–4; social effects, 240–41
Telford, Muriel, 235–6
Tempest, The, 5, **194–212,** 215–16, 229, 238, 241; structure, 201, 210; notions of language in, 196, 200–211 *passim.*; books, 201–9, *passim.*; playmaking, 196–7, 201, 209–12; Prospero as dramatist, 197, 209–12, 229, 238; as colonist, 211–12; and communication, 201–7 *passim.*, 241; and Ariel, 5, 216; Caliban, 198, 201; Caliban's language, 203–6, 208–9; his sexuality, 206–7; Ferdinand and Miranda, 207–8; ideas of the New World, 197–200; marriage, 206–8 *passim.*; date, 196; colonization, 195, 197–200, 207–8, 211–12
Terence, 67
Theatre, nature of, 4–5, 26–30, 125, 196–241 *passim.*; and literature, 32–3, 51, 71–2, 220–33 *passim.*; Elizabethan theatre, 51, 52, 71 n., 73–5, 91–2, 116–26 *passim.*, 211–12, 216–39 *passim.*; Restoration theatre, 231; modern theatre, 219–29 *passim.*, 231–41 *passim.*
Tillich, Paul, 115 n.
Time, 17, 21–2, 51, 53
Towneley Mysteries, 168
Tragedies, world view of, 105, 191–2, 226
Trager, George L., 11 n., 17, 22–3

Vocalization, and verbalization, 16

Wace, Robert, *Roman de Brut*, 169–71 *passim.*
Waller, Edmund, 198 n.
Watt, Ian, 75 n.
Wescott, Roger W., 20 n.
Whorf, Benjamin Lee, 11, 13, 49 n.
Wickham, Glynne, 51 n.
Willcock, Gladys D., 45, 59 n.
William the Conqueror, 44
Wilson, John Dover, 59, 69, 70
Wilson, Thomas, 42, 204
Wintu Indians, 12–13
World Cup, 232
Wright, Louis B., 45–6, 48, 197 n., 198 n., 200 n.
Writing, nature of, 16–32 *passim.*, 38–61 *passim.*, 70–2, 73–4, 103, 217 ff.

Yates, Frances A., 41 n., 44 n., 74–5, 116–17 n.

For Product Safety Concerns and Information please contact our EU representative GPSR@taylorandfrancis.com
Taylor & Francis Verlag GmbH, Kaufingerstraße 24, 80331 München, Germany

www.ingramcontent.com/pod-product-compliance
Lightning Source LLC
Chambersburg PA
CBHW071820300426
44116CB00009B/1386